Critical Perspectives on Canadian Theatre in English

General Editor Ric Knowles

2005

volume one	***Aboriginal Drama and Theatre***, ed. Rob Appleford 978-0-88754-792-8
volume two	***African-Canadian Theatre***, ed. Maureen Moynagh 978-0-88754-794-2
volume three	***Judith Thompson***, ed. Ric Knowles 978-0-88754-796-6

2006

volume four	***Feminist Theatre and Performance***, ed. Susan Bennett 978-0-88754-798-0
volume five	***George F. Walker***, ed. Harry Lane 978-0-88754-800-0
volume six	***Theatre in British Columbia***, ed. Ginny Ratsoy 978-0-88754-802-4

2007

volume seven	***Queer Theatre***, ed. Rosalind Kerr 978-0-88754-804-8
volume eight	***Environmental and Site-Specific Theatre***, ed. Andrew Houston 978-0-88754-806-2
volume nine	***Space and the Geographies of Theatre***, ed. Michael McKinnie 978-0-88754-808-6

2008

volume ten	***Sharon Pollock***, ed. Sherrill Grace & Michelle La Flamme 978-0-88754-751-5
volume eleven	***Theatre in Alberta***, ed. Anne Nothof 978-0-88754-753-9
volume twelve	***Collective Creation, Collaboration and Devising***, ed. Bruce Barton 978-0-88754-755-3

2009

volume thirteen	***Theatre Histories***, ed. Alan Filewod 978-0-88754-831-4
volume fourteen	***"Ethnic," Multicultural and Intercultural Performance***, ed. Ric Knowles & Ingrid Mundel 978-0-88754-832-1
volume fifteen	***Theatre Design***, ed. Natalie Rewa 978-0-88754-833-8

PLAYWRIGHTS CANADA PRESS

416-703-0013 • orders@playwrightscanada.com • www.playwrightscanada.com

Sharon Pollock

Critical Perspectives on Canadian Theatre in English

volume ten

Critical Perspectives on Canadian Theatre in English

volume ten

Sharon Pollock

Edited by Sherrill Grace & Michelle La Flamme

Playwrights Canada Press
Toronto • Canada

Playwrights Canada Press
215 Spadina Avenue, Suite 230, Toronto, Ontario CANADA M5T 2C7
416-703-0013 fax 416-408-3402
orders@playwrightscanada.com • www.playwrightscanada.com

This book would be twice its cover price were it not for the support of Canadian taxpayers through the Government of Canada Book Publishing Industry Development Programme, Canada Council for the Arts, Ontario Arts Council and the Ontario Media Development Corporation.

Canada The Canada Council for the Arts / Le Conseil des Arts du Canada ONTARIO ARTS COUNCIL / CONSEIL DES ARTS DE L'ONTARIO Ontario Ontario Media Development Corporation / Société de développement de l'industrie des médias de l'Ontario

Cover image: Jin-me Yoon, between departure and arrival, 1996/1997. Partial installation view, Art Gallery of Ontario. Video projection, video montage on monitor, photographic mylar scroll, clocks with 3-D lettering, audio. Dimensions variable. Courtesy of the artist and Catriona Jeffries Gallery, Vancouver.
Production Editor/Cover Design: JLArt

Library and Archives Canada Cataloguing in Publication

Sharon Pollock / edited by Sherrill Grace & Michelle La Flamme.

(Critical perspectives on Canadian theatre in English ; v. 10)
Includes bibliographical references.
ISBN 978-0-88754-751-5

1. Pollock, Sharon--Criticism and interpretation. I. Grace, Sherrill E., 1944- II. La Flamme, Michelle III. Series.

PS8581.O34Z86 2008 C812'.54 C2008-902837-6

First edition: May 2008
Printed and bound by Hignell Printing at Winnipeg, Canada.

For Aline La Flamme

Table of Contents

General Editor's Preface

Critical Perspectives on Canadian Theatre in English was launched in 2005 with the intention of making the best critical and scholarly work in the field readily available to teachers, students and scholars of Canadian drama and theatre. It set out, in individual volumes, chronologically to trace the histories of scholarship and criticism on individual playwrights, geographical regions, theatrical genres, themes and cultural communities. Over its first three years the series published nine volumes, collecting work on Aboriginal Theatre, African Canadian Theatre, playwrights Judith Thompson and George F. Walker, Feminist Theatre, Queer Theatre, Theatre in British Columbia, Environmental and Site-Specific Theatre, and Space and the Geographies of Theatre. I am very proud of this achievement, proud that these volumes have already been widely cited in subsequent scholarship, and proud that, although this is primarily a reprint series, essays newly commissioned for individual volumes have been nominated for and have won scholarly awards.

As the series continues, so do its original objectives. Each volume is edited and introduced by an expert in the field who has selected a representative sampling of the most important critical work on her or his subject since circa 1970, ordered chronologically according to the original dates of publication. Each volume also includes an introduction by the volume editor, surveying the field and its criticism, and a list of suggested further readings which recommends good work that could not otherwise be included. Where appropriate, the volume editors commission new essays on their subjects, particularly when these new essays fill in gaps in representation and attempt to correct historical injustices and imbalances, particularly those concerning marginalized communities. The volume topics have also been chosen to shed light on historically marginalized communities and work, while individual volumes have resisted the ghettoization of such work by relegating it to special topic volumes alone.

Volumes 10 through 15 carry on the work of the first nine volumes. They continue to address the work of individual playwrights, including Sharon Pollock, of geographical regions including Alberta, of genres including Collective, Collaborative and Devised Theatre, and of marginalized communities, here focusing on "Ethnic," Multicultural and Intercultural Performance. They also strike out in different directions, assembling a history of the criticism of Design in Canadian theatre, and reflecting on the multiple histories of Canada's theatre histories.

It is my hope that this series, in conjunction with the publications of Playwrights Canada Press, Talonbooks and other Canadian play publishers, will facilitate the teaching of Canadian drama and theatre in schools and universities for years to come. I hope by making available and accessible comprehensive introductions to some of the field's most provocative figures and issues, that they will contribute to the flourishing of courses on a variety of aspects of Canadian drama and theatre in classrooms across the country. And I hope that they will honour the work of some of the scholar/pioneers of a field that is still, excitingly, young.

Ric Knowles

Acknowledgements

It is a pleasure to thank all the contributors to this volume for permission to reprint their work and, in several cases, the publishers of books and journals for their cooperation: Blizzard Press, McGill-Queen's University Press, Talonbooks, the University of Calgary Press, *Canadian Theatre Review*, *Essays in Theatre/Études théâtrales*, *Theatre Research in Canada/Recherches théâtrales au Canada*, and the Stratford Festival.

First publication of these essays was as follows: Madonne Miner, "'Lizzie Borden Took an Axe': Enacting *Blood Relations*," *Literature in Performance* 6.21 (1986): 10–21; Denis Salter, "(Im)possible Worlds: The Plays of Sharon Pollock," *The Sharon Pollock Papers, First Accession: An Inventory of the University of Calgary Libraries.* Ed. Apollonia Steele and Jean F. Tener. Calgary: University of Calgary Press, 1989. xi–xxxv; Pat Quigley, "Musings of a Political Playwright: A Conversation with Sharon Pollock," *Stratford for Students.* Fall 1990. np.; Sharon Pollock, "Theatre Dead or Alive? Feeling the Pulse of Canadian Theatre," *Theatrum* 23 (April/May 1991): 12–13, and "Reflections of a Female Artistic Director," *Women on the Canadian Stage: The Legacy of Hrotsvit.* Ed. Rita Much. Winnipeg: Blizzard Press, 1992. 109–14; Rita Much, "Theatre by Default: Sharon Pollock's Garry Theatre," *Canadian Theatre Review* 82 (Spring 1995): 19–22; Jerry Wasserman, "Daddy's Girls: Father-Daughter Incest and Canadian Plays by Women," *Essays in Theatre/Études théâtrales* 14.1 (1995): 25–36; Rosalind Kerr, "Borderline Crossings in Sharon Pollock's Out-Law Genres: *Blood Relations* and *Doc*," *Theatre Research in Canada/Recherches théâtrales au Canada* 17.2 (1996): 200–15; Herb Wyile, "'Painting the Background': Metadrama and the Fabric of History in Sharon Pollock's *Blood Relations*," *Essays in Theatre/ Études théâtrales* 15.2 (1997): 191–205; Craig Stewart Walker, "Women and Madness: Sharon Pollock's Plays of the Early 1990s." Reprinted from *Sharon Pollock: Essays on her Work.* Ed. Anne Nothof. Toronto: Guernica, 2000, 128–50, and based on material in chapter three of *The Buried Astrolabe: Canadian Dramatic Imagination and Western Tradition*, Montreal: McGill-Queen's University Press, 2001; Anne Nothof, "Staging the Intersections of Time in Sharon Pollock's *Doc*, *Moving Pictures*, and *End Dream*," *Theatre Research in Canada/Recherches théâtrales au Canada* 22.2 (2001): 139–50; Cynthia Zimmerman, "Sharon Pollock: Transfiguring the Maternal," *Theatre Research in Canada/Recherches théâtrales au Canada* 22.2 (2001): 151–60; Sherrill Grace, "Imagining Canada: Sharon Pollock's *Walsh* and *Fair Liberty's Call*," *Performing National Identities: International Perspectives on Contemporary Canadian Theatre.* Ed. Sherrill Grace and Albert-Reiner Glaap. Vancouver: Talonbooks, 2003. 51–69; and

Anne Nothof, "Appropriated Voice in Sharon Pollock's *Angel's Trumpet*," *Theatre Research in Canada/Recherches théâtrales au Canada* 25. 1–2 (2004): 136–47.

I also wish to extend my warmest personal thanks to Mark Diotte for his work in preparing the manuscript of this volume and for his active interest in Pollock's plays; to Ric Knowles who began this series of critical perspectives and to whom all theatre scholars in Canada owe so much; to Michelle La Flamme who helped with the Pollock bibliography and who saw the need to discuss her plays in terms of First Nations theatre; to Angela Rebeiro, champion of Canadian theatre, enthusiastic supporter of all of us who work in the field, and a dear friend; to Apollonia Steele, Head of Special Collections at the University of Calgary, who gave her blessing to the reprinting of Denis Salter's important essay and who welcomes scholars warmly to her world of manuscripts in the Pollock *fonds*. I know I speak for everyone in this volume when I extend special thanks to Sharon Pollock for all she has given and continues to give Canada and the theatre. Life is short and art is long, and it is the plays that matter most.

Introduction: Placing Pollock – Past, Present and Future

by Sherrill Grace

Sharon Pollock began writing plays in the late 1960s and her first stage success came in 1973 with *Walsh.* Since 1973 she has written more than thirty plays for stage, radio and television, acted and directed, served as artistic director in two of Canada's regional theatres, run her own community theatre and mentored a generation of younger playwrights. Now in her seventies, Pollock is still writing, still making theatre and still mentoring. She is an iconic figure in Canadian theatre, especially for women playwrights, and her international reputation as a leading English-language playwright continues to grow. Ric Knowles, the general editor of this reprint series, recognized that it was time for an assessment of her work as a playwright and theatre practitioner, so when he approached me about the idea of a collection, I agreed. This volume provides an overview of her career that will, I hope, be of interest to all students of Sharon Pollock's career.

I use the word *career* deliberately because while the essays reprinted here demonstrate a range of critical responses to her published plays, both the critics and Pollock herself, in essays and interviews, comment more widely on the premieres of plays, on their staging, on Pollock's aesthetics and vision for the theatre, and on her themes and political commitments. These essays, like many others on her work, do not always separate the play text from production or from the strong views of the woman who wrote them. In making the final selection of what to include here, my co-editor, Michelle La Flamme, and I always kept this larger sense of the artist in mind because Sharon Pollock is not only a playwright; she has done every job in the theatre, including front of house, and her passion for theatre influences everything she does. We wanted to place Pollock in perspective or, more accurately, to trace some of the many perspectives from which her plays have been seen by others and by herself. The essays reprinted here began to appear in the early 1980s and continue right up to the present. Their chronological organization, which is central to the concept of this series, opens a fascinating window on many aspects of a playwright's work and, in Pollock's case, illuminates her constant development, her consistent belief in what constitutes the best theatre, and *our* (critics, scholars and students of her work) changing responses to her plays.

Understandably, we could not include every published study, but we are fortunate to have other critical resources to draw on. The two most important of these are Anne Nothof's *Sharon Pollock: Essays on Her Works* and Cynthia Zimmerman's three-volume edition of Pollock's plays, *Collected Works.* The only overlap we allowed in our selection is Craig Walker's essay, which was first reprinted by Nothof, but we decided to include this piece because, to date, no one else has examined the genesis of *Getting It Straight.* In her edition of the plays, Zimmerman includes her own substantial introductory essays and some of Pollock's previously unpublished plays—such as *Sweet Liberty's Call* and *Constance,* which both began life as radio scripts—and two of Pollock's most recent plays, *Kabloona Talk* and *Man Out of Joint.* She also begins each volume with one of Pollock's essays, thereby allowing the writer to set the stage for a specific period in her career. After some consideration we decided not to change our authors' page references to the plays by citing this new collected edition because Pollock makes revisions and our authors' comments often depend on the published version of a play available when the essay was written. My biography, *Making Theatre: A Life of Sharon Pollock,* will appear in 2008 almost concurrently with this collection of essays, and together these volumes constitute one of the most extensive explorations of a living Canadian theatre artist undertaken to date.

Despite this attention, there are gaps in the critical record. One of these has been filled by Michelle La Flamme's newly commissioned study of a little-known play called *The Making of Warriors.* This play also began as a radio script but has gone on to receive professional stage productions and, as La Flamme demonstrates, it sheds light on an important throughline in Pollock's work—the stories about First Nations people and their treatment by dominant history and culture—and it enables us to see Pollock's treatment of her subject (Anna Mae Pictou Aquash) in the wider context of First Nations playwrights' work. But there are other gaps, and not all of them could be addressed by commissioning new studies. Very little critical attention has been given to *Whiskey Six Cadenza.* It is discussed, in passing, by some of the authors included in this volume (Salter and Wasserman, for example), but the play—one of Pollock's personal favorites—deserves close study. Mark Diotte's essay, "The Construction of Masculinity in Sharon Pollock's *Whiskey Six Cadenza*" will appear in Anne Nothof's 2008 volume in this series *Theatre in Alberta,* and hopefully his discussion will spark new interest in this major work. *The Komagata Maru Incident, One Tiger to a Hill, Generations, Getting It Straight,* and the plays for children (two of the best are included in *Collected Works*) also deserve more critical attention.

Perhaps not surprisingly, the play that has most fascinated and intrigued scholars is *Blood Relations,* and anyone who reads this volume of essays through from start to finish will, I am certain, find a wealth of conflicting, complementary and challenging interpretations of this classic text. *Doc* has also been a favourite with scholars, in part because of its unusual structure and powerful characterizations, and in part because of its autobiographical dimensions. Fashions change, and fashions in critical theory are as fickle as in any other domain, but the theoretical development of autobiography studies over the past twenty-five years has provided an important new way of understanding how Pollock creates art out of life stories. *Blood Relations* and *Doc,* both winners of the Governor General's Literary Award for drama, are by no means Pollock's only excellent plays: I believe that future scholars will rank *Fair Liberty's Call* and *Moving Pictures* among her finest achievements. But predicting the future, especially with Pollock, is a tricky business because she is still writing, still looking for new "theatrical envelopes," and still presenting us with fresh "blueprints for performance."

Thus far I have mainly described what is not in this volume: so what is here? I do not wish to summarize each essay in turn; readers will make discoveries for themselves. Instead, I want to comment upon some of the capillary links that this volume highlights because it is these links, or themes, issues, and styles of presentation, that illustrate Pollock's development and the stages in our critical understanding of her work. One of the first things I see emerging here is the *shape* of her theatre career. When I stand back from the essays, I see them placing Pollock's plays in three stages – not categories, but *stages*. The early plays, from *Walsh* to *Whiskey Six Cadenza* (roughly 1973 to 1983), provided her with space to identify some of her most persistent themes and to articulate her subjects in an increasingly confident theatre language. *Blood Relations* began in this first stage but it opened up structural and thematic possibilities that Pollock continued to investigate during the eighties and early 90s, from *Doc* through *Fair Liberty's Call* to *Saucy Jack*. The eighties were also the years of her two appointments as an artistic director, and the lessons she learned from those experiences pushed her to formulate her views on the future of serious theatre—theatre that matters in our lives instead of theatre that is a mere rose on society's lapel—in the two essays reprinted here: "Theatre: Dead or Alive?" and "Reflections of a Female Artistic Director." From this point in her life she moved into what I call the Garry years, when she and her son Kirk Campbell joined forces to found the Garry Theatre in Calgary. This five-year period, from 1993 to 1997, cannot be segregated from her playwriting. During these years, she was practicing what she had long preached about serious community theatre, mentoring young actors and writers, and acting, directing and writing new work herself. When she emerged from the Garry years (barely emerged I might add), she required quintuple by-pass surgery, but she was also moving on into the next stage of creation (from 1998 to 2007)—a more reflective, philosophical stage—in which she revisited perennial concerns (*End Dream* and *Kabloona Talk*), assessed the artistic life and its costs (*Moving Pictures* and *Angel's Trumpet*), and addressed challenging contemporary issues (*Man Out of Joint*).

I describe these divisions in her work as stages, rather than categories, because other aspects of her work highlighted by these essays are their continuity with each other and their persistent recapitulation of core issues. At an earlier point in the critical assessment of the plays, it seemed as if Pollock had moved from political subjects and historical plays to family plays, and then to autobiographical work. Looking back from a later perspective, however, this categorization is clearly too limiting. None of her plays can simply be labelled a history play, even when actual events from Canadian history provide the starting point for her story—as in *Walsh* or later in *Kabloona Talk*—and her family plays are profoundly political: it is, actually, private, domestic politics that drives the family struggles in *Doc* or *Fair Liberty's Call*. Even her most personal work—*Getting It Straight* and *Moving Pictures*—situates the characters and their dilemmas in the context of social, economic and political pressures. Moreover, she has never relinquished her interest in the politics of being human or in the obstacles people (real or fictional) face as they try to fit in with or rebel against the dominant ideology and institutional authorities of their time. Another way in which scholars have been tempted to place plays like *Blood Relations*, *Doc*, *Saucy Jack* and *Moving Pictures* is to call them feminist, but I think the essays in this volume nicely problematize that label. Feminist theories and approaches can and have been used to elucidate Pollock's plays, but this only proves that there are many feminisms and that the plays are complex enough to reward a range of critical optics. The text that can survive everything from a close textual reading to a psycho-analytical one is resilient and satisfying.

Madonne Miner was among the first to read *Blood Relations* through the 1980s North American feminist lens of Cixous's reworking of Freud, and she concludes that Pollock's Lizzie is "a patriarchal woman par excellence." Denis Salter, the first to consider Pollock's *oeuvre* as a whole (at least up to *Doc*) saw *Blood Relations* as presenting "the self as a form of theatre." Salter was in the fortunate position of working with Pollock's papers and manuscripts when they were deposited with the University of Calgary, so he gained an early, intimate insight into the arc of her plays. But both Miner and Salter anticipate future approaches to *Blood Relations* and to the other plays in what strikes me now as almost prophetic gestures of analysis. A few years later, Jerry Wasserman returned to Lizzie and to other daughters in Pollock's plays to argue that underlying their stories was an incestuous father, and he analyzed *Blood Relations*, *Whiskey Six Cadenza* and *Doc* in the context of contemporary Canadian plays by women in which incest was a dominant concern. Rosalind Kerr employed feminist theory in her approach to *Blood Relations* and *Doc*, but this time, a decade after Miner, she combined feminist theories with autobiography theory to argue that Pollock's daughters must reinterpret and understand their roles in murdering their mothers because they have been complicit in the fathers' patriarchal plots. In other words, Kerr suggests that fictional biography exposes fictional autobiography and in doing so empowers the daughter, creates a voice for the mother, and makes the father's life story dependent on a larger, relational narrative. By focusing on the mother figures across a wide range of Pollock's plays, Cynthia Zimmerman talks back to Wasserman and Kerr and confirms that the mothers in these plays are pivotal characters. This is a fruitful approach to Pollock's work that warrants ongoing analysis because mothers—good, bad, murdered, mad, oppressed—haunt these plays and turn to their daughters, not their husbands or sons, to make things right: "Speak to your Mama," says the dragon to young Sarah in *Prairie Dragons* (226); "I place my faith in you," says the dying mother to her daughter in *Constance* (283); and it is the mother, Joan, who performs the ritual of belonging at the end of *Fair Liberty's Call*. Each of the later plays (*Moving Pictures*, *End Dream* and *Angel's Trumpet*) invites us to consider the role of the mother within a patriarchal order, and all could be said to throw a spotlight on the dilemmas faced by motherless and mothering women.

However, these are not the only contexts for Pollock's work or the only ways in which scholars have read them. Anne Nothof has always been especially astute in her discussion of play productions, so her descriptions of the premieres of *Moving Pictures* and *End Dream* provide an invaluable account of the ephemeral, collaborative art that is live theatre. Moreover, the premieres of Pollock's plays help us understand why she made certain changes to a play for publication or how she arrived at key decisions in her stage directions. In the second of Nothof's essays, she brings the discussion up to *Angel's Trumpet* but also draws attention to earlier plays in which Pollock examines artists' lives. Herb Wyile is well known for his analyses of history in the novel, but his study of *Blood Relations* as a metadrama that *destabilizes* our conception of history, rather than merely revising the historical record, marks a major advance in the appreciation of this demanding play. His is an approach that could be usefully applied to several other Pollock plays, such as *The Komagata Maru Incident*, *Saucy Jack*, *Fair Liberty's Call* and *End Dream*, and it brings me back to my earlier observation that Sharon Pollock does not write history plays or plays *about* historical events and figures so much as plays that probe the discursive and ideological practices of historiography. In my study of *Walsh* and *Fair Liberty's Call* I argue that these plays can be seen as parts of a contested national script because they interrogate so-called originary moments in shaping the identity of the Canadian nation, at least insofar as that script is contained by—and exceeds—the dominant historical record. Like Wyile, Kerr and Salter, I see Pollock asking us to understand that life is a performance, that we always play roles but that we have the power (and the responsibility) to add a line here and there, modify a gesture, and possibly even alter the outcome of the story. Whether or not the scholars represented in this volume dwell on Pollock's abiding interest in memory, all of them recognize what a crucial role memory plays in the thematics, aesthetics and politics of her work. Craig Walker is particularly emphatic about this aspect of her work because he links the process of remembering to the establishment of identity and sanity. Michelle La Flamme takes this business of memory a step further in her study of *The Making of Warriors* when she argues that through remembering the past we can transform trauma and, in the process, learn to accept our responsibility for the present and future.

The essays gathered here are not only about Pollock's plays. One of them is an important and little-known interview conducted by Pat Quigley on the occasion of the 1990 Stratford production of *One Tiger to a Hill*. Pollock has had three plays mounted at Stratford (the others are *Walsh* and *Fair Liberty's Call*), and yet this was the only time she was invited to discuss her work and her theatre philosophy for a Stratford Festival publication. In this conversation with Quigley, she makes some of her most forceful statements about the importance of having plays written by Canadians about Canada and she gives us many insights into her views on performance. To read this interview in conjunction with Pollock's two essays helps us to understand what motivates this Canadian woman theatre artist and why she remains here to live and work while her plays travel to Japan, the United States, Hungary, England and Germany. This brings me to Rita Much's short piece about the Garry Theatre, an endeavour that most Canadian theatre historians overlook and that some theatre practitioners describe as a come-down for an award-winning playwright like Sharon Pollock. I am convinced that the Garry experiment was a logical step for Pollock to take as an artistic director, a director and a writer. It was entirely consistent with everything she said in the Quigley interview and in her own essays. Much's "Theatre by Default" explains why.

Regardless of how we read or discuss Sharon Pollock's work—the theoretical concepts we use, the themes we consider, the contexts we place her in—the plays themselves bear eloquent testimony to the imagination of one of the most creative people living amongst us. The best way to appreciate this creativity, of course, is to attend a live performance, but if we cannot always manage that, then the next best thing is to follow Eddie's advice in *Fair Liberty's Call* to "look up close" (417) because when looked at closely these plays provide mirrors in which we can better understand ourselves as human beings (and as Canadians), and they present stories told with passion in language that is powerful, evocative and honest.

(2008)

Works Cited

Diotte, Mark Vincent. "The Construction of Masculinity in Sharon Pollock's *Whiskey Six Cadenza.*" *Theatre in Alberta.* Ed. Anne Nothof. Toronto: Playwrights Canada, 2008. 129–43.

Grace, Sherrill. *Making Theatre: A Life of Sharon Pollock.* Vancouver: Talonbooks, 2008.

Nothof, Anne, ed. *Sharon Pollock: Essays on Her Works.* Toronto: Guernica, 2000.

Pollock, Sharon. *Collected Works.* 3 vols. Ed. Cynthia Zimmerman. Toronto: Playwrights Canada, 2005, 2006, 2008.

———. *Constance. Collected Works*, vol. 2, 271–309.

———. *Fair Liberty's Call. Collected Works*, vol 2, 359–418.

———. *Prairie Dragons. Collected Works*, vol 2, 199–226.

"Lizzie Borden Took an Axe": Enacting *Blood Relations*

by Madonne Miner

In a famous passage in *Totem and Taboo*, Freud traces the beginnings of civilization to a mythic act of patricide: "One day the brothers who had been driven out came together, killed and devoured their father and so made an end of the patriarchal horde" (141). According to this myth, the ingestion of the father allows each of these hungry sons to "accomplish [an] identification with him" and to "acquire a portion of his strength" (142); further, the shared meal—and later totemic re-enactments of this meal—assuage feelings of guilt by enforcing the solidarity of the participants. This solidarity, then, provides for the beginnings of religion, morals, society and, at least according to some theorists, the beginning of drama. Without much difficulty, one might follow Freud in constructing a "history of the drama" that relies heavily upon Oedipal ambivalence for an understanding of both dramatic form and content. Freud begins such history himself, explaining that the hero of Greek tragedy suffers "because he was the primal father… and the tragic guilt was the guilt which he had to take on himself in order to relieve the Chorus of theirs" (156). As fascinating as such a history might be, it would surely perpetuate lacunae from Freud's originary myth. I refer specifically to a curious (or not-so-curious) omission of the female experience. Certainly women exist in this primitive clan, but they exist only as property: first, commanded by the Father and denied to the sons; later, exchanged by the sons for women outside the clan.

As feminists attempting to re-assess/revise drama and dramatic history, perhaps we need to construct new originary myths. In "*Aller à la Mer*," Hélène Cixous offers one such construction. According to Cixous,

> With even more violence than fiction, theatre, which is built according to the dictates of male fantasy, repeats and intensifies the horror of the murder scene which is at the origin of all cultural productions. It is always necessary for a woman to die in order for the play to begin. Only when she has disappeared can the curtain go up; she is relegated to repression, to the grave, the asylum, oblivion and silence. (546)

In other words, where Freud posits the Father as victim, Cixous posits "a woman" – more precisely, a daughter. Cixous insists that the victim in theatre "is always the Father's daughter, his sacrificial object, guardian of the phallus, upholding the narcissistic fantasy which helps the Father to ward off the threat of castration" (546). Cixous cites Electra and Antigone, Ophelia and Cordelia to support her claim.

Rather than reading Cixous as an alternative to Freud, we might more productively read her as illuminating and supplementing Freud. Her analyses suggest the likely fate of those women who are taken from the Father by former sons/new fathers. Since none of these new fathers "might ever again attain the Father's supreme power," each must be intent on bolstering his own power—not, of course, in competition with brothers, but in comparison to daughters. So, as Cixous explains, daughters are sacrificed to ensure the power of the phallus. Cixous' elaboration of Freud offers a fuller myth for understanding the dynamics of drama, the essential workings of performance.

Like Freud, Cixous falls short. She argues that a daughter must die for the play to begin; the man responsible for her death is a father. But patriarchal drama too often carries the victimization of the daughter beyond the boundaries of self. To enshrine the father's "fullness," this daughter must reject her mother's "lack"; that is, either passively or actively, the female victim must victimize other females. In order for Electra and Antigone, Ophelia and Cordelia to share center stage (no matter how temporarily) with fathers, these daughters leave mothers unspoken, unmourned, unacknowledged, unknown. Freud doesn't comment on this further victimization of daughters under patriarchy and Cixous does not include this dynamic as a component of "the murder scene which is at the origin of all cultural productions." Only by locating mothers and daughters, as well as fathers and sons, at the site of the murder scene, can we begin an exploration of the "blood relations" that structure patriarchal drama. After that exploration is underway, we can attempt to challenge and change these relations, to engage in new forms of interaction, performance, drama.

Sharon Pollock's play, *Blood Relations* (1980), initiates such an exploration. This play reproduces the patriarchal family's typical limitation of female roles to victim and victimizer, and then harshly denounces the bi-polar oscillation that this duality necessarily produces in female characters. Unlike much early feminist drama, which assumed that women eventually might trade the role of victim for a role of power and independence, *Blood Relations* insists that under patriarchy the woman who trades in her "victim script" will find herself just as fiercely trapped in the script of "victimizer." Further, whereas much early feminist drama attempted to slot women into the position of subject (formerly occupied exclusively by men), *Blood Relations* challenges the possibility of this position. Rather than valorize one woman's killing another to achieve "freedom" and "autonomy" promised to agentive subjects in an ideology of liberal humanism, *Blood Relations* deconstructs this ideology, offering characters who do *not* author their own meanings and actions, who do *not* originate their own histories (see Belsey 546).

In a Production Note preceding *Blood Relations* Pollock directs: "Action must be free-flowing. There can be no division of the script into scenes" (92). Despite Pollock's injunction, we might divide the play into two modalities for purposes of analysis. The first takes place in "the present" of the play—a Sunday afternoon in late autumn, 1902—and includes action among three characters: Lizzie Borden, Lizzie's older sister, Emma, and an unnamed actress who comes to Fall River to visit her "friend"

Lizzie.[1] This "present time" brackets and occasionally interrupts the play's second modality, what Pollock calls its "dream thesis." In the dream thesis, we watch as the Actress (playing Lizzie), Lizzie (playing Bridget, the maid), and various other characters re-enact events occurring in 1892, the year that Andrew and Abigail Borden were murdered, and Lizzie was tried for and acquitted of the murders.

I want to begin consideration of *Blood Relations* with analysis of this re-enactment. As the Actress "plays"/re-plays Lizzie, both the participants and the spectators realize that first, daughters in nineteenth-century patriarchal households read from scripts that allow them only two options—to be killed or to kill; second, if daughters elect the second option, their initial victims, almost inevitably, will be mothers (the relative powerlessness of a mother makes her more attractive as a target than a father); and finally, this option does not produce the results—autonomy, integrity, self-coherence—that it promises. Focusing on a woman whose own mother died in giving birth to her, a woman accused of murdering her stepmother, *Blood Relations* affords us the opportunity of laying out these oppositions in decidedly bold terms. Ultimately, however, *Blood Relations* is concerned not only with extremes, but also with the range of little murders and little deceits occurring daily in patriarchal households.[2]

Throughout the dream thesis characters repeatedly inform Lizzie of her infractions against the code of behaviour deemed appropriate for daughters. Each of these repetitions is intended to corset Lizzie more tightly in her role. Emma requests that her younger sister "be quiet"; Mrs. Borden suggests that her stepdaughter "discipline herself like a lady"; and Dr. Patrick coaches his neighbour in polite conversation: "The proper phrase is 'Good morning, Dr. Patrick', and then you smile, discreetly, of course, and lower the eyes just a titch, twirl the parasol—" (102). Undoubtedly the most important of Lizzie's many drama coaches, however, is Mr. Borden. It is he who articulates "the most natural thing" for a woman of Lizzie's age, class and culture: "Now... in most circumstances... a woman of your age would be married, eh? Have children, be running her own house, that's the natural thing, eh?" (105).[3]

Typically/stereotypically, Mr. Borden can envisage no other role for an adult daughter than that she leave his house on the arm of a husband. Despite Lizzie's protestations, her father cannot imagine that she might assume the role of a working woman:

> **LIZZIE.** Why can't I do something? ... Eh? I mean...I could go into your office...I ...could ...learn how to keep books?
> **MR BORDEN.** Lizzie.
> **LIZZIE.** Why can't I do something like that?
> **MR. BORDEN.** For God's sake Lizzie, talk sensible. (106–07)

Nor can he imagine that she might move out alone ("God damn it! I said you'll see Johnny MacLeod Tuesday night!" [107]); nor that she might be capable of caring for the property after his death ("I should make a will...moneywise I got to consider these things...it makes a difference no men in the family" [109]).

Despite such obvious limitations in his directorial vision, Mr. Borden maintains that he wants "what's best" for his daughter: that is, that she marry Johnny MacLeod and serve as stepmother to MacLeod's three children. But Lizzie knows that such a role, for her, would be death. First, she experiences extremely conflicting emotions about herself in relation to men. She manages these emotions by flirting only with "ineligible" men (those already married). Patiently, she explains to her father: "You have no idea how boring it is looking eligible, interested and alluring, when I feel none of the three. So I play games. And it's a blessed relief to talk to a married man" (106). And finally, most emphatically, Lizzie has no desire to revive a role played out by her stepmother:

> **LIZZIE.** You want me living my life by the Farmer's Almanac; having everyone over for Christmas dinner; waiting up for my husband; and serving at socials!
> **MR. BORDEN.** It's good enough for your mother!
> **LIZZIE.** She is *not* my *mother*! (106)

Buried immediately below and giving force to Lizzie's final assertion is another assertion: she is not me; I am not her; I am not going to *be* her. Lizzie has seen what it means to *be* a mother in this culture—to be ignored, patronized, employed in the service of male family members—and she wants none of this death-in-life.

And yet what alternatives does she have? Emma, Mr. and Mrs. Borden and Dr. Patrick all insist that Lizzie partake of the slow death prescribed for her by Miss Cornelia's School for Girls, the Farmer's Almanac, and nineteenth-century patriarchal culture. Lizzie, however, looks elsewhere for options. The play provides her with at least two: both enacted by females, both socially acceptable, both finally rejected by Lizzie as requiring too great a sacrifice.

Bridget articulates the first option as she relates the adventures of Mary, a cook for a wealthy family. According to Bridget, Mary is much beloved by her employer; the lady of the house "swore by her cook, finest cook in creation, yes, always bowin' and scrapin' and smilin' and givin' up her day off if company arrived" (108). But the whole time Mary is bowing and scraping and smiling, she's also spitting in the soup, cutting up hair for an omelette, and serving mutton stew "when it's off and gone bad." In other words, one way for a nineteenth-century female to cope with situations that demand docility and servility is to don a mask, to put on a performance, all the while sabotaging the situation. Although Lizzie shows interest in Mary's tactics, when Bridget concludes her story and admonishes Lizzie, "You should try bein' more like cook, Lizzie. Smile and get round them. You can do it" (108), Lizzie retorts, "it's not...*fair* that I have to" (108). Lizzie is right: it *isn't* fair that she should *have* to perform, to run the risk of losing her self in the performance. The more often one dons the mask, the more likely the mask will shape one's features, will affect one's vision of self and world. Lizzie's experiences indicate that men are allowed to appear in public with faces exposed; Lizzie wants to do the same. Yet, as Bridget points out, this simply isn't an option. She tells Lizzie, "Be sensible," then asks, "What could you do?"

> **LIZZIE.** I could–
> **BRIDGET.** No.
> **LIZZIE.** I could–
> **BRIDGET.** No.
> **LIZZIE.** I ...dream. (108)

Bridget forces Lizzie to acknowledge how tightly limited her "life choices" are. If she does not play the game straight, according to Miss Cornelia's rules, or play it subversively, according to Mary-the-cook's rules, she simply cannot play the game at all.

"Not playing" is the second option offered to Lizzie in *Blood Relations*' dream thesis. This option, enacted by Lizzie's mother, comes to Lizzie in Act II. Having seen Mr. Borden slaughter her birds and make arrangements to sign over the family farm to Harry, brother to Mr. Borden's second wife, Lizzie feels betrayed, trapped, caught in a snare. At this point, in conversation with Mr. Borden, Lizzie muses about the first Mrs. Borden. She asks her father if he loved her mother ("Of course I did, Lizzie"), then asks if he hates Lizzie for killing her ("I was born and she died...Do you hate me for killing her?"). Mr. Borden's reply, ("You don't think of it that way, it was just something that happened") prompts Lizzie to deflect responsibility for this death from herself to her mother. She says:

> Perhaps she just got tired and died. She didn't want to go on, and the chance came up and she took it. I could understand that...Perhaps she was like a bird, she could see all the blue sky and she wanted to fly away but she couldn't. She was caught, Papa, she was caught in a horrible snare, and she saw a way out and she took it. (115)

It is Lizzie, of course, who most resembles a bird, who wants to fly away like a bird, whose pet birds have just met their deaths at the hand of Mr. Borden. Lizzie is caught in a horrible snare, sees a way out, but is not going to take it. The first Mrs. Borden, a gracious, genteel woman, may very well have bowed out after giving birth to her second daughter; or perhaps in birth mother and daughter struggled against each other for oxygen, for blood, for that precious matter that sustains life. In either case, the daughter won. So, in 1892, when Lizzie again feels as if her life is in danger, she rejects the "genteel option"; she refuses to fade out unobtrusively. Lizzie concludes her musings on her mother with the observation: "Some people have small wrists, have you noticed, mine aren't..." (11). In other words, Lizzie's wrists are not made for cutting. She does not intend to perform her life as a victim, or according to the more subversive script of cook Mary; she intends to live.

But what script remains? How might Lizzie avoid the life of victim? The events of 1892, played by Lizzie and her actress friend, seem to lead, inevitably, to victimization status: Lizzie is denied a voice in who (if anyone) shall court her, is denied the fellowship of her birds, is denied a future stake in the farm she loves. She is told, instead, that she will be "cared for"—if not by a husband, then by Harry, the brother-in-law adopted by Mr. Borden as surrogate son. Harry and Mr. Borden, two men, demand the sacrifice of her "self" as they carve away at her life. Harry goads Mr. Borden into disciplining Lizzie ("If a man can't manage his own daughter, how the hell can he manage a business—that's what people say" [104]), proposes that Mr. Borden transfer title of the farm to Harry's sister ("I wouldn't want to be in a position where Lizzie would be havin' anything to do with that farm" [109]), and hands Mr. Borden the hatchet with which he will slaughter Lizzie's birds. Mr. Borden agrees to each of Harry's proposals—no matter that each takes a toll in blood from his daughter. One might assume then, that as Lizzie battles for her life (a battle that mandates—sadly—that she carve away at others to prevent them from carving away at her), she would turn on her father and Harry. To a limited extent, this is true. Lizzie readily engages in verbal and physical bouts with her father and succeeds in upsetting the household royally during Harry's infrequent visits. But Lizzie directs the greatest part of her animosity to Mrs. Abigail Borden. In early dream thesis sequences, Lizzie characterizes her stepmother as a "fat cow," "an elephant who never forgets." By the end of the dream thesis Lizzie has determined that either she or "that fat cow in there" must die. Stepdaughter kills stepmother.

On the one hand, Lizzie's identification of Mrs. Borden as her major adversary seems strange. Why should Lizzie murder a woman who is nearly as powerless as she is, a woman who has as little say in her future as Lizzie does? On the other hand, Lizzie's choice makes perfect sense. In patriarchal culture, wives serve as conduits between father and sons; wives are responsible for producing male heirs so "the family" may continue. The second Mrs. Borden commits no such transgression. Although not herself a mother, she brings a "son" into the Borden family. When encouraging Mr. Borden to sign over the farm, Harry supports this conclusion: "the farm will still be in the family, 'cause aren't I family" (109). As "mother," Abigail must suffer the wrath of Lizzie, a daughter displaced in her father's affections by Abigail's "son." Further, the very power of the Father—a power that attracts Lizzie to him—discourages expressions of anger against him (one wants his love and approval). Thus, rather than lash out against Mr. Borden, the most appropriate, most immediate object of her anger, Lizzie directs her hostility toward Mrs. Borden. In a conversation with Emma not long before the murders, Lizzie comments: "I can't talk to him anymore… I hate him, no. No I don't. I hate her" (113). Power dynamics within patriarchal cultures (dynamics that position the mother as lack to the father as fullness) encourage daughters to deflect anger away from fathers, toward mothers. Emma will not listen to such comments. Adopting the strategy of her long-dead mother, she beats a hasty retreat, leaving Lizzie alone in her struggle. Watching Emma's departing figure, Lizzie muses, "I want to die, but something inside won't let me…inside something says *no*" (113). Once more, Lizzie affirms her refusal to sacrifice herself.

But tensions have reached a breaking point in this family, and if Lizzie is not going to give, someone else must. The second Mrs. Borden is a prime candidate. However, before picking up the infamous axe, Lizzie debates the relative values of life with Dr. Patrick. She pushes him to make a hypothetical determination of whom he would save if confronted with two dying people: "come on, it's a game. How does a doctor determine? ...If one were a bad person and the other was good, was trying to be good, would you save the one who was good and let the bad person die?" (107). The doctor cannot answer her questions. As Lizzie backs him into a corner, confronting him with one hypothetical situation after another, it becomes clear that the decision she is asking him to make is between her life and that of Mrs. Borden. According to Lizzie, for one to live, the other must die:

> **LIZZIE.** *My Life is precious!!*
> **DR. PATRICK.** To you.
> **LIZZIE.** Yes, to me, are you stupid!?
> **DR. PATRICK.** And hers is to her.
> **LIZZIE.** I don't care about her! *(Pause.)* I'm glad you're not my doctor you can't make decisions, can you? You are a coward. (117)

On that note, Dr. Patrick, like Emma, flees from Lizzie.

Lizzie kills Mrs. Borden. For reasons associated with plot and performance, the murder scene does not occur onstage (the audience must never know positively that Lizzie "did it"; also, having to watch the "40 blows" might do us in). We listen, however, as Lizzie tells Mrs. Borden how she would kill someone, if she wanted to do so. And we watch as Lizzie initiates her plan of action, hiding the hatchet in a pile of clothes and stalking Mrs. Borden up the stairs. When Lizzie descends the stairs, she is a picture of quiet triumph: "She seems calm, self-possessed" (119). She claims Mrs. Borden's chair as her own, and tells Bridget, "He would never leave me the farm, not with her on his back, but now I will have the farm, and I will have the money, yes, to do what I please!" (119). But Mr. Borden arrives home too soon (Lizzie had planned to concoct a "break-in" as explanation for Mrs. Borden's death) and Lizzie realizes that she must kill him as well. A short exchange between Lizzie and her father clarifies her reasons for shedding more blood:

> **LIZZIE.** I could never stand to have you hate me, Papa. Never. I would do anything rather than have you hate me.
> **MR. BORDEN.** I don't hate you Lizzie.
> **LIZZIE.** I would not want you to find out anything that would make you hate me. Because I love you. (120)

To hate the father and to provoke his hatred places the daughter in an extremely perilous position; she risks being disinherited, orphaned and rendered homeless. Therefore, Lizzie denies her hatred for him (easily transferring it onto her step-mother), insists that she loves her father, and concludes that she must kill him to retain his love. One would like to assume that Lizzie might establish a non-victimized sense of self without becoming a victimizer. The logic of the play, however, will not support this assumption. Rather, it insists that if Lizzie is to avoid the role of victim, she must assume that of victimizer; if she is to avoid being acted upon, she must act.

Her act results in an investigation and an accusation. In June 1893, Lizzie is tried for the murders of Andrew and Abigail Borden. A jury of twelve men finds her not guilty. Thus, with regard both to her act and its consequences, Lizzie "wins." She rescues her "self" from the threat posed by Mr. Borden and Harry. Or does she? Incidents that occur in both the dream thesis and the frame play radically undermine Lizzie's apparent victory as they force the audience to confront questions about who this "self" is, and how and why it acts as it does. In other words, *Blood Relations* is preoccupied with relations between mothers, daughters and fathers as these relations encourage the construction of female "subjects" within the parameters of nineteenth-century patriarchal discourse. *Blood Relations* first introduces questions about the subject with regard to Lizzie's misrecognition/misconstruction of self as "other-than-normal-woman." Further questions about the subject arise with regard to men's misrecognition/misconstruction of Lizzie as "innocent."

Throughout the dream thesis, Lizzie consistently identifies, authors, and recognizes herself as "other," "different from other women." Just as consistently, the play disputes the authority of Lizzie's identification, highlighting her similarity to other women. Two instances will illustrate such construction/deconstruction. In the first, Lizzie muses that perhaps she was born defective:

> Do you suppose...do you suppose there's a formula, a magic formula for being 'a woman'? Do you suppose every baby girl receives it at birth, it's the last thing that happens just before birth, the magic formula is stamped indelibly on the brain – Ka Thud!!...and...through some terrible oversight...perhaps the death of my mother...I didn't get that Ka Thud!! I was born defective... (104)

Lizzie would like to attribute her "difference" from other women to the natural death of her mother. In patriarchal culture, however, the formula for "being a woman" mandates that the daughter cause the death (most often, the symbolic death) of the mother. In this culture, "being a man" and partaking of the powers accorded to men by the culture is preferable to "being a woman." But daughters cannot hope to be "the man/the father." Therefore, they set their sights on second best: to be desired by the father, to be "the mother." This goal necessarily sets them at odds with the person who occupies the mother position. Thus, rather than being an anomaly, Lizzie is a patriarchal woman par excellence.

In the second instance of construction/deconstruction, Lizzie once again muses on her own "difference," as she tells the story of a puppy ostracized by its mother and siblings:

> They ignored it, that puppy didn't exist for the others...I think it was different, and the mother thought the difference she sensed was sickness...and after a while...anyone could tell it was sick. It had nothing to eat!...And papa took it and drowned it. That's what you do on a farm with things that are different. (111)

Here, too, rather than providing evidence of her difference from other nineteenth-century women, Lizzie underlines her similarity to them. Women generally are perceived as "sick," incapable of leading "normal" (men's) lives. As a result, they receive little sustenance (in the form of attention, affection, trust, etc.) and truly become sick.

Further questions about the validity of Lizzie's authority in claiming to be different arise as the Actress responds to Lizzie's story about the puppy. The Actress, who has been playing Lizzie in a re-enactment of the events of 1892, asks, "Am I different?" Lizzie, who has been playing Bridget, responds "You kill them" (111). How are we to read these lines? Does the Actress speak "in character," in Lizzie's voice, or is she speaking out of character, in her own voice? When Lizzie responds "'You kill them,'" does the "you" refer to herself, or does it refer to the Actress, who, in the course of the dream thesis, takes up an axe against Mr. and Mrs. Borden? These ambiguities reaffirm the "non-defiance" of Lizzie's acts; such acts might be committed by any nineteenth-century woman—and, as a matter of fact, *are* committed by the Actress. Furthermore, the ambiguities suggest the oscillation of "self" in the play: who is "I"? who is "you"? The words mark slots available for interpolation. As characters slide from one to the next, the slipperiness of "self" is underscored. By presenting presumably coherent individuals engaged in numerous and varied acts of transformation, *Blood Relations* raises questions about the very possibility of some "essential self." Contrary to Lizzie's assumptions, this play argues that "self" is not something that may be "won."

Both of the preceding examples clarify ways in which Lizzie misrecognizes herself as different from other women. One final example from the dream thesis highlights male authorities' misrecognition of Lizzie—and, by implication, of all middle-class gentlewomen—as "innocent." Defence, judge and jurors, all nineteenth-century middle-class men, *must* find Lizzie innocent; their discourse cannot contain her guilt. Like all discourse, that of the nineteenth-century middle-class operates with a limited number of subject positions (allocations of which vary according to sex, class, race, age, etc.). Despite the lack of fit, despite gnawing contradictions, speakers articulate one another within the available subject positions until contradictions thwart speech altogether, forcing change. Arguing on behalf of Lizzie's innocence, the defence props up a system that is cracking. Refusing to grant that Lizzie *might* be guilty, he wards off an extremely troubling possibility, that the concept of "gentlewoman" no longer holds. As he says in his concluding statement:

> Gentlemen! If this gentlewoman is capable of such an act—I say to you—look to your daughters—if this gentlewoman is capable of such an act which of us can lie abed at night, hear a step upon the stairs, a rustle in the hall, a creak outside the door… Which of you can plump your pillow, nudge your wife, close your eyes, and sleep? Gentlemen, Lizzie Borden is not mad. Gentlemen, Lizzie Borden is not guilty. (105)

The Defence speaks within the logic of the day. Sane gentlewomen do not murder their parents; Lizzie is a sane gentlewoman; hence, Lizzie did not murder her parents. To question the initial premise would call too many other premises into question. Therefore, Lizzie must go free.

And yet, what "freedom" is this? Who has been set free? Is it the "Lizzie Borden" who delivers thirty-two blows to the head of her stepmother, then picks up the axe once again to bestow thirteen blows to the head of her beloved father? If not this "Lizzie," then who? Perhaps the "Lizzie" who, according to the defence, is "the youngest daughter of a scion of our community, a recipient of the fullest amenities our society can bestow upon its most fortunate members" (105)? Is it the same "fortunate member" whose birds are axed, whose claims to the farm are denied? I raise these questions because I read *Blood Relations* as a play obsessed with relations among mothers, father and daughters under patriarchy, but also, obsessed with conceptions of the self, the subject—especially the female subject. In *Blood Relations*, the two obsessions cannot be separated. The play shows how patriarchal institutions encourage women to believe that they may achieve the status of subject by eliminating other women. Having vanquished her mothers and distanced herself from maternal "lack," Lizzie expects a fullness, a wholeness, a unity of self. By manipulating role playing and by playing with misrecognitions *Blood Relations* casts doubt on the integrity of presumed subjects. This integrity comes under even more debilitating attack in the final sequences of the frame play.[4]

The dream thesis ends in a tableau. The Actress raises a hatchet high over Mr. Borden's head, preparing to strike him. The lights go out, and children's voices sing:

> Lizzie Borden took an axe,
> Gave her mother forty whacks.
> When the job was nicely done,
> She gave her father forty-one! (120)

As the lights come up, Lizzie stands behind the Actress; she reaches up and takes the hatchet from her. The Actress "whirls around to face Miss Lizzie," then backs away from her presumably to demarcate an area of difference—difference that the dream thesis has effaced. At that point, the play returns to the "present," a Sunday afternoon in 1902, and the audience is confronted with a more radical effacement of boundaries between presumably "individual subjects"—specifically, between Emma and Lizzie. On the basis of Lizzie's decisive "directorial" presence within the dream thesis, it is tempting to read her as authoritative subject, individualized "self." Final exchanges among Lizzie, Emma, and the Actress in the frame play, however, require that we question the identity of this subject.

Emma initiates these exchanges by asking the question, "Lizzie, did you?" (121). In her response, Lizzie focuses not on *act*, but on *agency*: "Did you never stop and think that if I did, then you were guilty too?" (121). This response requires that we ask who Lizzie is, who Emma is, and what relationship the two women share. Lizzie continues:

> It was you who brought me up, like a mother to me. Almost like a mother. Did you ever stop and think that I was like a puppet, your puppet. My head your hand, yes, your hand working my mouth, me saying all the things you felt like saying, me doing all the things you felt like doing, me spewing forth, me hitting out, and you, you—! (121–22)

Listening to Lizzie describe this relationship between mother and daughter, puppeteer and puppet, the actress makes the connection between her enactment of Lizzie's desires in the dream thesis and Lizzie's enactment of Emma's desires in history. Having just witnessed the breakdown of boundaries between the Actress and Lizzie, should we be ready to believe Lizzie's articulation of a similar breakdown between her "self" and Emma. When Emma hedges, arguing, "I wasn't even here that day," Lizzie agrees. Precisely because Emma wasn't "here that day," Lizzie became Emma. The play concludes with a final statement of breakdown.

> **EMMA.** You didn't... did you?
> **MISS LIZZIE.** Poor...Emma.
> **ACTRESS.** Lizzie. Lizzie, you did.
> **MISS LIZZIE.** I didn't. You did.

Who is this "you" in Lizzie's last line? Emma? The Actress? The Actress impersonating Lizzie? The audience? The play will not say, *cannot* say. It denies the integrity of "self" assumed by liberal humanism. Further, as it enacts this denial, the play casts serious doubt on goals of liberal feminism—to be an independent, free self—and calls for a more radical analysis of the ways in which these goals are effects of language and ideology. *Blood Relations*, then, illustrates not only how patriarchy manipulates an ideologically-constructed desire for "self" to set woman against woman, but also the impossibility of ever achieving this desire.

In an afterword to *Blood Relations* Sharon Pollock locates the "origin" of her play in personal experience. While living with an abusive man, she used to plot "murderous schemes" to get rid of him. On leaving this man, she realized "that in all likelihood I was cast as the murderee, not the murderer, in my drama." She goes on to say that if she had stayed with this man, she might've ended up killing him, not to prevent physical injury to herself, but "to maintain my sense of self, to prevent a violation that was far more frightening and threatening than any blow, and of which physical violence against my person was only the outward manifestation. And so it is with Lizzie" (124).

Pollock's comments simultaneously operate within and express the contradictions of the liberal humanist ideology that her play undermines. That is, she talks about maintaining her "sense of self" and yet her acknowledgement of confusion—"was I the murderer or the murderee"—suggest that she misrecognizes her "self," that this "self" is in flux, that perhaps there is no essential "self." Further, her attribution of a "sense of self" to Lizzie reveals how eminently appropriatable these "selves" are. The playwright *constructs* the self that she names "Lizzie," "Lizzie" does not precede the playwright. Finally, Pollock's play provides overwhelming evidence of "self" as mask, "self" as position marker into which we are slotted—not as something we make, but something into which we are made. As the Actress "is made" Lizzie, Lizzie "is made" Emma....

(1986)

Notes

[1] The absence of a name suggests the absence of a unified, stable, coherent "self." Hence, it is important thematically that the Actress remain unnamed. I should note, however, that the Actress is grounded in history. After her acquittal, Lizzie became involved with Nance O'Neill, a popular actress of the day.

[2] Again, see Belsey for commentary of the conjunction between liberal humanism and patriarchy.

[3] Reference to "the natural thing" provides characters with one strategy for ignoring the cultural constructs under which they live. Dr. Patrick, for example, "explains" the interest shown by neighbouring boys in Lizzie's birds as "a natural thing" (103).

[4] One of the most frightening images of internal absence occurs in Lizzie's description of a dream that she attributes to the Actress, but to the actress as she plays Lizzie, so that the audience is left, as usual, with serious doubts about the "authority" and "origin" of this dream:

> You're wearing a mask, a white mask like the mane of the horse, it looks like your face except that it's rigid and white...With each flick of the lights, the expression, it changes, but always so rigid and hard...And each time you go round, your hands rise a fraction nearer the mask...and the music and the carousel and the horse...they all three slow down, and they stop...You can reach out and touch...you on the horse...with your hands so at the eyes...You look into the eyes! There are none! None! Just black holes in a white mask. (109).

Works Cited

Belsey, Catherine. *The Subject of Tragedy.* London: Methuen, 1985.

Cixous, Hélène. "*Aller à la mer.*" *Modern Drama.* 27.4 December (1984): 546–48.

Freud, Sigmund. *Totem and Taboo.* New York: Norton, 1950.

Pollock, Sharon. *Blood Relations. Plays by Women III.* Ed. Michelene Wandor. London: Methuen, 1984.

(Im)possible Worlds: The Plays of Sharon Pollock

by Denis Salter

"I believe that every play has a politic," Sharon Pollock declared in a 1982 interview. "I believe that 'Three's Company' has a politic. The fact that most people don't recognize it makes it a far more dangerous politic than any politic I could put on the stage" (Wallace and Zimmerman 122). By politic she is referring, I gather, to a play's ideological patterns, the definitions which it gives, both explicitly and implicitly, to the sociopolitical assumptions characteristic of a group, culture or individual. As a "committed playwright" (to cite Malcolm Page's apt designation), she is using the theatre to expose deception, to probe the origins of behaviour, to weigh the truth of a character or situation, and to determine people's responsibilities for their actions. She is using the theatre, in other words, as an instrument of moral inquiry, to project (though seldom to achieve) a better world with a better set of values by which to live. Some of her earlier plays, including *Walsh* (1973), *The Komagata Maru Incident* (1976) and *One Tiger to a Hill* (1980), lean towards simplistic ideas and holier-than-thou didacticism; but her subsequent works—*Generations* (1980), *Blood Relations* (1980), *Whiskey Six Cadenza* (1983) and *Doc* (1984)—treat her subjects and her audiences much more respectfully: "The theatre is not a classroom, the playwright is not a teacher," Pollock has explained, "but a good play should provoke intelligent discussion about an issue or theme pertinent to our lives" (Rubin and Cramer-Byng 134).

Her concern that audiences might not recognize, let alone understand, a play's ideological conclusions is a recurring theme in several interviews. It seems to have influenced her decision to work as a cultural activist (with groups such as the Playwrights Union) and as the artistic director of several theatre companies including Theatre Calgary (where, characteristically, she resigned over a point of principle) and more recently Theatre New Brunswick. It has also influenced, I will argue here, her commitment to experiment with different techniques of dramatic engagement. Audiences cannot respond passively to a Sharon Pollock play. They must respond actively, coming to terms not only with the play's politic but with how the playwright (not unlike a politician) is trying to direct their emotional, intellectual and moral attitudes. Typically, audiences find themselves located inside the points of tension which Pollock, always a tough-minded idealist, insists that we should think about. In what I consider her most significant plays (*Blood Relations*, *Whiskey Six Cadenza* and *Doc*), she relies on modified presentational techniques, among other things, to draw her audiences directly into the dramatic action, so that they become, together with the characters, the main subjects of the playwright's ethical investigation.

I

Walsh (1973) began life as a conventional history play. Skeptical of the myth of the peaceful settlement of the Canadian West, Pollock started reading standard historical accounts and soon grew angry over what "the historians hadn't told me" (qtd. in Page 104). She undertook her own research, concentrating her attention on Major Walsh of the Northwest Mounted Police who had attempted to prevent Sitting Bull and the Sioux from being sent back from Canada to the United States, ostensibly to stand trial for the death of General Custer and his men at the battle of Little Big Horn. As Pollock pursued her subject, she confronted a tissue of lies in the newspaper accounts and diary entries of government commissioners. Keen to make use of virtually everything she had uncovered, she overburdened the early 1973 version of the play with historical information which is delivered with impersonal authority by voice-overs at the start of every scene. During revisions, Pollock became less interested in historical documentation and more preoccupied with Walsh's moral dilemma: "For me, Walsh is a man who knows that there is a nobility to his struggle, but he abdicates responsibility as an individual" (Wallace and Zimmerman 121). The fourth (and evidently final, 1983) version of the play has dispensed entirely with the voice-overs. History exists much more effectively through character-interaction, dramatically motivated direct address, and the essential details of time and place. The emphasis is on a psychologically-determined social analysis of why, how and to what ends Walsh was forced—against his better judgment—to sacrifice his own high principles.

The voice-overs might have worked in Piscator or Brecht's kinds of political theatre. But for Pollock, who was developing a different kind of political theatre, they simply got in the way, and failed to provide the kind of historical and psychological context which is essential if we are to understand not just the political forces (British, American and Canadian) which Walsh is up against, but also the fullest dimensions of his character. The final version begins with a traditional induction-scene, set in the Klondike in 1898 long after Walsh has betrayed both Sitting Bull and himself. Placing the entire play into a retrospective frame of reference, this induction-scene allows Pollock to pose, and to some degree answer, her central question: "How did the man change from 1873 to 1898?" (Wallace and Zimmerman 119). As a direct projection of Walsh's degenerated state of mind, the scene relies on psycho-dramatic techniques of role-playing to underscore the various contradictions and paradoxes in Walsh's behaviour. Walsh plays himself. But all the other characters (with the notable exceptions of Harry the wagon master and Clarence the young recruit) are played by actors who assume a different set of roles in the main play. This doubling establishes a number of ironic contrasts which comment indirectly on the perilous uncertainty of life and on the possibility of being defeated by the reversal of life's idealism. Louis the Métis scout and Colonel MacLeod, who, like Walsh, is a member of the NWMP, are both cast as poker players; Mrs. Anderson, a self-righteous white woman who gets indignant over Walsh's sympathy for the Indians, is cast as Jennie the whore; and, most significantly of all, Sitting Bull is cast as the Prospector.

Despite just playing himself, Walsh is nevertheless portrayed as a man who has had to assume many roles to survive. Appearing "in civvies, impeccably dressed," his own past as a member of the Force is made evident by the presence of Clarence wearing the "red tunic" and standing just outside the scene observing Walsh (*Walsh*, revised 9). Clarence serves both here and in the main play as Walsh's double, a younger version of his idealistic self, still believing in the values of honesty and dignity symbolized by the tunic before being overtaken by mid-life disillusionment. From their juxtaposition in this induction-scene, Pollock summarizes some of the main contrasting moral values of her play: innocence and experience, courage and cowardice, private beliefs versus public actions, moral engagement versus moral evasion, etc. Moreover, in his role as Walsh's conscience, Clarence reminds us that Walsh is not merely a man of action but a man who is prepared to reflect upon the meaning of his life. His unusual degree of self-awareness is disclosed in the climax of the scene. When the Prospector (i.e., Sitting Bull) begs for some money for the boy, Joeie (i.e., Sitting Bull's son, Crowfoot), Walsh says repeatedly, "I can give you nothing." Then, in despair, "Walsh hits him in the face, knocking him down. As he goes to get up, he plants a foot in his back, sending him sprawling" (*Walsh*, revised 15). This precipitates a primal scream from Clarence who is standing, with symbolical aptness, in the shadowy area at the edge of the scene. Walsh has descended at this moment as low as he can go, literally to a point of nothingness. The moment is a mirror-image of the scene in the main play where Walsh, overcome by his inability to help Sitting Bull and enraged by the Indian's stoical courage in the face of adversity, hits him again in exactly this way. This technique of visual repetition, with its concentration of effect, enables Pollock to dramatize Walsh's inner turbulence clearly and swiftly, and to suggest that he is paradoxically the victim of his own strong character. A lesser man would simply have acquiesced to government authority and then conveniently have forgotten about it; but Walsh, having acquiesced, is now destroyed by the very code of honour which he has so passionately upheld. Overall, the induction-scene functions as both theme and structure suggesting that the roles we play are invariably suspect and provisional, directed not by us but by historical and psychological forces much more powerful than we are.

Clarence's long scream heightens the significance of the tableau in which Walsh stands ready "with his hand upraised to hit the Prospector" one more time while the other characters are grouped around in typical attitudes (*Walsh*, revised 16). Since Clarence is no longer just a self-referential observer, Harry the wagon master (who also plays just himself) now assumes this role, coming forward to address the audience with a long exposition about Sitting Bull, the Sioux, General Custer and how "the 'merican Army was out to avenge the 'Custer Massacre'" (*Walsh*, revised 19). Although this darkly ironic speech is over three pages long in the published edition, it is not merely dry as dust historical evidence but is sustained by the dramatic energy which Pollock has released in the scene, by the striking contrast between the role-playing tableau in the background and the immediacy of Harry's "real" personality in the foreground as he tells us what appears to be *the* historical truth, and by our curiosity about the historical and psychological circumstances which have caused Walsh's degeneration. The play is therefore not an historical chronicle, docudrama, or piece of Brechtian revisionism; but, like the historical dramas of Schiller, Goethe and Lessing, it chooses to examine its historical crisis by means of a powerful central personality.

Nonetheless, history is by no means secondary to Pollock's intentions. The premise of the induction scene is that the assumptions of the present will serve for the investigation of the past, as long as we understand what Pollock came to understand as she conducted her own historical research. The past is not merely a stable body of evidence but an ever-shifting set of so-called facts, which are ostensibly objective but in effect prejudiced by the ideological values with which we interpret them. The main play, alas, doesn't live up to the promise of the induction scene. Where the latter is problematic, the former tends to be a schematic moral outline. Walsh is the well-meaning but ultimately ineffectual white man whose potentially tragic stature is undermined by his decision to renege on his responsibility to the Sioux; Sitting Bull is a variant of the noble savage, given to speaking in parables and the kind of sententious phrases which Charles Mair made a source of embarrassment in our dramatic literature almost a century earlier in *Tecumseh*; and the Indians, as in a formulaic Western, are the good guys while the American soldiers and government lackeys are of course the bad guys. Clarence's idealism, maintained to the end despite the corruption he witnesses, is an ironic parallel to Walsh's moral decline and varies the controlling moral equation somewhat. But this is not enough to bring the play to a level of sustained moral debate. Since everything has been pretty much decided beforehand, the dialectical possibilities of the induction scene are pretty much left undeveloped as the play follows its predictable linear direction. This means the audience is put into a limited position. We empathize (and perhaps even sympathize at key moments) with Walsh, largely without qualifications; we valorize Sitting Bull and the Sioux, again largely without qualification; and we can luxuriate, if we wish, in a deep emotional bath of anti-imperialism. When Walsh accedes to his government's demands and sends Sitting Bull to his certain death in the United States, we regret his weakness, but this is essentially another form of empathy, allowing us the easy way out. Worse, the simplistic moral pattern encourages the audience to feel morally superior to every single character, Sitting Bull and Walsh included. This negates our sense of idealism, and relegates the moral problems of the play to the once-upon-a-time with absolutely no relevance to the present. Pollock is right: there is a large element of "historical pageant" (Wallace and Zimmerman 119) to this play; enough, in fact, to subvert the complexity of moral argument which the induction scene had led us to expect.

Stylistically, however, the play is on much surer ground, an object lesson in how an experimental playwright is constantly sharpening her dramatic methods. Each published version is increasingly economical and more precisely focused; characterization is elaborated without losing its central purpose; and, most important of all, she becomes more confident in her use of visual and aural synecdoche, as in the example of Clarence's Munch-like scream which brings the whole course of Walsh's life vividly into perspective. Through this technique of poetic compression, Pollock generalizes her themes by developing symbolical connections between various characters and situations. The symbols engender a kind of internal language which is conditioned by subjective values. Pollock is in effect exhuming the past, with our assistance, as a form of collective memory (dense, suggestive and elusive), and not as a body of historical evidence to be marshalled and subjected to rigorous analysis. In the induction scene, for example, Billy the harmonica player at key moments plays "Garryowen," which Harry the wagon master identifies as Custer's marching song. Although Custer doesn't actually appear in the main play, only a few strains of this song are needed to make him and the battle of Little Big Horn as real a presence as any of the onstage characters. Thus, when Harry whistles the song after the scene in which Colonel MacLeod has made it clear that Walsh *must* order the Sioux back to the United States, Custer's death, Walsh's unavoidable decision, and the eventual murder of Sitting Bull together with his family and people are *all* concentrated into the compelling intensity of a single moment.

Similarly, through a kind of network of inferences, Walsh's role as a victim of political machination is established and developed by assigning moral values to places which are never seen but often referred to. The United States is dangerous, aggressive, barbaric—a place where deals are made and where people die. Britain, as the centre of imperial policy, is byzantine in its complexity, remote and all powerful, able to colonize any form of political opposition at the mere stroke of a pen. Ottawa is similarly remote but also weak, a mere pawn of British and American foreign policy. Glengarry, however, where Clarence comes from (the Ralph Connor allusion is a nice touch), is an ideal world. So, too, is Brockville where Walsh's wife and two daughters live, emblems of his private integrity, kept intact despite the duplicity of his public responsibilities. The West, in stark contrast, is portrayed as the romantic cliché of new world hopes and noble savages, but it has been polluted by debased political values irreversibly brought to bear from centres of power located elsewhere.

Near the end of the play, Walsh and his men are assuming yet another set of roles: they are planning to dress up as Indians to make mock attacks on trainloads of Eastern visitors coming to see the last best West. Thus, in the image patterns that the play's geography has been articulating, even the West cannot be taken at face value—appearances to the contrary, it is no longer the genuine article. At the close, Walsh takes off his red tunic and gun as he tries to dissociate himself from the role that has destroyed him. But he cannot do so. Clarence has just reported the brutal murder of Sitting Bull ("They shot him twice and put the boots to him…and Little Crow says the soldiers dropped him in a pit of lime, so's his people couldn't bury him proper" [*Walsh*, revised 128]); meanwhile we hear the voice of Sitting Bull, from earlier in the play, talking of his own inevitable death ("My cup is broken. It has passed away" [*Walsh*, revised 129]). The West itself, as both a real place and a state of unimpeachable moral worth, has also "passed away": Walsh can of course do nothing, as we had discovered in the induction scene, and so he "slams his hands down on his desk" as the action shifts to a final emblematic blackout (*Walsh*, revised 129).

II

The Komagata Maru Incident (1976), like *Walsh*, has many of the trappings of a history play and again provides the playwright with an opportunity to probe some of our smug assumptions about the peaceful settlement of the West. Her main subject is racism. In 1914 the Canadian government prevented a boatload of East Indian immigrants from entering Canada even though they were entitled to do so as British citizens. Their boat remained moored for two months in Vancouver harbour while negotiations took place and the Indians suffered from hunger and inadequate living conditions. Pollock's research into the incident again made her reappraise the ways in which our history has been written. "As a Canadian, I feel that much of our history has been misrepresented and even hidden from us," she has observed in a Note to the published text. "Until we recognize our past, we cannot change our future." Her play is the theatrical equivalent of the kind of task force inquiry which the government should have commissioned to find out what was really going on; but, as she also observes in her Note, the whole affair was soon "overshadowed by the outbreak of World War I" (iii). The retrospective frame of reference in *Walsh* allows us to treat its indictment of racism as an isolated historical event. But in *The Komagata Maru Incident*, the playwright is using much more direct presentational strategies to engage the audience's attention, to persuade it to take responsibility *now* for the pattern of racial prejudice found throughout our history.

The early versions of *Walsh*, as noted, suffered from too much historical documentation. As a moralist, Pollock seems to have believed that the truth is to be found in the so-called objective record. Even the later versions of *Walsh* are to a degree hampered by her self-assumed responsibility to publicize what she had found out about his life and times. *The Komagata Maru Incident* is an important stylistic departure, as clearly explained in her prefatory Note: "*The Komagata Maru Incident* is a theatrical impression of an historical event seen through the optique of the stage and the mind of the playwright. It is not a documentary account although much of it is documented. To encompass these facts, time and place are often compressed, and certain dramatic licence is employed" (iii). There are three playing areas, different in theatrical style but also interrelated in a number of significant ways. The main area is a brothel where two prostitutes, Evy and Sophie, entertain their lovers—Georg, a shady German immigrant, and William Hopkinson, an Immigration Department Inspector who struggles throughout the play to come to terms with his own deeply interiorized racist attitudes. Behind and surrounding the brothel is a runway where the Master of Ceremonies, T.S. (which possibly means The System), plays a number of different roles, creating the atmosphere of a carnival or seedy German-style cabaret. At the back, on a higher level, there is "an open grill-like frame" which Pollock says is meant to convey "both the impression of a cage, and of the super-structure of a ship" (iv). This section is reserved for an East Indian woman and her child who together represent all the Indians on shipboard whom we never see.

Pollock has dispensed with the conventions of theatrical illusion. Characters remain onstage throughout the play and simply move into the acting areas whenever necessary. There are no blackouts to simulate the passing of time; scenes are sequential, overlapping or simultaneous; characterization is not meant to be psychologically grounded but exists as the projection of interchangeable roles. We are never allowed to forget that this is a highly theatrical, non-illusionistic investigation of a continuing social problem. As both judge and jury, we are in effect being asked to pass judgement on ourselves.

Pollock has acknowledged that the play is an important point of departure in her career: "I started to explore structure, and it was exhilarating, and I decided that I never wanted to write a naturalistic play again" (qtd. in *Canadian Literature: A Guide* 139). But the exploration, though consistently interesting, is often problematic. There are still too many loose ends, several key moments are awkwardly handled, and there is an overall discrepancy between intention and result. The juxtaposition of different theatrical styles is in itself not a problem. As an instance of rough theatre, it has extraordinary vitality, the power to disconcert, and a kind of edgy playfulness—coming mostly from T.S. as he shifts all too cleverly from one identity to another—which puts us on the defensive. Her main difficulty is the failure to establish a set of theatrical priorities. The sinister ringmaster T.S. steals the limelight, so that the real-life characters—Hopkinson and Sophie, Georg and Evy—tend to become merely pawns in his own manipulative games. This works to good effect when he is playing Hopkinson's superior in the Department of Immigration. But as a controlling theatrical technique, it is of limited use apart from the expedient of imparting historical information without boring the audience to death. The revisions to *Walsh* are instructive: the awkward voice-overs got replaced by functional characters like Harry the wagon master; T.S. is still somewhere between these two possibilities. The so-called everyday reality of the brothel is to a certain degree overwhelmed by T.S.'s grandstanding routines; and as a metaphor for the ways in which Hopkinson prostitutes himself, it seems both pedestrian and overstated. The Woman is a moving emblem of suffering and endurance but, as with Sitting Bull, the decision to portray her as a type-character robs her of much of her humanity and makes the painful experience on shipboard seem distant rather than immediate. She's like one of those symbolical characters in a drama by Andreyev or Maeterlinck: you know what she's supposed to represent but you have to work harder than you should to maintain your interest in her.

Pollock has explained that in writing this play she "wasn't so interested in character" as she was in later plays like *Generations* (qtd. in *Canadian Literature* 139). Notwithstanding the honesty of her remark, her perhaps unwitting preoccupation with the characterization of Hopkinson is incompatible with the investigative presentational style established by the regular foregrounding of T.S. and his performances of various characters. As in the exposition of a naturalistic play, we gradually learn—through implication, innuendo, strenuous denial, subtextual registers and then sudden disclosure—that Hopkinson's racist behaviour can be attributed to his heredity. Although his father was British—and proud of it—his mother was a mere Indian. Hopkinson has never been able to reconcile this split in his racial identity: hence the destructive forces at work inside his moral code.

Pollock uses some vivid theatrical techniques to render his obsession with hiding his real identity, not just from others but also from himself. During an attempt to board the *Komagata Maru*, Hopkinson's face gets covered in coal dust when the Indians hurl the ship's cargo down on him and his men. As Robert C. Nunn has neatly put it: "Through a neurotic oversight the meticulous civil servant has placed himself where he will be overwhelmed by the dark-skinned men in whom he refuses to see himself, until his skin too is dark" (76). Once Hopkinson is back in the brothel with his prostitute Evy, he is desperate to wash the dust off. Here both setting and character business interact effectively to underscore the extent to which he is prepared to lie to himself and to others. Yet this kind of symbolical evocation is the exception, as Pollock concentrates her attention on a more prosaic and derivative kind of characterization. True to the naturalistic premise, Hopkinson cannot go on resisting the dark weight of the past. In the court room scene at the end, he admits to his own part in enacting the government's racist policy, and as he recites a hymn to Shiva the Destroyer out of the depths of his racial memory, he is shot dead by an Indian as an act of revenge. Pollock's sentimental attitude towards her leading character is unmistakable:

> I am very fond of Hopkinson; I see him as a far finer man than Walsh. Hopkinson is a person who has a guilty secret that is used against him by people in power. He atones for his actions by the manner of his death. When he says, yes, I'll testify, he accepts fatalistically the manner of his death in the nature of a Sikh, his mother's religion. He accepts responsibility for it and, to me, that's not despairing; that's a high point. That's why I have him say, "I open my arms" towards death, and speak the verse that is that part of his background. (Wallace and Zimmerman 121)

This kind of reductive approach to the character and the issues which he is meant to embody denies the audience a number of insights which the juxtaposed theatrical styles had in fact promised to deliver. We are being asked to think of racism as caused largely by personal neurosis. It can be, of course; but the broad sociological dimensions of the play had suggested that we were going to undergo a more complex, thorough and possibly analytical examination of the origins and effects of racism in Canadian society both in the past and the present. The emphasis on individual psychology, with its concern for the dignity of atonement, gives the audience relatively little to think about, beyond something lame or perhaps even self-righteous (e.g., "too bad he had such trouble accepting his mother's race"; or, "oh well, everything's all right now that he's able to come to terms with himself and behave properly by dying for his cause"). The audience is in effect left off the hook: it doesn't need to pass judgement on itself, since it can all too readily pass judgement on him. As instructive experiment in political dramaturgy, the play is ultimately frustrated by its surrender to naturalistic conventions and by its inability, for whatever reasons, to explore fully the presentational techniques in which, at one level, it seems interested.

Overly simplifying the very issues it purports to treat also causes a whole set of interrelated problems in Pollock's *One Tiger to a Hill* (1980), a hostage-taking prison-drama, loosely inspired by several real-life incidents but in no sense meant to be taken as a docudrama. The main character, a lawyer named Everett Chalmers, winds up mediating between the prison officials and the prisoners with their hostages. A well-meaning ordinary man, Chalmers' strong but untested sense of social responsibility means that, like Walsh, he cannot stand idly by when injustices are clearly taking place. He has to get involved, no matter what the personal cost.

Pollock uses the moral changes which Chalmers goes through to bracket her entire play. At the start, he stands inside the sinister, multi-levelled "medieval fortress" of a prison as he describes it, and explains directly to the audience that he has been going past this prison for nine years, always interested in but always unwilling to think too hard about "what it was like being inside, locked up" (76). To drive his point home he likens himself to those Germans who during World War II deliberately turned their backs on all kinds of atrocities ("Would I be any different in essence from all those good Germans who passed Dachau and Buchenwald, and never asked questions?" [76]). And when he has an opportunity to compensate for his own guilt, he does so, believing, however naively, that maybe one person, after all, can really change the system. As our guide to the inside, Chalmers is meant as a kind of surrogate for the audience; as Pollock has explained, "My hope is that the next time the audience reads about a hostage-taking event, I'll have given them a touch of Chalmers..." (Wallace and Zimmerman 122). At the end of the play, Chalmers again stands inside the prison, looking directly at us. But now everything has changed. The guard Hanzuk has just shot the Métis prisoner Tommy Paul and the social worker Dede Walker. As they lie dead on the floor behind him, Chalmers tries, however hesitantly, to account for what has gone wrong and what he will do next ("...Is everything lies?...tomorrow... I said...I will have breakfast...drop...the kids off at school...on Friday...I'll go to the Y...*he weeps* [137]). Pollock wants the scene to move us—"I want the audience to come away having been touched by that theatre incident so that the next time they read the paper, it isn't just the headlines and they don't say, oh those fucking psychopaths, we should lock them up and throw away the key"—and, at the same time, she recognizes that despite its clear agitational objective the play will probably not lead to social change, for audiences are of course entitled to do nothing ("But I don't think they're going to be moved to action") (Wallace and Zimmerman 122). The play's idealistic commitment to social justice, its determination to examine contemporary rather than historical issues and its impatience with mere finger-pointing reveal a kind of moral seriousness which is all the more valuable for being so uncommon. But here, as in *The Komagata Maru Incident*, there are several dramaturgical problems which make it hard for her to realize her consciousness-raising intentions.

The main difficulty is Chalmers himself. As Nunn has rightly argued, "his part in the action is so peripheral that it will not bear the weight of the anguish he informs us he is suffering" (80). He only addresses us at the beginning and the close. For the rest of the play, he is simply one character among many, with a dilemma which seems almost insignificant in contrast to what the other characters are going through. Brutal though it sounds, it is uphill work to care much about Chalmers. His worry over not being able to do much looks like a self-indulgent posture, even though this is *not* the impression that the playwright intends to create.

As for the main play, Nunn is again right: it borrows too extensively from "the clichés of television melodrama" and the final piling up of dead bodies is a routine taken "out of pure soap opera" (80–81). Being derivative is no bad thing—the theatre, after all, is a derivative art form—but if borrowed strategies are awkwardly handled or inappropriate to what the playwright is trying to achieve, the results are bound to be pretty much unsatisfactory. To use Pollock's own term, it is hard to figure out the controlling politic of *One Tiger to a Hill*, apart from her quixotic statement that audiences will pay close attention the next time that they learn about a real hostage-taking incident. Pollock's own remarks on the play she meant to write are more interesting, in my view, than the play she has in fact written. She thinks that the left-wing social activist Lena Benz "is as ineffectual and weak as the Warden because she's given up"; that the Head of Security, McGowen, is sympathetic "because he's the ordinary person who has to do all the shit work"; and that the rehabilitation officer Soholuk "has the clearest idea of what's occurring" in contrast to the rehabilitation officer Dede Walker who, despite audiences' need "to make her a heroine," is in fact "the ultimate villain in the piece...that well-meaning person who causes the shit to hit the fan" (Wallace and Zimmerman 121). But the play is so action-oriented and sensationalistic, so overburdened by crude characterization, and so weakened by dialogue alternating between the banal and the hyperbolic, that it doesn't seem much better than the average TV mini-special purporting to treat a controversial issue.

The play is more important, I think, for what it tells us about Pollock's thematic preoccupations and the contours of her imagination. Despite the way the play sets him up as concerned observer, Chalmers is mostly in a psychological prison of his own making. Confined by his daily routines and bourgeois morality, and alienated from a life-threatening cause, he feels compelled to make the kind of weighty moral choices which his marginal status in the play serves to deny him. He is a character who wants to radicalize himself by throwing off the dead weight of the past and by embracing a different set of moral assumptions in order to set himself free from all forms of tyranny—social, political and psychological. He is, by accident as well as design, the prototype of the central characters in Pollock's subsequent plays: the Nurlin family in the naturalistic *Generations*; Lizzie Borden in the extended psychodramatic game of *Blood Relations*; Johnny Farley, Mr. Big and Leah in the mythic dream-play *Whiskey Six Cadenza*; and his namesake, the physician Ev Chalmers, in *Doc*, a 'realistic' study in time remembered.

III

The Nurlins have been farming in Alberta for three generations. Old Eddy, now in his late seventies, emigrated from Europe in 1908 and has been working hard ever since to create a place of lasting value ("And when I go, what I'm leavin' is land, not money" [Pollock, *Generations* 193]). His son Alfred has accepted this legacy somewhat reluctantly, and though now in his mid-fifties still wonders if he should have made a different kind of life for himself. His wife Margaret, harbouring no such misgivings, content in her traditional role as wife and mother, gives him the strength to carry on. Their two very different sons focus the play's main conflict: whereas Young Eddy wants to sell off part of the farm to buy his way into a legal practice in the city, his younger brother David wants to retain every part of his grandfather's legacy and commits himself to running the farm in spite of government interference and stupidity. Young Eddy's decision is also motivated by his recognition that the land will ultimately try to possess those who try to tame it. He wants, instead, to have a more independent kind of life; so, too, does David's girlfriend Bonnie who leaves David near the end of the play. Afraid that she will simply become another version of Margaret, she will probably not come back, even when she has found herself.

As this summary suggests, *Generations* is a case study in naturalistic conventions. The setting of the New Place, where the family now lives, is realistically detailed and through inference tells us everything we need to know about the Nurlin family. Characterization relies on individualizing minutiae and psychological development; the dialogue is believable *conversation*, suitable to its time and place; and the land is a character in its own right, "revealed," as Pollock notes in the stage directions, "by the light and shadow it throws on the Nurlins' lives" (141). Heredity, too, is a significant determinant of behaviour. Whereas Alfred and Young Eddy are temperamentally unsuited to a farmer's life, Old Eddy and David are governed by what David can only gropingly describe as the awesome "*power*" (196) which the prairie seems to contain, and by a phallocentric desire to make the land submit to their will.

When I saw Cecil O'Neal's production of the play at the Tarragon Theatre in 1981, I was struck by how every aspect of the naturalistic style contributed effortlessly to the pervasive lifelike impression. Nothing seemed old-fashioned or contrived. Even something as ordinary as making the morning coffee managed to convey something small but important about the characters. The only drawback was that the apparent naturalness sometimes verged on the prosaic, and once the basic dramatic situation had been established, some of the developments—Old Eddy's ability to endure disappointment, Bonnie's departure, David's obsessive pursuit of his manly ethos and Margaret's benign acceptance of *everything*—seemed entirely predictable, close to the formulaic. But, ultimately, none of these things really mattered. The evocation of a sense of place was so keenly observed and honestly rendered that I could readily understand why naturalism, even now, can have the kind of radical impact that it had in the nineteenth-century. *Generations*' mimetic truthfulness makes an audience pay attention, as though for the first time, to a group of people whose lives have mostly been ignored by the theatre. Naturalism perhaps succeeds better than any other theatrical style in not only acknowledging but also authenticating their existence. Like Gwen Pharis Ringwood's sympathetic studies of prairie life, Pollock's drama—despite some of its reservations—is a celebration of the rural values of hard work, independence, self-discipline and moral certitude as it confers a kind of heroic dignity on those who struggle daily with the immutable forces of nature. Its dominant politic urges us to believe that the kind of traditional sacrifice to a larger cause made by Old Eddy, Alfred, Margaret and David is a more powerful form of self-realization than anything which Bonnie and Young Eddy can achieve through the single-minded pursuit of their own shallow interests.

The naturalistic style is made to look easy. But it gave the playwright no end of trouble, particularly during rehearsals for the premiere in 1980 at Alberta Theatre Projects. As Pollock explains, naturalism doesn't succeed unless the real-life illusion is perfect in every single detail: "once you're in the kitchen, you've got all the stinking things you've got to do in the kitchen, like cook the food" (Wallace and Zimmerman 120). Naturalism, despite its bad press, is a highly imaginative form of theatre. By giving us just part of the setting, it invites us to imagine the rest. Here we can readily transform the kitchen into the credible reality of the entire house. The naturalistic setting suits the development of her domestic themes and situations, but it seems to have frustrated her large intention of making the land itself into a living thing, as full of life as any of the characters. "You can't put the Prairies on the stage so you have to find another way of doing the outside scenes" Pollock argues (Wallace and Zimmerman 120). And although the solutions never really satisfied her, they were undeniably inventive, and tell us a good deal about the naturalistic paradox of using artificial means, not just to simulate reality, but to hint at the existence of a kind of omnipresent symbolical reality which is much harder to define.

She calls in the stage directions for a setting with a double perspective. From the vantage point of the New Place, we can see across the prairie to the Old Place, the original homestead where Old Eddy started his dream of a better life for his family. It is represented—or suggested—by a run-down porch with some worn steps and a few remaining posts. The Old Place, so clearly the victim of time and weather, brings the destructive force of nature within the naturalistic frame: the prairie landscape is thus portrayed as an eternal brooding presence, not just influencing but in fact controlling the lives of the Nurlin family. Moreover, the Old Place, as an enduring connection between the old and new worlds, has a kind of mythic dimension, summarizing the family's history in a single vivid image which is more poetic than real.

Fittingly, it is at the Old Place that the normally taciturn Old Eddy opens himself up a little to his oldest friend, an Indian named Charles Running Dog, who is not merely a character but an embodiment of the land itself—ancient, wise and full of insights denied to the more literally minded white man. The differences between these two friends are culturally determined: whereas for Old Eddy the land is "some kind of monster a man had to wrestle and fight," for Charlie "it's like a woman, you gotta woo her and win her" (163). The Indians have cut off irrigation water to the farmers because the government hasn't paid them enough for it; and Old Eddy, as a practical farmer, above all else, tries to get Charlie to convince the Indians to change their minds. As the two of them sit within the mythic aura of the Old Place, talking knowledgeably about the passing of time, the coming of death and the life-enhancing properties of water, they take on the stature of demi-gods from a distant legendary time, and the land surrounding them seems informed with the kind of awe-inspiring beauty which David ascribes to it. Thus, through the suggestive interaction of character, symbol and locale, the play's naturalism establishes a convincing illusion of contemporary farming life on the prairies and also manages to explore the kinds of ineffable themes and feelings which normally lie deep below the surface of human experience.

IV

Whatever the style of play, Pollock's characters are invariably challenged by the possibility of transforming themselves with a kind of idealism, a protean energy which verges on the mystic. To use the kind of theatrical metaphor which turns up in one form or another in all her plays, *if* we wish, we can perform ourselves into a different kind of existence—freer, less rule-bound, much more imaginative and much more connected with natural impulses. The self as a form of theatre: this is the controlling metaphor in *Blood Relations* (1980), Pollock's ambiguous, multivalent and in some ways dangerous retelling of the story of Lizzie Borden. The ideological assumptions of the play are meant to be unsettling. As a Conradian glimpse into our collective heart of darkness, the play suggests that the family and personal identity are *never* stable, *never* to be trusted, and that the desire to commit murder is a product of socio-economic and psychological factors over which a single individual might have very little control. "I'm saying that all of us are capable of murder given the right situation," Pollock has observed. "The structure [of the play] is a way of maintaining the ambiguity. You see, I don't say that Lizzy did it. The defence says she's not guilty. The Actress says she's guilty" (Wallace and Zimmerman 123).

The first version of the play, entitled *My Name Is Lisbeth*, was a conventional linear approach to the story and Lizzie's guilt was never in doubt. After the premiere in Vancouver in 1976, Pollock started to revise the text, coming up with the novelty of a double time-frame which adds a remarkable degree of psychological and dramaturgical complexity. The revised play, evocatively entitled *Blood Relations*, is set in Fall River near Boston in 1902. (What apt place-names for a play about repressed desire, guilt and ostracism, together with the possibility of being 'rehabilitated'!) Lizzie and her Actress-lover visiting from Boston while away the boredom of a Sunday afternoon by acting out some of the key events from ten years earlier in 1892, leading up to but stopping just short of the actual murders. Pollock herself describes this re-enactment as a "dream thesis" (*Blood Relations* 13), but Ann Saddlemyer has more precisely described it as a "psychodramatic game" (85). Lizzie plays the Borden's Irish maid, Bridget, who testified at Lizzie's trial because she was home on the day of the murders; the Actress meanwhile takes up the challenge of playing Lizzie herself. The psychodramatic game is not, I think, a play-within-a-play. Instead, the events of *both* 1902 and 1892 are juxtaposed throughout, to create a number of concurrent and interactive blood relations, many of which are ironic and threatening. Through this technique, the past, the present and (by implication) the future, are all made to bear on one another. Unlike *Walsh*, the play cannot be treated as mere history play—it has a kind of timeless urgency which *must* be answered.

The Actress is not named but given generic status so that she can readily assume Lizzie's identity and so she can function (like Chalmers in *One Tiger to a Hill*) as the audience's guide, taking us inside the house and eventually inside Lizzie's claustrophobic mind. This game is made to look like fun—at first—but it soon proves to be deadly serious. Its power to disclose what is normally hidden from view can cause permanent psychological damage, not only for the characters but for the audience as well. Once the audience has agreed to participate in the game, it cannot of course change its mind, even when it find itself being asked to take some responsibility for what happens to Lizzie.

Moving effortlessly back and forth from 1902 to 1892, *Blood Relations* has many of the thematic and structural features of a *fin-de-siècle* play. Victorian faith in normalcy, family life and traditional roles for women are being disrupted from within by repressed desires, independent thinking, aberrant behaviour and (covert) lesbianism. Whereas Lizzie is the wayward daughter who must pay a price for her unconventional ideas and actions, her sister Emma is the dutiful daughter who embodies the traditional moral values we are supposed to admire. Because Lizzie's mother died in childbirth, Lizzie is being raised by her loving but weak-willed father who is regularly overruled by Lizzie's wicked stepmother who of courses hates her adopted daughter. Lizzie demands her rightful share of the family inheritance, but Mrs. Borden is trying to persuade Mr. Borden to sign everything over to her villainous brother, and together the parents are trying to marry Lizzie off to a respectable widower with three children. Lizzie will of course have nothing to do with this nonsense. As in an Alice Munro story, our interest is not fundamentally in the scrupulous attention paid to the surface period-details of clothing, domestic architecture and etiquette as regulated by Mrs. Beeton, but in the Gothic nightmare which is buried deep within the subtext. We watch with fascinated horror as it is gradually dug up, brought to the surface and acted out with frightening vividness by the Actress. At this psychological level, the play is full of images of being locked inside and of trying, however unsuccessfully, to break out. Lizzie is imprisoned both figuratively and literally inside the house by her parents and never gets free, even when they are safely dead. Lizzie's pet pigeons, symbols of her own caged identity, are padlocked inside the garden shed, until her father chops their heads off with an axe. Lizzie gets their blood all over her hands, an indelible symbol, like her flaming red hair and the red sores and scabs on her knees as a child, of her murdered self as it is ritualistically sacrificed on the altar of social convention. In demanding her fair share of the estate, Lizzie, like many women in the 1890s, is demanding her right to be her independent self, to escape from lifelong imprisonment in the role of a contemptible Victorian spinster.

The play isn't grounded in the clichéd assumption that there is a *real* and healthy Lizzie, intact and knowable, just ready to emerge from beneath the mask of her adopted identity. Lizzie's greatest fear is that underneath her role there is nothing, an abyss from which a complete sense of herself might never emerge. "I'm supposed to be a mirror," she says to her impatient father, "I'm supposed to reflect what you want to see, but everyone wants something different." And then she reaches a startling conclusion which is not resolved, least of all at the end of the play: "If no one looks in the mirror, I'm not even there, I don't exist!" (39). Her father of course doesn't understand, and neither does anyone else in her patriarchal society. So she gets her stepmother to look directly into her eyes, and asks what she sees; but the answer, predictably, is "...Myself" (64). Lizzie keeps returning to this nihilistic theme, imagining herself as an expressionless face ("Just black holes in a white mask" [44]) going up and down with all the uncontrollable energy of a carousel horse; and throughout she seems a figure always on the edge of an identifying context, trapped, as Pollock notes, in a "bell jar effect" in which she is being forced "to fulfill other people's expectations of 'normal'"(55). Inhabiting their social reality instead of a room which she can call her own, she becomes obsessed with the eyes, both dead and alive, of animals and people, an obsession which dramatizes the eye/I connection and calls her own tenuous identity even further into doubt. Since she can't belong, and since she has no real identity in her isolation, is there anyone there who will answer to her name? Empowering the Actress to play the *part* of Lizzie is a dangerous decision. Lizzie is surrendering, if only for the time being, the limited amount of authority she has over herself, and runs the risk that the Actress, through the witchery of her art, will create an autonomous version of Lizzie which will wipe the *real* Lizzie completely out of existence.

The Actress is brought just to the point of committing murder. As in *Walsh*, a vivid tableau imprints the full significance of the moment on our collective conscience. While the Actress stands with the hatchet upraised, completely absorbed by the unleashed desire to kill, Lizzie breaks the spell, as it were, by touching her, and the Actress, terrified by this controlled encounter with her own demons, "whirls around to face Miss Lizzie who is left holding the hatchet." At this climactic moment, Emma calls down from upstairs, immediately returning the action to the so-called normal atmosphere of 1902. When Emma comes downstairs and sees Lizzie with the hatchet, she poses the question which she has asked repeatedly, like a haunting leitmotif, over the last ten years: "Lizzie, did you?" Lizzie replies that *if* she did, Emma, as a kind of mother to her, must bear some responsibility as well. The Actress, who has been watching this exchange, comes forward to tell what she has discovered during her investigation into the demoralizing environment in which Lizzie had been trapped in 1892: "Lizzie, you did." It is Lizzie, however, who has the final word: "I didn't," she says, and then as the "Actress looks to the hatchet—then to the audience," Lizzie says (cryptically), "You did" (70).

What might at first seem an enigmatic sidestepping of the issue is nothing of the kind. The last line encapsulates the full complexity of the murders, and draws everyone into the act of judgement. It was indeed the Actress, and not Lizzie, who was about to commit murder: as in psychotherapy, she is not allowed to make Lizzie into a scapegoat, but must assume responsibility for her own powerful destructive feelings. At the same time, we the audience, as participants in the game of re-enactment, must be willing to take on our responsibility, not just for what happened to Lizzie but for what can always happen, even in our own time, whenever we insist that both men and women adapt themselves to a rigid standard of behaviour. We remember that in a critical scene earlier in the play Lizzie asks Dr. Patrick what he would do if he could only save one person when two were in fact dying (61). What she is really asking is which life is more precious: hers? or her parents? She is struggling with the kind of irresolvable paradox found in a classical tragedy. If she is to live, her parents must die; if her parents are to live, she must die, psychologically if not literally. The doctor cannot answer her question, beyond giving a stock answer ("What I do is try to save lives…." [62]). This kind of unanswerable dilemma means that the play can never really end. The break in the frame of dramatic action at the close to address both us and the Actress carries the play out of the theatre into life itself where it is much harder to avoid answering the kinds of difficult questions which Lizzie's situation poses to us.

What is most disturbing about *Blood Relations* is the way it undermines our normal expectations of dramatic character. The faithful recreation, at one level, of Victorian society might lead us to think that the play is mostly concerned with empirical reality: certainly Pollock followed her usual approach of doing a good deal of historical research, and some of the lines spoken in the text by the Defence are taken directly from actual transcripts of her trial. However, once Pollock had introduced the double time frame and the role-playing, with their multiple levels of dream, memory and reality, she made a commitment to a different kind of characterization from which she hasn't turned back. Who *is* Lizzie Borden, we might well ask? Despite the attempts to contain her, Lizzie eludes definition. Like the proverbial madwoman in the attic, she is a prisoner of her own thwarted desires and cannot enact her sexual difference with the kind of absolute authority which will release her from the constraints of the past. Present but absent, visible but invisible, she is a fleeting image in the performance of a play written and acted not by herself but by someone else. Thus, it is not surprising that the essential indeterminacy of human character is what becomes the central theme of Pollock's next two plays, *Whiskey Six Cadenza* and *Doc.*

V

Whiskey Six Cadenza (1983) takes place during the fall and spring of 1919–1920 in the coal mining town of Blairmore, Alberta, "a small, distant town that might-have-been," as Pollock points out in her stage directions. A place of uncertain identity, located high up in the enveloping mists of the Crowsnest Pass, Blairmore is caught between multiple borders (Canada and the U.S., Alberta and B.C.) and therefore resembles not a real place but a dream-world in which "images and figures often appear fractured, refracted, fragmented" (141). So-called normal reality is but a pretense here; characters move easily in and out of focus as though they, like Blairmore itself, feel compelled to resist permanent definition; and with all the fluency of film, multiple perspectives are superimposed, fade from view and then magically re-appear in strange new forms. This is what the West has come to: it is no longer a promised land (as in *Walsh* and *Generations*) but rather an evanescent state of mind, idealized on one level, but treacherous on another.

At the start, Johnny Farley returns from Toronto where he couldn't find a job; like many of Pollock's characters, he *must* return home to confront his own self within the context of the past. Eager to escape from his mother's suffocating love and from the coal-dark prison of the colliery, Johnny gets himself adopted by the local rumrunner, Mr. Big, a master of gamesmanship whose greatest pleasure is to direct, enact and applaud his own performance as a self-made romantic existentialist. Standing outside the normal constraints of the law, conveniently glossing over his shady past in the East in order to embrace the self-fulfilling myth of the West, he moves easily across borders (both real and psychological) in his legendary car, the Whiskey Six of the play's title. As the sole proprietor of the aptly named Alberta Hotel, Mr. Big is answerable to no one but himself, and his rhetoric is as inflated as his mythic pretensions, studded with talismanic words like "radiance," "incandescence," and "illumination," which he delivers with such philosophical panache that they *almost* seem true. Mr. Big is carefully watched over and harassed by Sergeant William Windsor of the Prohibition Police. Known locally by his nickname of Bill the Brit, he is the symbol of British political power as it extends its rigid moral codes to the farthest parts of the Empire. As in *Walsh*, *The Komagata Maru Incident* and *Blood Relations*, these prohibitive moral values are portrayed as retrogressive, a form of old world tyranny which robs people of their right to an independent and visionary set of beliefs. Mr. Big and Johnny are placed in the kind of situation which recurs in Pollock's work, between imprisonment in the past or self-realization in the future; between impossible and possible worlds as they come into conflict to form what is essentially a morality play.

Mr. Big has also adopted a girl known only as Leah, an orphan who, like her namesake Leah the Forsaken, symbolizes fallen innocence just awaiting redemption. In making Johnny and Leah into members of his self-created family, Mr. Big creates permanence from change, meaning from nothingness, a sense of belonging from alienation, and becomes, as he explains to Leah, "like God descendin' to take his Chosen up into heaven in a fiery chariot!" (157). Despite our instinctive admiration for Mr. Big's histrionic style, we come to distrust him as a dangerous mythmaker whose fanciful stories and grandiose ideas about a new age about to dawn are largely corrupt and self-serving. Leah, it turns out, is not merely his so-called daughter but a Lolita, inciting his passion but also, in the end, victimized by it. Johnny, now in love with her, finds himself pitted in a moral struggle with a man to whom he owes his freedom. Like Lizzie in *Blood Relations*, Johnny is living out an irresolvable dilemma. If he remains with Mr. Big, he will be an accomplice not just in the crime of rumrunning but in the bigger crime of a life-lie, and in the repression of his own natural passion for Leah. If he betrays Mr. Big to Bill the Brit, along with the demi-Eden which Mr. Big has managed to create, he will have to descend into the mine which has killed his brothers, and return home to a mother whose burden of guilt and apocalyptic visions of hellfire are certain to destroy him.

Mr. Big, like a tragic hero, comes to recognize that he has been betraying his own ideals and that, to cleanse himself, he must take responsibility for his own actions. The ending is intentionally ambiguous: Leah, weary of what she calls their game of pretense, gives Mr. Big a pistol and says: "Now—make it right" (246). As she runs out of the Alberta Hotel towards Johnny, Mr. Big shoots her in the back, and as she dies, the scene shifts imperceptibly to a version of the dream-like dance involving all the characters (except Bill the Brit and Johnny) with which the play had begun. Johnny, now older, enters in front of this kaleidoscope of memory to comment on the paradoxes of what has transpired. The pictorial arrangement of past, present and future encloses the continuum of memory for both our contemplation and his in a series of ever-shifting moments which are mostly self-referential. Johnny won't deny the persuasive authority of Mr Big's rhetoric—"It may all have been lies, but that still doesn't mean it weren't true"—nor Leah's significance as "livin' proof a transcendence" (247). Lying *is* a form of truth, if one wants it to be so; Mr. Big, inspired by Leah, indeed answered to his name by sacrificing what he had created in order to set them all free. In the flickering light we see Johnny about to take the train that had brought him home to go…who knows where? It doesn't matter. What does matter is that he has now become the player of his *own* cadenza, occupying the borders of past, present and future at one and the same moment, in an "illuminated" state of being which is his rightful legacy from his father, Mr. Big.

Doc (1984) is also a play about the self-referential encounter of parent and child. Catherine, a writer in her mid-thirties, goes home to see her father, Ev Chalmers, the Doc of the play's title. Recovering from a bad heart attack, he is suddenly feeling old, and is only partly flattered to think that a new hospital is being named after him to honour a lifetime of dedicated service to his community. Unlike his namesake in *One Tiger to a Hill*, Catherine's father has been a man of determined involvement throughout his career who has saved many lives but at the expense of his family. His wife Bob loses her tenuous identity inside the straitjacket role of the doctor's wife, becomes an alcoholic and eventually commits suicide; his doctor-friend Oscar turns into a stranger; his mother commits suicide by walking into a train; and his children only know him as a distant figure who sometimes comes home briefly in the middle of the night. The main question of the play—was this sacrifice in fact worth it?—is too complex for a definitive answer, although there is a lingering sense that he was not acting as a compulsive egoist but knew exactly why he had made this choice.

Realistic only in its observed detail and lifelike conversations, the play has a non-linear structure, exists simultaneously on multiple levels of dream, memory and reality, and ranges widely through time and space. Katie, Catherine's "younger self" as Pollock describes her (*Doc* iii), also appears onstage: Catherine/Katie can talk to and for each other, as two generations inherent in the same personality, both of them needing to come to terms with their parents' failing marriage and with their self-realization independent of their father's indomitable will. The main objective, as in *Blood Relations* and *Whiskey Six Cadenza*, is to exorcise the ghosts of the past, to allow past, present and future to co-exist without damaging each other. As an investigation of both personal and public forms of (moral) accountability, the play is full of images of the body as either sick, dying and self-destructive, or as healing itself, becoming its own doctor, repairing the traumas of childhood which have been carried irresistibly into adulthood through the obsessions of memory. The house itself becomes a symbol of how so-called normal reality is controlled from within by ever-shifting states of mind. I remember that in the 1984 premiere at Theatre Calgary, the house seemed, on one level, a poetic spatialization of a Gothic labyrinth of black and white lines into which Catherine's mother Bob was gradually swallowed up as her daughter Katie called plaintively again and again for the mother whom she had never really known.

Catherine's greatest fear is that she will fall victim to the family malady of suicide, that as a woman she will be destroyed by her powerful father. But by leaving and by coming back with an autonomous identity as a writer, she can risk the investigation of the past and remain (unlike Lizzie Borden) in absolute control of herself. At the end, she asks her father if he will now open his mother's letter (which he has been holding in his hand throughout much of the play) to find out why she in fact committed suicide. But he says, in effect, that he doesn't need to ("I know what's in it" [122]), and neither does Catherine/Katie, for together they have just spent the play talking themselves through the psychological demons which it contains. And so Catherine lights her letter, and as the play fades to black, the last image is of "the dying flame from the letter" (126) as the lies of the past are sacrificed to the clarity of the here and now. Father and daughter are reconciled, to a certain degree, and Catherine can leave home without, as it were, taking it with her this time.

The self-reflective divided character has turned up in one guise or another in all the plays examined in this introductory survey. The earlier plays emphasize public forms of ideology in which figures of authority must be destroyed if the central characters are going to succeed in liberating themselves. Hopkinson in *The Komagata Maru Incident* kills his father, embraces his mother, and thus integrates the two sides of his racial identity which he has been struggling to keep separate; David Nurlin in *Generations* sets the prairie on fire to protest against government inaction and fights physically with Old Eddy who is angered by his grandson's behaviour—in these rites of passage, David is relinquishing the old ways and establishing his authority as the rightful head of the family farm. If, however, the authority figures cannot be destroyed, the central characters pay a high price: Walsh ends his days as a drunk, watched over with contempt by the idealistic Clarence; and Chalmers in *One Tiger to a Hill* can only stand on the outside of the prison, weeping at his own failure to change the system from within. The more recent plays, in contrast, emphasize personal forms of ideology, a politic of the self, in which acts of self-annihilation *might* lead to personal freedom. Lizzie Borden in *Blood Relations* is no longer controlled by her parents, but in playing the reconstructive game with the Actress is perhaps substituting one psychological prison for another; Johnny Farley in *Whiskey Six Cadenza* denies *and* affirms Mr. Big's self-serving myth and in this way paradoxically manages to become himself in the future; Catherine/Katie in *Doc* observe themselves in the mirror of the past and at the end, as an integrated adult character, they manage to stand free of the father whose authority they had so deeply interiorized. Parent and child together, judging each other and eager to be free; experiencing the world as it is, but suggesting the world as it ought to be: this, finally, is the recurring moral politic at the centre of Sharon Pollock's dramatic imagination.

(1989)

Works Cited

Bessai, Diane and Don Kerr, eds. *NeWest Plays by Women.* Edmonton: NeWest, 1987.

Canadian Literature: A Guide. Council of Ministers of Education of Canada, 1986.

Nunn, Robert C. "Sharon Pollock's Plays: A Review Article". *Theatre History in Canada/Histoire du Théâtre Au Canada* 5:1 (1984): 72–83.

Page, Malcolm. "Sharon Pollock: Committed Playwright". *Canadian Drama/L'Art dramatique canadien* 5:2 (1970): 104–11.

Pollock, Sharon. *Blood Relations. Blood Relations and Other Plays* Ed. Diane Bessai. Edmonton: NeWest, 1981. 11–70.

———. *Doc.* Toronto: Playwrights Canada, 1984.

———. *Generations. Blood Relations and Other Plays.* Ed. Diane Bessai. Edmonton: NeWest, 1981. 138–98.

———. *The Komagata Maru Incident.* Toronto: Playwrights Canada, 1978.

———. *One Tiger to a Hill. Blood Relations and Other Plays.* Ed. Diane Bessai. Edmonton: NeWest Press, 1981. 71–137.

———. *Walsh.* Vancouver: Talonbooks, 1973.

———. *Walsh.* Rev Ed. Vancouver: Talonbooks, 1983.

———. *Whiskey Six Cadenza. NeWest Plays by Women.* Ed. Diane Bessai and Don Kerr. Edmonton: NeWest, 1987. 137–47.

Rubin, Don and Alison Cranmer-Byng, ed. *Canada's Playwrights: A Biographical Guide.* Toronto: Canadian Theatre Review Publications, 1980.

Saddlemyer, Ann. "Circus Feminus: 100 Plays by English-Canadian Women." *Room of One's Own* 8:2 (1983): 78–91.

Wallace, Robert and Cynthia Zimmerman, eds. *The Work: Conversations with English-Canadian Playwrights.* Toronto: Coach House Press, 1982.

Musings of a Political Playwright: A Conversation with Sharon Pollock

by Pat Quigley

Pat Quigley: How did you feel in 1973/74, when you first heard that the Stratford Festival was interested in presenting *Walsh*?

Sharon Pollock*:* I remember John Wood had either come through town and seen the show or had heard about it in some way. Michael Bawtree called me up and mentioned that Stratford would like to do the show, and I was surprised, and happy. I suppose I was probably ecstatic.

Pat: Stratford hadn't done many Canadian plays at that time.

Sharon*:* John Wood had done *Billy the Kid* the year before, and it had been very successful. The year that *Walsh* was done, I believe they did a children's play at the same time so there was a little push for more Canadian work then, although our company, as I recall, was quite isolated down at the Third Stage.

Pat: So you did come to Stratford and work for a while with John on the play?

Sharon: John and I had several sessions here in Calgary, as a matter of fact. We talked about the piece, and I did a fairly extensive rewrite on the basis of that. I also came to Stratford. I was there during the rehearsal period, although I really only sat in on the read-through the first day, and a couple of times was consulted on this or that.

Pat: You have spoken about the playwright feeling isolated from the play once the director starts to work with it. Is that how you feel?

Sharon: Well I believe that one of the terrible things about this country is that the playwright often does feel that way. I don't think he or she should. And I think that part of the problem is that we seem to have no idea of who the playwright actually is. That's partly because we were raised on foreign work where the playwright was dead or safely removed.

Pat: Did you feel at the time that you were having input with *Walsh*? Did you feel valued as a playwright?

Sharon: Well, I guess I did in some respects. Of course, once a play has been up and running I think that the playwright has to let the play live on its own. And even in those first rehearsals, the responsibility is to the script. To what I call "the document." The play begins to grow in rehearsal. And the most difficult thing for the playwright is to want to contain it to the thing that he or she knows, as opposed to letting it go free and become that which it evolves into as a result of the input of all of these other creative artists.

Pat: And now, Stratford is producing your *One Tiger to a Hill*, with the same director, John Wood. Do you still feel, as a playwright, isolated from the process?

Sharon: When I talk about feeling isolated or removed from the rehearsal process, in actual fact I'm not talking about myself. I'm very fortunate, because I work in other areas of the theatre, and I really have never felt that isolation—partly because I feel as if my opinion has been respected. One of the reasons why it is respected, I think, is because I've worked so much as a director (and sometimes as an administrator and as an actress) that I have some view of the overall picture of things and I understand the mechanism of which, in a way, the rehearsal of the play is only one part, although it's the most important part. So I don't know that I have ever felt really removed, but I do know that my situation is unique. Writers are still signing contracts that say that if they're asked to leave the rehearsal, they will. Or that one can attend a rehearsal only if one is invited to do so. Or that one will attend a rehearsal as an observer and keep one's mouth shut. Now, nobody wants to interrupt rehearsals, but if you have a problem with something that's occurring that isn't working, nothing should prevent you from, at the appropriate time, voicing that to the director, not necessarily in the middle of the rehearsal.

Pat: It's been a long time since *Walsh*, and you've done lots of writing and all kinds of directing in the interim, but how do you feel now that Stratford is producing *One Tiger to a Hill*?

Sharon: Well, of course I'm happy because it's a play of mine that has not seen many productions, although I know it works and I think it's a good play. The other thing that makes it a very happy occasion is the nature of that particular work, the subject matter. This is a piece that deals in a contemporary sense with a political issue. And I think that for David William to produce that play and to support that play, gives a very important signal to Canadian playwrights, and also to the theatre community—that Stratford will not shy away from that kind of work. This particular piece, because of its subject matter, I think, is a choice that says something beyond producing a play of mine.

Pat: It says that it's all right to do large cast and obviously political plays and have them accepted by a large establishment like Stratford.

Sharon: That's right.

Pat: All your writing is political, isn't it? *Blood Relations* and *Doc*, although more intimate, are still political. But this play makes a very obvious political statement. Is this important to you as a playwright—to write plays and make obvious political statements, for instance, like *One Tiger*, which says something about prisons, the penal system and legalized violence?

Sharon: I believe that the kind of theatre that I want to work in deals with the world around us or the world inside us. I somehow don't like the kind of work that is non-critical, anti-intellectual, almost nostalgic, emotional—by that I mean that the audience is carried along on a great wash of emotion, but it's not really based on any real questions being asked about whatever it is that's being written about. So, I see my work as a playwright as being my work as a political person. You know, I live in a world that's full of things I don't understand, and sometimes I'm trying to make some sense out of it, using the specific to try and find some general answer to something. I very seldom find answers; usually all I get are questions. But even framing the question is very important. So *Doc* or *Blood Relations*, I think, are political plays, but people don't see them as such because the power and the politics are disguised in the family, and we don't like to think that within families there are politics, there is a hierarchy. But with *One Tiger to a Hill*, I lived in Vancouver when the real incident happened, and in fact I lived basically across the street from the B.C. Pen. It was impossible to live there at that time and not ask yourself, "What's happening here?"

Pat: Of course, I'm sure one of the criticisms that will be made by some of the patrons this summer is that the play is depressing.

Sharon: I don't see art as being decorative. And the only reason why some of the audience is happy with *Hamlet* and *Macbeth*, and don't see them as depressing, is that time has safely removed them from us. I always feel that we should meet that criticism absolutely head-on. All too often we allow people to say, "After a hard day's work, I don't need to go to the theatre and be depressed." I always say to them, "Why did you think you should go to the theatre that night? Stay away. Come to the theatre when you're prepared to participate. When you are prepared to be, in a way, challenged." And I believe the reason why we see audiences falling off, in a general sense, in a wide range of theatres, is that we are trapped into programming increasingly conservative work: work that allows the audience to become increasingly passive, and does not touch them any place where they live. I don't think you necessarily have to feel depressed. I do think that you should come out questioning some of the things that have been raised in the play.

Pat: And if the questions are challenging for us, then perhaps we'll empower ourselves to take action to find answers.

Sharon: That's right. When *Walsh* was being produced, I actually thought that would happen in a more direct way. That was, if you remember, the early seventies and late sixties, when everybody was acknowledging that Geronimo was a freedom fighter for the Apache people, and not the bad guy that we've seen in the movies. We were looking at Wounded Knee and understanding that a policy of real as well as cultural genocide had been carried out against the Aboriginal people here. And I suppose that with *Walsh*, I thought that we actually were on the verge of accepting responsibility for what had happened in the past and making a difference in terms of the situation of native people. It didn't happen. But the theatre's job, it seems to me, is to empower people. It's not to succumb to the many pressures that exist that want us to re-create the television experience. There are many different kinds of theatre, but the theatre that I think is important is the one that asks you to feel and think. I also believe that the theatre should have a cross-section of productions available too. However, the Stratford Festival, or our major regional theatres, should be dealing with large and important issues. I'm going there to feel more alive than I do when I sit at home and watch television.

Pat: And to be challenged with the hard questions.

Sharon: Yes, and in fact, I enjoy that. If everyone who had gone to *Hamlet* had said to Shakespeare, "Well, really, this is a bit depressing," we might not be doing him today.

Pat: Another question I wanted to ask you about *One Tiger* concerns the women in the play, Dede Walker and Lena Benz. For me, anyway, the women in the play don't seem to have any more particular solutions than the men do. And I read somewhere you had said at one point that you sometimes had difficulty writing women.

Sharon: I don't feel that I have that difficulty anymore. *One Tiger* was written about the same time as *Blood Relations.* I think that these plays are definitely a step forward, if you compare them with *Walsh*, for example, or *The Komagata Maru Incident.* I saw theatre, and I still do, as being about dramatic action, and in the world that we live in, women are often not in a position to initiate action. I couldn't find a way in *Walsh*, or even in *Komagata* to explore that. But I think as I've grown older, I've grown quite comfortable in terms of writing women. The only statement I can come up with in terms of *One Tiger to a Hill*, in a personal way, is that we have far more to fear from legalized violence than we have from the insane acts of a few people. I am frightened much more, in a societal sense, by what Wallace and McGowen do, or allow to have happen, than I am by what Tommy Paul and Gillie have done. Because Wallace and McGowen exert the power of the State, all of us are potential victims of what it is that they do.

Pat: Not just what they do to Tommy Paul and Gillie, but what they did to Dede Walker, whose worst crime, I suppose, was that she was well-meaning.

Sharon: Yes. When I researched this play, I had a great deal of difficulty, and for a long time I couldn't write it. I kept thinking that I had to figure out somehow who was right. At one point I was pulled very much toward Tommy Paul, or a figure like Tommy Paul, and then the next moment I would think, "My God, he should be shot, they should execute him. He is a walking time bomb." I had spent a lot of time with a broad cross-section of ex-cons and rehabilitation officers. I went around with a drug dealer for a period of time, around The Main in Vancouver, and on occasion, I would feel such a wash of sympathy for these people whose lives had been so terrible from the time they were small. I didn't see how they could turn out to be anything else other than what they were. Then the very next day I would feel, "My God. We have to get these people off the street," and that they were like Tommy—they were very dangerous individuals. It was only naïveté that allowed me to sort of "hang out" with them. They knew that I was doing something on that hostage-taking situation, so I think that they were fairly honest with me. But what I began to see was that really it's our own confusion that we feel. In my mind, if there's a villain in the piece, it's partly Dede Walker, the sort of "white-assed" liberal. I agree with Soholuk who says, "You think screwing Tommy Paul is a political act." And there's a whole wash of women who indeed believe that that's true—prison groupies, and people who believe that all you have to do is be really nice to somebody. But with the power structure that exists in society, that is not a solution. You have to do more than that.

Pat: And Lena Benz has sort of given up, hasn't she?

Sharon: In a way. I see her as being the very same as Wallace. Both of them play the game. Now Wallace has more power than Lena does, but we see her at a moment of doubt. When she talks to Wallace, she's being honest about how she feels, and with her own doubts about what she's committed her life to. Wallace has tried to really change things within the institution, and she has tried to change things outside of the institution. And neither one of them has been successful. What she is, I think, and what is commendable, is that she is honest about it. She tells Chalmers what she thinks is happening.

Pat: Is Chalmers the only hope then at the end of the play? The fact that he is now thinking differently than he was before, and that he's remembering it and trying to come to terms with it?

Sharon: I've often wondered where Chalmers is and who he's telling this story to. I've always thought of it in either one of two ways: I've thought there is an inquiry happening as a result of the incident, and Chalmers is basically talking to somebody in a formal situation who is examining what has occurred, which to me is a slightly more positive thing, because at least somebody said, "This isn't right"; the other thing I think is that he's gone to a psychiatrist about what's happened to him. However, there is a third possibility, which is perhaps the one which I like the best: I think of Chalmers as being some ordinary person who got caught up in this, and who this actually happened to, and he's standing up and telling the people who are there in the theatre, "This is what happened to me." I think of Tom Wicker who wrote a very interesting book about the Attica prison. He was very much like Chalmers insofar as he was a left of centre journalist whom the prisoners as Attica asked to become part of the negotiating team. He went through the whole negotiating process and began to suspect what was going to happen, and eventually it did happen: a number of the guards were being held hostage, and they were all killed by the bullets of the force that came in to free them. Nobody was knifed to death. At any rate, his reaction to that was to write a book about the whole situation. And so I think of Chalmers as someone whose reaction to it has been to create a play. I think of him as an ordinary person who has been up at the front of a group like Alcoholics Anonymous and said, "This is something that happened to me." And as he's telling us, because it's the theatre we're in, we then begin to re-enact it, as opposed to simply standing there talking about it. But in real life he would be explaining in prose what occurred to him. All I want, I suppose, is for an audience to look at surface and substance; what people say and what people do are often different.

Pat: Is it important that students see this play?

Sharon: Well, I think it's important that kids see theatre. I think that *One Tiger* is a good choice particularly for young people, who tend to be very conservative. I think that the play is more grey than black and white. Even though Hanzuk seems to purposely shoot Dede Walker, we still understand that we, society, have put him in a terrible position. How is it that we make people take jobs like that? There was a situation in one of the New England states where several lawyers and judges were put into an institutional setting in which half of them got to be guards and administration, and the other half got to be prisoners. And within forty-eight hours it had degenerated into real cruelty happening. When anybody is given complete control over another individual, quite often, it seems to me, unacceptable behaviour ensues.

Pat: Students seeing the play might begin to see that it's the absolute power in itself that one ought to question and think about, as opposed to putting the blame on any one individual. They start to ask those questions about authority and power.

Sharon: I think the play, although it deals very specifically with a particular situation that has political over- and undertones, at the same time is also, perhaps in some small way, a metaphor for a larger societal problem, in which we have "throw-away people"—the people who have done terrible things. I think of Tommy Paul and Gillie as throw-away people.

Pat: And even Dede Walker turns out as a throw-away person in the end.

Sharon: That's right. But, of course, she makes the mistake of appearing to be on the wrong side. And she forgets that it's more important to cover your ass; I mean some of the things that McGowen says, I think apply: "They sign the chit and we shovel the shit." I think that anyone who works in a large institution usually feels that way.

Pat: I'm interested, too, in the fact that the play is by a Canadian, and based on a Canadian incident. Not so much in the most obvious sense, but in the sense that it has an ambiance, a feel to it. The characters express themselves in certain ways that are unique to people who live in Canada, whatever those ways may be. Do you have a sense that it's important that kids see plays like that as well as Shakespeare?

Sharon: Yes I do. I think that when you recognize something as truthful because your ear tells you it's so, it is a wonderful moment. Not only do you have the enjoyment, the engagement with a wonderful piece of theatre, but inside you, something is legitimized. The place you live is part of some larger scheme of things.

Pat: And you experience that moment of recognition, which gives you a sense of belonging.

Sharon: That's right. A person's life is a small part of the tapestry which has some larger universal meaning, and if you never ever have your life experience played back to you, as part of that larger tapestry, then you only live in this time and at this one moment. And that's why it's so important that we have a theatre written by Canadians.

Pat: Well it strikes me it's important for future Canadian playwrights. There could be one in the audience that afternoon—a seventeen-year-old who goes, "Oh! That's my voice. I hear it. I recognize it, and now I can write it too."

Sharon: I was doing a show a couple of years ago, and two young women came up to me. They had seen *Doc* in Toronto, and according to them, it had changed their lives. They both wanted to work in theatre but the way that they thought theatre could happen had altered as a result of seeing that show. And indeed there may be that playwright sitting there. Unfortunately, I do feel that the person who has the largest responsibility with students in some respects is in fact the teacher. It's always disturbing, because when you meet *Macbeth*, not necessarily on the stage, but even in the classroom, the attitude of the teacher towards that work and how he or she feels about the work is often very, very important.

Pat: So we need teachers to be sympathetic to Canadian work and to understand its significance themselves, and to pass that on to students.

Sharon: That's right. But often they're quite willing to go with the stamp of approval that time has given, and they don't see that work can be very important in a particular time and place even though it may not live past that time and place. It seems to me that universality is what time determines. If a play is around a hundred years from now, then I guess it's truly universal; but a playwright must always work from a specific location or constituency. I belong to a constituency of outsiders by the simple fact that in Canada, in the west, you are on the periphery, removed from the centre of power. And I'm sure that's why most of my plays are about outsiders. It's got something to do with the fact that I live in a country that has a centralist coalition that's really two provinces that use the rest of us as sort of colonial outposts.

Pat: It's important, then, for students, to see and to read these plays, whether or not they're universal, just to know that it's acceptable to write about who you are and what's happening now.

Sharon: That's right. How many of them go and fidget through Shakespeare? No matter how universal it is, you can't go to them afterwards and tell them that they really enjoyed the play because it's a great work that has transcended time and has something to say to us today. They can go and see what is perhaps a lesser work, but be moved and touched by it.

Pat: And that's important in the theatre, too.

Sharon: Well that's all that lasts in the theatre. I mean, I see the theatre as performance art, and because of that, it exists only in the time it exists in, and every performance is different.

Pat: You've directed a lot of contemporary playwrights from around the world. Did directing these plays have an effect on your work as a playwright?

Sharon: I think that directing is about communication. How do you reveal and communicate the play, the story, and then what it means? When I'm directing other people's work, I'll come across something that I think is clever or works well; of course I don't attempt to imitate that, but I think it's certainly an advantage when I go to write myself, just knowing other work from the inside out. Some of the nicest parts about directing a master like Sam Shepard or Harold Pinter is that you discover their little black holes. It makes you much more generous to other work that you might do. You realize that every play has the parts that work better than the other parts.

Pat: You're more generous with yourself once you recognize that.

Sharon: Yes. And you're not afraid to take chances.

Pat: What do you hope for in the director of one of your plays?

Sharon: Someone who can find a way of subliminally endorsing what the play is about, without being heavy handed about it. That's quite an art.

Pat: For instance, a director who creates stage pictures that live on in the memory of the audience, enhancing the ideas that are already in the play, without overstating them.

Sharon: That's right. The secret is not to be literal; it's to find a thing that stands for something and makes what it stands for grow, and I think that John Wood does that.

Pat: Yes, I do as well. He demonstrated that art clearly with *Henry V*, which he directed here at Stratford last year, and I am certain he will do the same for *One Tiger to a Hill.*

(1990)

Dead or Alive? Feeling the Pulse of Canadian Theatre

by Sharon Pollock

Distinguishing the difference between the living and the dead in the human species is fairly easy; it's far more difficult to trace the passage and discern the difference between the lively and the moribund when it comes to institutions and ideas, attitudes and structures. If I may mix a metaphor, things generally start to smell before the light dawns.

When I think of the 60s and 70s, I think of the struggle of Canadian directors and playwrights to gain access to the stages of this country; of Canadian actors to speak in their own voice as opposed to using some mid-Atlantic vocal hybrid on those stages; of artistic directors to produce Canadian plays as opposed to providing a platform or "repeater station" exclusively for the plays of other times and places; I think of the struggle both for and by Canadian audiences who wished to see their own specific revealed, legitimized, universalized on the Canadian stage.

The difficulty of storming the major cultural bastilles resulted in the birth of workshop organizations dedicated to workshopping (with its many meanings and applications) but seldom or never producing Canadian work; and of "alternate" theatres committed to the production exclusively of Canadian plays. The larger institutions, whose greater human and financial resources should have enabled them to act as natural flagships for change, were often the last to mount Canadian work. And too often they did so in response to the carrot of subsidy held out by public funding bodies and specifically targeted to commissioning, premiering, the second production, the workshopping, of such work or for the residency (usually short-term), or rehearsal presence of a Canadian playwright.

All activity took place within the non-profit structure for it was deemed the most appropriate for the creation and dissemination of theatre as an art form. As well it was one within which the ability to generate revenue was not the prime factor in decision-making (although it naturally constituted a factor), thus the legal entity of "non-profit." Other motives of community and societal value were paramount.

Back then it seemed self-evident that the nature of theatre was to court peril, to take risks; and if its practitioners were to work honourably in the theatre s/he must do likewise. That wasn't too difficult, for to assume and to act on the assumption that Canadian plays were worthy of creation and production was a revolutionary act in and of itself. Any Canadian play, no matter how benign its content or form, was identified as "experimental" and "high risk" by its PR, theatre professionals, boards, reviewers, academics and government agencies.

A quarter of a century has passed, and I find it reasonable and necessary to pause and take stock, to sniff the air, to assess the liveliness of the theatre, and of those structures and processes we've created as a result of those early struggles.

Many of our non-profit theatres appear to have abdicated their responsibilities, obligations, *raison d'être* as non-profit structures. They have become alternate commercial theatres, as opposed to an alternative to a profit-driven commercial theatre. Non-profit status has mutated into nothing more than an acknowledgement of the inability to turn a profit rather than being the mark of a value-driven, not-for-profit organization. And instead of embracing social service, people support, and grassroots organizations and workers as members of our extended family, theatres cuddle ever closer to corporations and multinationals for financial support and operational models.

The targeted subsidy has not resulted in the integration of a budget line reflecting the financial and artistic implications of creating and supporting new work, new ways of looking at old work, into the regular operating budget. When the carrot of targeted subsidy is not available, innovation does not occur.

The financial chip for reduction of expenses to balance a budget is almost always artistic—choice of a "safer" play, smaller cast or set, cheaper costumes or artist.

Audiences are aging and programming is increasingly conservative. Joint and touring productions result in conceptual and creative homogenization as well as in a decrease in individual work opportunities (fewer artists work longer contracts). Emphasis is placed on larger market share as opposed to market expansion, and demographic profiles of theatre patrons dictate market strategy which assures growing elitism. Marketing and fundraising increasingly drain human resources and energy, and seize focus within an operation. We have become crisis-oriented; and our process of choosing and rehearsing plays is not conducive to creativity or to our sense of community.

In many cases the "alternate" theatres have revised their mandates to include work from the historical and international canon. The nature of their "alternate" state is increasingly defined by the size of budget rather than by any substantial alternative creative or administrative process as compared to that of the major theatres.

Workshops easily slip into "make work" activity; time constraints severely limit creative exploration of text; works of little substance benefit most; works of real substance are boiled down by hasty input; works which explore form or which do not rely on literary values or psychological analysis of characters are short-changed.

As a profession we run the risk of becoming increasingly isolated, insular, incestuous, with the work we create becoming increasingly self-centred. Plays about making plays, neurotic dramas about neurotic families, and biographical reconstructions too easily crowd out the new, the expansive, the other-worldly. Denial and dishonesty play a role. Read the press releases. Listen to a company's reaction to negative-comment. Honest and constructive self-assessment seems missing. Our denial even extends to the multi-racial nature of this country, for we exclude plays and players which speak to that reality from the majority of our stages. We label their art and artists "folk," or "multicultural," meaning not the "real" culture which needs no prefix.

Theatre as an art form, which was founded in spirituality, and began as a place to celebrate, question and challenge the gods, is in danger of losing its soul as we increasingly identify what we do as a commodity. The original impulse, that creative and communal spirit, is being replaced by the struggle to survive in a progressively deteriorating system.

Perhaps we didn't notice in that earlier struggle to gain access for Canadian audiences to Canadian work and Canadian artists to Canadian stages that the institution of theatre and the ideal form of theatre are in opposition, and we as theatre workers must be ever vigilant against its slide into cultural irrelevance. We must admit the tendency of theatre, aided and abetted by the very structures set up to serve it, to transform itself from a performance art, the immediate function of which is to entertain while engaging its audience in questions of substance, into a rose on society's lapel, from an immersion in life to a diversion from life.

As we enter the 90s, let us not expend our energies in maintaining at all costs the institution of theatre as a "cultural industry," nor be diverted by a struggle for power and control between artists and the boards, unions, media, audiences, administrators, granting agencies and government departments that inhabit the institutionalized theatre arena. Let us move on to the rediscovery and examination of our need for theatre—our need as a society, an audience, an artist, a community, in this time and place. And let us be guided in the creation, production and dissemination of work by what we discover through the exploration of that need.

And if we can admit that we often fail to achieve what we aspire to in the creation of a truly living theatre, the theatre will survive and so will we.

Otherwise, I'm not so sure.

(1991)

Reflections of a Female Artistic Director

by Sharon Pollock

"Women! This is men's realm," someone has said. "If you insist on invading it, unsex yourself, and expect the road to be made difficult."

No in-depth survey is required to ascertain the pervasiveness of the male in Western Theatre. It has been men's realm and exclusively so. Prior to the mid-seventeenth century boys played women's roles, men played men; and women weren't allowed on the stage nor in the director's chair. In Canadian theatre less than a decade separates us from entry into the twenty-first century, and things aren't so different. Women do play women (and men play women); women do write plays, direct and design, and women are over-represented in the theatre's administrative, management and support systems (or so the latter appears to one who has not taken a formal survey but who has worked for twenty-seven years as an actor, playwright, director and artistic director); however, the talent, and vision, of women is so circumscribed, diminished and diluted by the male's primary position as artistic director in the realm of mainstream theatre as to render their contribution essentially insignificant.

As a woman who, through a combination of fate, desire, and perhaps perverseness, invaded that realm, I share the following observations, in the hopes that others who follow may find something of use.

We know that there is a push in our society for the casting or the embodying of the deepest comprehensions and truths in the male character in the play or the male voice in the theatre. It is deemed to have greater significance, import and impact on the audience member, the critic, the corporate patron, the public funding body, the board of directors, and in the theatre community itself. This affects the work, the programming of the work, the interpretation of the work, the creative process whereby the work is produced, and the structures within which we create, finance and market the work.

Female directors in Canada are most often found in the smaller alternate theatres. Generally the creation of the companies has sprung from one of two impulses. They have grown out of consciousness raising (which is not necessarily grounded in a feminist ideology) and seen their major impact as political; or they have been formed in response to artistic frustration, and their goals are primarily artistic goals. There is overlap and combination of these two goals. Women artistic directors are attracted to and highly visible in the support and creation of new work by both male and female playwrights. Often women's dramaturgical experience has led to directorial experience and thus to artistic directorships. I leave it to you to determine if this is a manifestation of the constant channelling of women's actions and energies into the becoming of themselves and, if so, whether the impact on their contribution to play-making and theatre-building be potentially more or less positive as a result.

I believe that the preponderance of women artistic directors with such companies reflects a profound interest in discovery and creation as well as a more integrated view of theatre and the life of the world around it. Artistic and political commitments are interconnected and interdependent, with the strength of the theatre determined by the extent to which it touches the lives of its audience, and the life of the larger community.

The absence of the female artistic director in the larger regional, national and mainstream theatre companies reveals more than the obstacles to be overcome in the employment practices and biases of boards. It also reveals women's recognition of the male-dominated theatre establishment's obsession with theatre as commodity, as a diversion from life rather than an immersion in life, as a thing to be manufactured and marketed using corporate, hierarchical and patriarchal models. There is a contradiction between women's and men's view of the making and sharing of theatre, and there is a difference in the perception of men and women as to what constitutes compromise, and what constitutes capitulation in the making and sharing of theatre.

In other words, I believe many women have chosen not to enter men's realm of the artistic director in establishment theatre for they see or sense the inherent contradiction between themselves and the structures which they must direct and within which they must function, and the betrayal and denial of self which may be asked or demanded as a result.

"unsex yourself"

"made difficult"

Within men's realm of the theatre, there is subtle pressure and conditioning to deny profound female life experiences, comprehensions and processes as legitimate or important or appropriate or useful, or even interesting, as the raw material on which to base decisions. I believe receptivity and openness to female impulses, and women's ability to receive, and to make something of what is received, is often mistaken in both boardroom and rehearsal hall for indecisiveness, weakness, lack of vision or purpose. The style and substance of male assertiveness is used as a gauge for leadership and creation. If one is to be a good artistic director in such organizations, one must first deprive oneself of identity as a female, and manufacture the style, if not the substance, of those with higher status—act like a man. Unless, of course, you have been contracted because as a female you are seen as more malleable to the will of the board whose theatre it is seen to be. The father/child model shall then determine the relationship between board and artistic director.

Deeply ingrained male ways of seeing and doing impact on far more than board room relationships and dialogue. Company activities may be prioritized quite differently by the male and female artistic director. The male impulse to see creativity as output, and the female's to view it as a medium for growth and development, are, in my opinion, the basis for the discrepancy. For the male, if there is no product at the end, there is no process, process being harnessed only to product. In major theatres in Canada, product is the subscription season. While I see this as the most visible manifestation of a company's activities, I do not see it as the foundation or raison d'être or soul of the company. However, subscription seasons are finite and knowable, and this gives comfort to some. They are the "what" of the company. The female artistic director is more interested in the "why" and "how" from which "what" will emerge. Female-run companies are often identified by community outreach, and the exploration, research and development of plays and artists—taking more chances on work and on people is more the operational norm.

A woman's life teaches her many things: to trust less the exterior and seek the interior; not to fear multiplicity, having multiple selves within herself; to be suspicious of certainty; and to entertain ideas of contradiction, and diversity, along with unity and singularity. This makes her a positive enabling force. And it requires first an acknowledgement that one is not complete to begin with, and that totality may not be knowable. Receptive thinking and collaborative actions in the theatre do not represent failures of imagination, energy or intellect. I see the compelling need to believe that all is contained within, and that, in essence, one generates alone, as male motivating forces in the creation of work, and the administration of companies.

The betrayal of self, the denial of impulse, intuition and belief can be accompanied by pressure to deny equality of opportunity for other women. In my experience the predominance of male directors was never questioned; however, when more than one freelance woman director was hired in a season, it was not uncommon for me to be asked both publicly and privately to defend such a choice of directors. The quality of work was not the issue, but gender. When plays were programmed whose cast lists had more women than men, I was accused by the board of producing "too many women's plays," no matter what the content of the work. When I asked for clarification as to what constituted "woman's plays," and whether they were suggesting that the programming of "men's plays," which I would like defined, was preferable, I was informed that I knew what they meant. I didn't really, although I suspected much. Such pressure may find many forms, but I believe the mindset it reveals is alive and well in mainstream theatre operations.

While the male artistic director views tenure at a small alternate company as a station stop on a career path spiralling ever upwards towards the nirvana of Stratford, the female artistic director views her similar situation as a destination for that particular point in time. The position held is the centre at that moment, and not the means to a professional end to be achieved at some future point in theatrical history.

Perhaps because women have been invisible to those who write histories, and our faces, names and stories ignored, we are more aware of that which is not stated and those who do not appear in historical honour lists, cultural or otherwise. Knowing the fiction of fact frees the female from the onus of "place in history," and removes the burden of assessing future generations' assessment and interpretations of work and actions. This is not to say that what we do shall be lost, for I do not think that is so, nor would one desire it; but that, as a result of our previous exclusion, the possibility and the nature of inclusion do not wear on us. Notions of ambition or success or even "art" have more to do with the empowerment of others and our relevance to now.

We are more concerned with what things are than what they appear to be. For centuries the quality of our lives has been dependent on seeing into things and people, and making something of what we saw because our very lives depended on it. We have learned the lesson well. However, as the theatre moves more and more towards façade and surface with appearance replacing substance, the ability to access the latter becomes a liability to be suppressed for it serves only as reminder to those who control our theatre of what might have been.

And always it seems that despite—or perhaps because of—the great challenges should exciting ground-breaking work occur, media and public focus are on the femaleness of the artistic director as opposed to the quality or artistic philosophy of the work, thus endorsing the image of the successful artistic and organizational woman as being unique among her sisters.

"invade"

May women storm the bastions of men's realm of the theatre establishment? Despite the inhospitable environment, there is dire need of their talent and insight, for the female artistic director is one with the true nature of theatre, and at home with non-profit status (which supposedly is that of the majority of Canadian theatres), more so than her male counterpart. She is better able to articulate the values that replace revenue as the prime factor in decision-making in the not-for-profit structure, for her personal ability to generate monies has not been the standard by which worth is determined in the female world, nor the means by which she has survived and triumphed. The male artistic director, captive in a world where economic worth is the value standard, and inheritor of power, control and privilege by way of his maleness, is weaker in defining and speaking of those values which replace profit and the generation of revenue. This being a time when most of our theatres are incurring large financial deficits as a result of falling revenues, with subsequent pressure for bottom-line thinking to determine all decision-making, the need to define and defend the not-for-profit arts organizations in this country has never been greater. Those who are seen as the appropriate persons to mount such a defence, artistic directors of the major and regional theatres, are those least able to do so, and the theatre suffers accordingly. Its most eloquent spokespeople are silenced, muted, or find no platform.

This can not be the way of the future if theatre is to survive.

(1992)

Theatre by Default: Sharon Pollock's Garry Theatre

by Rita Much

When her play *Fair Liberty's Call* was in rehearsal at the Stratford Festival in July of 1993, Sharon Pollock casually announced over a drink in a local bar that she had started her own theatre in Calgary, the Garry. The small venue, only 236 seats, is run like a cooperative, she explained, receiving no public or corporate subsidies and, she added with a nervous laugh, it might just bankrupt her. My first reaction was one of astonishment. Why, I wondered, would a senior Canadian artist, a multiple award-winning, internationally-respected playwright choose to embark on such a breath-taking but stressful theatrical venture during dire economic times that saw some theatres in the country close and most in retrenchment? There was no question that the enterprise was gutsy, but was it also foolish?

Upon reflection I concluded that Pollock's founding of the Garry was, in terms of her artistic vision and practical experience, an inevitability, that there was a logical progression from the work Pollock did as an actor, director and playwright in the late 1960s and 1970s in her effort to establish an authentic Canadian dramatic voice and the Garry's modest launch with Canadian classic *Billy Bishop Goes to War* on October 22, 1992. Upon reflection I realized that the artist who is on record as saying she eschews conventional terms of success and that she has never been satisfied with anything in her life could hardly have done otherwise.

In hindsight Pollock's abruptly terminated (and highly publicized) appointments in the 1980s as artistic director of two established not-for-profit theatres were clear markers of the direction she would take in the 1990s. The fact that she was the first female artistic director of a major western theatre did not carry much weight with Pollock. In 1984 after only three months at Theatre Calgary, Pollock resigned. Brian Brennan in *The Calgary Herald* cites "duality of management" as the official reason, which translates into Pollock's unwillingness to allow her artistic vision to be compromised by a general manager concerned with finances who held joint authority in running the theatre. According to Brennan, Pollock's objection was that "the present operational structure...doesn't allow for the centrality of the artist." In 1988 she returned to her native Fredericton to head Theatre New Brunswick, excited at the prospect of running a theatre that toured province-wide. It was the input from audiences of diverse communities that appealed to her, for it is her belief that theatre should be "part of the quality of essential life—like hospitals and social services—rather than something you just went to five times a year to be entertained" (Godfrey). Two years later she left, frustrated by the difficulty of meeting the needs of significantly differing kinds of audiences (a difficulty which resulted in a substantial decline in the number of subscribers) and by the Board of Governors' priorities of box office revenue and drama that entertained rather than challenged (Mullaly 23). Pollock's strongly-worded reaction to the Board's profit-driven model for theatre was that theatre practitioners should "abandon the cultural palaces as our home" (Rempel 57).

In the spring of 1991 Pollock elaborated on her concerns about the state of dramatic art in Canada in an article she wrote for *Theatrum* called "Dead or Alive? Feeling the Pulse of Canadian Theatre":

> Many of our non-profit theatres appear to have abdicated their responsibilities, obligations, raison d'être as non-profit structures. They have become alternate commercial theatres, as opposed to an alternative to a profit-driven commercial theatre. Non-profit status has mutated into nothing more than an acknowledgement of the inability to turn a profit rather than being the mark of a value-driven, not-for-profit organization. And instead of embracing social service, people support, and grass roots organizations and workers as members of our extended family, theatres cuddle ever closer to corporations and multinationals for financial support and operational models. (12)

The article goes on to predict the death of theatre as an art form in Canada unless artists stop viewing it as a commodity, as a "cultural industry" (13), and begin to rediscover its spiritual provenance.

Pollock proceeded to demonstrate how to go about doing this by founding her "own damn theatre group" (Hutchinson, "Somewhat" 50), the Calgary-based Performance Kitchen which served primarily as a workshop for actors and writers. Then, at the instigation of businessman John Kerr, Pollock and her son Kirk Campbell took over a former porn cinema on Garry Street in Calgary's rather seedy neighbourhood of Inglewood as part of a general community effort to revitalize the area. The Garry's financial survival was to be dependent upon a low rent, theatre rentals, and volunteer labour (particularly on Pollock's part) and it was to be a "people's theatre," close to "the pulse of the community" (Pollock, Interview by Rena Cohen 35). Halfway through the Garry's first season Pollock succinctly articulated the challenge that lay ahead: "If we fail to make this work… there is no one to blame but ourselves. If we succeed, we know that value-driven theatre has a future" (Hutchinson, "Staging" 43).

By the end of the second season the Garry still wasn't making a profit from its own productions and the Canadian Actors' Equity Association had issued a Defaulting Management Notice due to the $800 owed in members' benefit levies. Recently in the upstairs offices of the Garry Theatre, Pollock paused to take stock of her theatrical experiment (1994). I asked her if she felt the space is integrated into the larger community life of Inglewood in the way she and its owner, John Kerr, envisioned.

Pollock: I think so, in part because from the start the Garry was part of the process of revamping the neighbourhood. Actually, for a while I was worried that Inglewood might become too upmarket, but the improvement is slower and longer term. What originally attracted me to the area was its diversity—the diversity of age, the diversity of income, the diversity of business—all of which makes for a very interesting place to create theatre in. I don't ever want the increasing homogenization of class, age and economic and social elements you see in other parts of town to happen here, and I doubt it will. The area itself is pretty finite, bounded on one side by the river and on the other by the railroad tracks. The corporate city presses on us to the west and in the east we run into Blackfoot Trail.

I also think that the strong role the Garry has assumed in the community over the past two seasons is due to our relationship with the building's owner. We don't see a lot of John and his wife Oreal but we aren't just tenants to them. They care tremendously about what happens to the theatre and support us as much as they can, and if we are late with the rent because we don't have the rentals or we have a show that doesn't do well, they're understanding.

Much: *With what have you have replaced the corporate operational model? How is the Garry administered?*

Pollock: Kirk is sort of General Manager, I guess, and he's the only one who draws a salary which he gets from the rentals, an amount considerably below poverty level, less than minimum wage in terms of the hours that he puts in. He's the liaison with the groups that come in, he's the person who looks after the financial management of the space, and he's the one who has to be here every day. I don't take any money out of the place. I sometimes put "Director" beside my name on the program because people keep asking me if I am the Artistic Director. People keep insisting we have titles and we hate that. We refer to ourselves as the "Garry team," or the "artistic team," because we don't like to think of ourselves as administrators. We like to think of ourselves as theatre workers who do various jobs. Besides Kirk and me there's Tim Culbert, a university drama student by the name of Kristian McInness, and an actor called Jarvis Hall, which makes five of us who are here on an on-going basis, who are in and out and who work in some capacity and for little or no money on almost every show—acting, designing lights, running lights, stage managing, working front of house. All of us are cleaning.

Much: *In your first season you produced John Gray's* Billy Bishop Goes To War, The Other Side Of The Pole *by Stephen and Marney Heatley and Edward Connell,* Macbeth, *an Australian work called* Jack's Daughters *and your own piece,* A Death In The Family. *Your second season consisted of* Come Back To The Five and Dime, Jimmy Dean, Jimmy Dean*;* Death Of A Salesman*; Kirk's* Heading Out*;* Nurse Jane Goes To Hawaii *and* Saucy Jack, *another new work by you. Are the decisions regarding programming made collectively?*

Pollock: Lots of suggestions are made and anyone can put forward suggestions, not just the people I've mentioned. Someone on the team might have a burning desire to do something, or an actor who seems to fit into the way we operate might propose to play a particular role, or a director might turn up at the door with an idea. We want to preserve flexibility and reduce burn-out, so we solicit input as much as possible.

Much: *Is programming also determined by an official or formal mandate?*

Pollock: What we see ourselves as doing is trying to balance producing work that is close to the pulse of our community and close to our own pulse as theatre workers. So we wouldn't do plays that we hate but we have to consider or acknowledge up front (because we don't have public funding or ask for it) that if we want to do such and such a show that probably nobody is going to come and see it and that we will pay very directly for doing it.

What we started to do last year is to program a large enough variety of choices to satisfy those who come here regularly, the ones who are the most reliable and who tend to be between the ages of 30 and 50, and to do other work for an audience much less loyal and not necessarily from the area.

We sometimes see an artificial line between professional and community actors (I prefer the word "community" to "amateur") that some people see as a quality judgement or a commitment judgement. We don't want to look at that line. We want to provide an opportunity for people to do roles they believe in, that stretch and challenge them, and that they might not get a chance to do (whether they are Equity actors or not). There are some great actors around who can't for a number of reasons commit themselves to acting as their only source of income. A part of what we do is blur that line a little so everyone is equal when they come in. We see ourselves as providing an opportunity for people in or coming out of drama programs—at the University of Calgary, for example—to get another take on theatre that more accurately reflects what they might be facing after they graduate and leave that rather hothouse situation.

We also see ourselves as providing inexpensive artist-and people-generated, community-generated projects. Sometimes when groups don't have enough money to rent the space we help out if we're able to do so. We try to be open to whatever comes up out of the community.

Much: *Is the fact that you must rent out the space between shows to survive a selling point, as it makes the Garry a venue for a large range of activities, theatrical or otherwise, within the community?*

Pollock: Absolutely. In fact, we just had a fashion show in here, "There's No Business Like Sew Business," run by a woman who teaches sewing to young people, kids even. I think the Garry has established its identity securely enough that people aren't confused to find out there's a fashion show on instead of a play. I think people feel we fall into the middle ground between a movie house and a theatre in terms of the formality of the Garry. Often people will just call and ask, "Oh, what's on tonight?" or simply drop in, willing to go to whatever is being staged. We also act as a kind of clearing house for information. People phone us and say, "I'm looking for a Black actor. Do you know any?" or "I need to have a fire on stage and I don't know what to do about that" or "I've friends coming to town from overseas. I know there's nothing playing at your theatre but what do you think I should take them to see and where should we eat?" I know it sounds corny, but when people come in and find me selling tickets they'll say, "Hello, Sharon" and talk about what I've written. They like the fact that an actor they've seen on stage is selling concessions, perhaps, or answering the phone. They don't respect the work any less. It seems to me they feel the work belongs to them in a different way.

We're always having people dropping by to give us costumes and set pieces. The informality of the atmosphere here attracts them. The artistic event isn't distanced or removed from the pattern of daily life as much as it is in other theatres. In fact, some people who remember the Garry as a cinema or who haven't attended the theatre often enough to understand the conventions actually get up in the middle of a performance to go to the bathroom. We're much more flexible than other theatres in terms of accommodating people, I think. If someone doesn't have enough cash for a ticket we can say, "Oh, that's okay. Drop by later in the week with the rest." And we appeal to those people who don't want an evening out at the theatre to be a "big event" involving two weeks of planning and dressing up and great expense. When people ask if we have a dress code we say, "Well, you have to wear something," and our top ticket price is about $12.

Much: *Did the ban by Equity come as a surprise?*

Pollock: Yes, but in retrospect I'm glad it happened. Though Equity makes concessions to other theatres our size they kept rejecting our requests for a concession and since we couldn't afford to continue to pay union scale, the Defaulting Management Notice forced us to confront the problem head on. I've said from the start that if an actor has an opportunity to play *Macbeth* at the Garry and he can't even get on stage at the Centre for the Performing Arts and he would like that opportunity, couldn't it be his business? Is it better for an actor to earn $200 a week washing someone's hair in a beauty salon than to play a part she'd love to play at the Garry? I think it's a matter between membership and Equity. The actor should decide if she wants to make an investment in her career. It's not a loss.

No one wants to hear this, but there are a lot of very good non-Equity actors around, as our reviews this year prove. The fact that they don't have an Equity card has got more to do with who has chosen to employ them and how many times and what their financial situation is than with talent.

Maybe Equity wasn't supportive because we don't fit into their pigeonhole of how a professional theatre operates. I think of us as evolving into something that falls between an amateur or community theatre and the professional theatre. The thing that binds us together is the work and that can be a new play or a classic, like *Salesman*. What there has to be is some kind of equity between the way people interact, less ego, less silliness.

We won't replace existing forms of theatre but there should be room for us—and more theatres like us.

(1995)

Note

This article was written with the assistance of the Ontario Arts Council.

Works Cited

Brennan, Brian. "Pollock suddenly quits TC." *Calgary Herald* (23 August 1984): F1.

Godfrey, Stephen. "Pollock pulling up stakes at Theatre New Brunswick." *The Globe and Mail* (18 October 1989): C11.

Hutchinson, Brian. "'Somewhat democratic' theatre." *Alberta Report* 18:36 (30 September 1991): 50–51.

———. "Staging a comeback in Inglewood." *Western Report* 7.51 (18 January 1993): 42–43

Mullay, Edward. "The Return of the Native." *Canadian Theatre Review* 63 (1990): 20–24.

Pollock, Sharon. Interview by Rena Cohen. *NeWest Review* (December 1993/January 1994): 33–35.

———. "Dead or Alive? Feeling the Pulse of Canadian Theatre." *Theatrum* 23 (April/May 1991): 12–13.

———. Personal interviews by Rita Much (Spring-Summer 1994).

Remple, Byron. "Not a Diplomat." *Western Report* 4.42 (6 November 1989): 56–57

Daddy's Girls: Father-Daughter Incest and Canadian Plays by Women

by Jerry Wasserman

> How, as women, can we go to the theatre without lending our complicity to the sadism directed against woman, or being asked to assume, in the patriarchal family structure that the theatre reproduces ad infinitum, the position of victim? Who is this victim? She is always the Father's daughter … (Cixous 546)

By a quirk of history the same decade that saw the rise of the contemporary feminist movement also gave birth to modern Canadian theatre. Ironically, although shaped by many of the same cultural forces that helped mould the first phase of late twentieth-century feminism, the new Canadian theatre that emerged in the late 1960s and early 1970s included few women's voices. The most notable women's stories it told were by men—George Ryga's *The Ecstasy of Rita Joe* (1967) and Michel Tremblay's *Les Belles-Soeurs* (1968). In the paradigmatic Canadian play of the era, David French's *Leaving Home* (1972), a young man breaks free of paternal tyranny to assert his selfhood and independence: a male parable of the Canadian nation itself in the euphoria of post-Centennial nationalism.

By the late 1970s, as the "women's liberation" phase of feminism gave way to an awareness that women suffered from a deeply rooted and internalized systemic oppression, history (redefined as her/story) came under increasing re-examination. To uncover the sources of oppression, one line of investigation pursued her/story back to its most personal source—the construction of woman within the patriarchal family. Around this same time, a strong contingent of women playwrights emerged from the second wave of contemporary Canadian theatre, playwrights who would explore the Canadian dramatic landscape from a feminist perspective. For their characters, daughters rather than sons, leaving home had to be preceded by revisiting and re/presenting the site of their journey's origin: the father's house. And like much of the non-dramatic women's literature of the period, what many of these dramatists found hidden away there was a terrible family secret: an epidemic of child abuse, particularly sexual abuse, including father-daughter incest.

This revelation has given impetus to a critical reappraisal of Freudian assumptions about the psychosexual development of girls in early childhood and adolescence, in particular Freud's recanting of his own initial conclusions about the widespread reality of incest. Jeffrey Masson and others have accused Freud of an "assault on truth" for having distorted clinical evidence in his investigations of childhood sexual traumas in order to conclude that "although all my women patients told me that they had been seduced by their father I was driven to recognize in the end that these reports were untrue and so came to understand that hysterical symptoms are derived from phantasies and not from real occurrences" (Freud 120). An extensive body of literature for and about victims and survivors of childhood abuse has developed, from groundbreaking clinical work like Judith Herman's *Father-Daughter Incest* (1981) and Diana E.H. Russell's *The Secret Trauma* (1986) to self-help best-sellers by the likes of John Bradshaw and Gloria Steinem, not to mention a flood of flavour-of-the-week TV movies. Scholarship has been affected by feminist rereadings of literary biography, such as Louise DeSalvo's controversial *Virginia Woolf: The Impact of Childhood Sexual Abuse on Her Life and Work* (1989), and a constant stream of high-profile women—Rosanne Barr, LaToya Jackson, and Lawrence Durrell's daughter among them—have offered autobiographical confessions revealing sexually abusive relationships with their fathers. The inevitable backlash has brought with it accusations of "false memory syndrome," mockery of the self-help rhetoric, and a general subsuming of the complaints of women against men under the all-purpose demonization of "political correctness."[1] But there is no doubting the power of the shattering accounts by Canadian women of their own incestuous childhoods and subsequently scarred adulthoods in books like Charlotte Vale Allen's *Daddy's Girl* (1980), Sylvia Fraser's *My Father's House* (1987), Elly Danica's *Don't: A Woman's Word* (1988) and Trysh Ashby-Rolls's *Triumph: A Journey of Healing from Incest* (1991).

Within this context Canadian playwrights Joanna M. Glass, Sharon Pollock, Betty Lambert, Judith Thompson, Linda Griffiths, Jackie Crossland, Connie Gault, Kim Morrisey[2] and others have dramatized the relationship between daughters and abusive fathers or father-surrogates. Even where literal, technical incest is not the issue, the plays exhibit what Sandra M. Gilbert has called "the submerged paradigm of father-daughter incest" (273).[3] The structure, symptoms and consequences of that paradigm prove a useful template for understanding the patterns of behaviour exhibited by female characters in these plays, as well as the theatrical strategies chosen by the playwrights for dramatizing their women's stories.

Many of the common denominators of the non-dramatic literature manifest themselves in the plays. The most important of these, as described in Ellen Bass and Laura Davis's *The Courage to Heal*, involves the abused child's "splitting" her childhood self and later, as an adult, reintegrating the "child within" (42, 111–15). "The panties come off," Elly Danica writes. "He doesn't notice that my skin comes off with them" (53). Less graphically, Sylvia Fraser describes how, at the age of seven, "I created a secret accomplice for my daddy by splitting my personality in two…In future, whenever my daddy approached me sexually I turned into my other self…She loved my father, freeing me to hate him. She became his guilty sex partner and my mother's jealous rival, allowing me to lead a more normal life" (15). Charlotte Vale Allen named her split selves "The One" and "The Other": "The One was evil, mean, capable of everything bad. The Other was the little girl who played hopscotch…and was in love with her entire family" (97). The "child within" may be either the self-as-innocent before the abuse or the self as guilty sex-partner, but in either case, as long as that self remains other, the abused daughter carries into adulthood acute self-hatred and a profound sense of personal fragmentation. The child-self needs to be rediscovered, acknowledged and forgiven in order for the healing process to begin. As therapy, Trysh Ashby-Rolls writes letters to her inner child, "Mary Patricia," and fills her a Christmas stocking. Sylvia Fraser recounts how "the adult me comforts the child, holds her hand, pities her suffering, forgives her for her complicity, assuages her guilt" (223).

The split that characterizes the abused daughter's sense of self is equally evident in her feelings towards her parents. Her mother often seems to her more guilty than her father—guilty of betrayal, desertion, or complicity—even as the daughter understands her mother is simply powerless, an absent presence. "Oh my poor baby, I'm so sorry. I wouldn't help you," laments the ghost of Medea's mother in Jackie Crossland's play *Collateral Damage: The Tragedy of Medea*, after her attempt to warn Medea of her father's sexual predation comes too late. Medea remembers her mother's death in terms of her own increased vulnerability: "I was terrified" (32). The staging of the first production underlined the ghostly mother's impotence by casting her as a ten-foot-tall puppet (13).

The abusive father himself is generally the object of extreme ambivalence on the part of the daughter. In her study of the victims of father-daughter incest, Judith Herman found that "in adult life, their only possible source of self-esteem was to maintain an identification with their powerful fathers. But more often, on a deeper level, they identified with the mothers they despised, and included themselves among the ranks of fallen and worthless women" (103). For the abused daughter, forgiving the father—and the mother too—appears to be a prerequisite for moving on. Fraser concludes her memoir: "I forgive my father so I can forgive myself...I also forgive my father because I love him" (241).[4]

In the drama, the phenomenon of the split self and the impulse to embrace the child within frequently inform structure as well as character and theme. The genre of choice is usually the memory play, with the female protagonist split between her adult and childhood selves, sometimes played by different actresses. Revisiting the past becomes a way for the character to reconcile herself with the inner child (literally the child within the memory frame), a way to re/member the split self, to re/collect the fragments of a shattered life.[5]

All this can be vividly seen in American playwright Marsha Norman's 1977 drama *Getting Out*, the first instance of this kind of play I know. Norman intercuts the story of Arlene, an adult woman just getting out of prison, with the story of her younger self, called Arlie, from whom she is completely estranged. The initial appearance in the play of Arlene's mother triggers a flashback to Arlie's just having been raped by her father, only one in a long line of men who abuse and exploit her in and out of prison. Later we learn that in prison Arlene attempted suicide—the tendency of an inordinately high percentage of adult victims of childhood incest (Herman 99; Blume 91)—as she tried to kill Arlie, "her hateful self" (Norman 74). At the end the actresses playing Arlie and Arlene come together for the first time, sharing a gesture, a line of dialogue, and a laugh, as Arlene finally begins truly getting out of the incest victim's trap of self-hatred by accepting her child within. A more recent British play, Sarah Daniel's aptly titled *Beside Herself*, provides another compelling example of this kind of incest drama.

Sue-Ellen Case has argued that the split subject in plays like *Getting Out* is a function of the contradictions inherent in woman's assuming the male position—the subject position—in discourse. "She cannot appear as a single, whole continuous subject as the male can because she senses that his story is not her story" (131; see also Schoeder 107–08). Making his/story her/story is precisely what the incest survivor does in reclaiming herself for herself, in refiguring herself from being the object of another's discourse—daddy's girl—to self-created subject, her own inner child. This process involves an important element of the alternative dramaturgy inscribed in feminist plays: "the performance of transformation" as opposed to Aristotelian recognition (Keyssar, "Drama" 93), a dynamic that Helene Keyssar calls "the theatrical manifestation of *metamorphosis* of contexts, actions and, most crucially, of characters" (*Feminist* xii; emphasis added).

Father-daughter incest in recent Canadian drama by women is literal and overt in at least a few instances. Rose, the epileptic welfare mother in Judith Thompson's radio play *Tornado*, describes her father's anal and oral rape of her as a child (87–88). And the woman called SHE opens Linda Griffiths's *The Darling Family* with a graphic account of her father's "shov[ing] his thing up me like a kitchen knife, like a knife so far up…I think it's going to rip me in pieces…" (11–12), although whether this is fantasy, dream, or memory remains uncertain. In Connie Gault's *Sky*, young Blanche tells her simple-minded husband that the father of her child-to-be was God, but she has in fact been made pregnant not by the Heavenly Father but by her own. All three of these women are pregnant; all literally carry a child within. In *The Darling Family* SHE is also split between the self that speaks to her partner, HE, and the self whose interior monologues or articulated subtexts are available only to the audience (though HE shares this same split). Played by two actresses, the woman in *Sky* is physically split, Old Blanche looking on silently from the memory frame at her younger self. But nothing ever comes of this relationship. Old Blanche's observation is not in any way essential to the unfolding of the interior drama. She never intervenes in her own life. Perhaps not coincidentally, the child within young Blanche will be stillborn.[6]

Joanna M. Glass's autobiographical *Play Memory*, while less overt in its suggestions of incest, has far more resonance psychologically and dramatically. The central character, Jean MacMillan, controls the action from her adult position in the memory frame, going back thirty years to revisit her father's house during the first fifteen years of her life. At the centre of her retrospection is her father, Cam. A proud Saskatchewan sales manager, Cam becomes an alcoholic after losing his job as a result of a betrayal by his "boys," three salesmen who fill his need for surrogate sons, and he vents his frustrations on his loyal wife and only child. As Cam literally sells the house out from under them to support his alcoholism, he grows progressively more abusive.[7] He regularly hits Jean in the face and beats her so badly around the kidneys that even as a teenager she wets herself. His verbal abuse reveals his profound misogyny. He enjoys telling his ten-year-old daughter how the collapse of his self-esteem and identity began not with the loss of his job but with her birth: "You can't imagine how I wanted a boy to carry the name." he tells her. "I sat in that delivery room, I was in a cold sweat, and then he came. Dr. Kincaid. Do you know what he said?" "Dad, please," Jean begs him, but Cam ignores her. "He said, 'Sad tidings, MacMillan, sad tidings. It's got a cloven crotch'" (24).

The situation comes to a head the night Cam slips in to fifteen-year-old Jean's bedroom and removes her beautiful hand-carved antique closet door to trade to the bootlegger for two bottles. The scene has all the qualities of an incestuous seduction: the bedroom, the darkness, Jean sitting up in bed and watching silently, alienated from the experience, split from herself, as her father slowly, symbolically deflowers her.[8] For two weeks after this Jean refuses to speak or eat or get out of bed until, with Cam's encouragement, she and her mother Ruth move out of the house. Cam meanwhile locks himself away and drinks himself to death.

For all its horrors, the play is largely positive in its outlook, due mainly to Jean's adult perspective. The first time we meet her as an adult we see her smiling at a memory of her father. The stage directions describe her as wearing "*a fine woollen suit, silk blouse, [and] high heels.*" Dressed for success, she is "*dignified and assured....One feels that she has achieved a healthy perspective on her past*" (6). We learn nothing about the thirteen years since her father's death, but Jean's appearance and the playwright's editorial comment clearly imply that she has somehow outgrown her childhood trauma and, as a successful adult, can afford to be generous and forgiving. In fact she reveals many of the symptoms of what Robert Ackerman calls "perfect daughters" in his study of the survival mechanisms exhibited by adult daughters of alcoholics (see also Blume 115). Nevertheless, Jean does appear less severely split than other such survivors of childhood abuse, one indication being that a single actress plays her as both child and adult. Slipping easily back and forth between the narrative frame and interior story, Jean illustrates the continuity between the child within and her adult self. At least outwardly exhibiting an already firm and coherent self-possession, she appears to have little need for re/collecting.

But Jean chooses to exercise (and in so doing exorcise) her memory, and with characteristic ambivalence. She constructs in the flashbacks a strong, sympathetic mother who, while not overtly collaborating with the father, attempts nevertheless to preserve the status quo of family respectability as long as possible. Even Cam accuses Ruth, "You teach [Jean] *acceptance*" (55), and in the end has to beg her to remove their daughter from his destructive presence. Jean's portrait of her father is deeply complex. The Cam she remembers is not only abusive and hateful but also charming, articulate and loving. Like Linda Loman's eulogy for Willy, Jean's final memory of her salesman father flatters him with the most positive possible reading of his life. His last act, to "let us go," was his "most admirable" (61). In the play's concluding tableau we see Jean flanked by both her smiling parents as she repeats her mother's words: "'the truth of people isn't where they are now. It's the space between them, and where they came from'" (61). The space between her mother and father is precisely where Jean has come from; she is very much the daughter of *both* parents, deeply implicated in her father's life through the symbiosis of abuse. Her eagerness to understand and forgive him comes from the urge to reaffirm her own self-worth. I find in this final tableau a strong resemblance to the dust jacket of Germaine Greer's *Daddy, We hardly Knew You* (1989), a book about her search for the truth about her dead father whose emotional neglect scarred her as child and adult. The front cover photo of the father and rear photo of the author/daughter mirror one another: the eyes, the set of the mouth, the tilt of the head. Bound by love and abuse, father and daughter are doubles. Only by laying his ghost to rest can she move on.

For all its emotional complexity, the unresolved father-daughter relationship in *Play Memory* is far less disturbing than the similar situations in Sharon Pollock's plays *Blood Relations*, *Whiskey Six Cadenza* and *Doc.* Though the substantial critical attention received by *Blood Relations* has focused largely on the feminist slant in Pollock's retelling of the Lizzie Borden story, and on its metatheatrical form,[9] the play makes most sense when seen as a dramatization of the abused daughter's fragmented self and her ambivalent "blood relations," maternal and paternal.

Blood Relations portrays Lizzie as the victim of an oppressive patriarchal system. She wants her independence but can't have it without money. Her father won't let her work and tries to force her to marry. Her uncle Harry is conspiring with his sister, Lizzie's stepmother, to get control of the family estate, threatening Lizzie's inheritance, her only hope for eventual economic freedom. And Lizzie's sole family ally, her older sister Emma, runs at the first sign of a fight. Feeling trapped, Lizzie considers suicide. But she decides that if someone had to die, she should not be the one. So she chooses murder, in self-defence as it were, as her way out.

All this is presented ten years after the events of 1892 by her friend the Actress, who plays the role of Lizzie in her own dramatic reconstruction and interpretation of Lizzie's memory play or "*dream thesis*," as Pollock calls it in her stage directions (13). Lizzie is fragmented into three selves: Miss Lizzie in the frame, Lizzie playing the servant-girl Bridget in the re-enactment, and the Actress playing Lizzie. Lizzie and Emma are not only sisters but also comprise the incest victim's classic bad girl/good girl split. Further complicating the psychological dynamic, Lizzie has to contend with three "mothers": her birth mother who died when Lizzie was a child, leaving a legacy of guilt and insecurity ("I was born and she died," Lizzie tells her father. "Did you hate me for killing her?" [57]); the stepmother whom Lizzie loathes; and Emma, who has long been her surrogate mother but who, like the other two, deserts or betrays Lizzie in her time of greatest need.

At the centre of the play, again, stands the father. Lizzie adores him. And though he loves his daughter, Mr. Borden is incapable of deviating from the strict patriarchal codes that his society demands fathers enforce upon their daughters. To her plea that he let her "do something" like learn to keep his books, he responds: "For god's sake, talk sensible" (40). But he also abuses Lizzie more insidiously. He infantilizes her.

When she refuses to see the man he wants her to marry, he tells her three times to "Get the hell upstairs to your room!" and three times she says no (41). He grabs her arm and shoves her to the floor; twice he slaps her face. These are scenes not uncommon between parents and children except that Lizzie, the child within this play, is 34 years old.

At the end of the first act Mr. Borden takes brother-in-law Harry's hatchet and kills Lizzie's birds. As well as prefiguring Lizzie's own ostensible act of murder, in the symbolic structure of the play this is the phallic violation. Lizzie tells Emma: "I felt their hearts throbbing and pumping and the blood gushed out of their necks, it was all over my hands" (53). The conflation of the father with Harry is significant. In Harry's first interaction with Lizzie (in her role as Bridget), "*He grabs her ass with both hands*" (21). Throughout the play Harry is associated with horses (his plan, once he takes over the Borden farm, is to "run horse auctions and a buggy rental" [44]), and in a dream Lizzie describes to the Actress, she rides a carousel horse that "goes up and comes down" in a sexual rhythm, its red horse flesh "so rigid and hard." In terms similar to those used throughout the incest memoirs describing how the child would split herself during her father's attacks, Lizzie tells how in her dream "you watch…watch yourself on the horse. You're wearing a mask,…it looks like your face except that it's rigid and white…" Ultimately, she recognizes, the mask has eyes like those of her birds (43–44).

Just before she kills her father, Lizzie reminds him that he wears her ring, a symbol of their oedipal marriage. "And you gave it to me and you said, 'it's real gold, Lizzie, it's for you because you are very precious to me.'…[A]nd I put my ring on your finger and said 'thank you, Papa, I love you.'" She then re-enacts the incest scene. He lies down, "*[s]he kneels and undoes his shoes,*" and she receives his kiss. As she raises the hatchet, the scene reaches its climax in a blackout and silence out of which comes her "*wordless sound of hysteria*" (67–68).

In *Daddy's Girl* Charlotte Vale Allen remembers recognizing, as a teenager regularly abused by her father, her own capacity for murder. "If I were ever to release the control I held over the two distinct halves of my self, I'd kill. I'd walk calmly into the kitchen, pick up the bread knife and kill my father, perhaps my mother too" (Allen 98). Allen did not kill her father, and long after his natural death she continued wrestling with his demons. Lizzie does—or, rather, the Actress-as-Lizzie does in the scenario she constructs—but whether Lizzie is much better off for it, whether she has moved on, is debatable. Ten years later she sits in the same chair "where I have always sat" (19), in the house where her father and stepmother were butchered,[10] across from Emma who asks her the same old questions. Her relationship with the Actress seems trivial and superficial. Lizzie appears emotionally numbed, and the fragmented self no less fragmented.

But if Lizzie were to plead self-defence to justify the murders of her parents, arguing from necessity that she had to kill in order not to die herself, Pollock's *Whiskey Six Cadenza* might support her argument, for in that tragicomic fantasia the incestuous father kills the daughter. Set in an Alberta mining town during the prohibition 1920s, *Whiskey Six Cadenza* features Johnny, a miner's son who aspires to something better. Going to work for Mr. Big, the local bootlegger with the patriarchal name, Johnny is on his way to becoming the surrogate son until he gets to know the adopted teenage daughter, Leah. Mr. Big literally snatched her off the street when she was eleven—"like God descendin' to take his Chosen up into heaven in a fiery chariot!" in Mr. Big's self-mythicizing language (157), though later he will admit that his rhetoric served just "to legitimize…an on-going affair…with a child" (242).

When Johnny and Leah fall for each other, and he learns that she and Mr. Big are lovers, he confronts the adoptive mother. She proves classically complacent and accommodating, arguing that Leah would "have run from here if she hadn't been happy" (209). But later, when Mr. Big asks Leah to go for a ride with him on an imaginary errand to a make-believe place—their obvious code for a sexual encounter—Leah's resistance and subsequent capitulation make clear the real nature of the relationship.

> **LEAH.** …I…I'm sorry…I hurt you, I made you feel bad.
> **MR. BIG.** No.
> **LEAH.** We…we…can go tomorrow.
> **MR. BIG.** That's what we'll do.
> **LEAH.** …We…could go today – later today – if you want.
> **MR. BIG.** We'll make it tomorrow.
> **LEAH.** You won't be mad that we don't go today? (220)

This is the scene replayed in all the incest memoirs: whatever her reluctance, daddy's girl always eventually gives in. He has all the power. She has none. Unlike Lizzie or Jean, Leah hasn't even any access to the therapeutic power of the meta-narrative; her/story remains the story. "Did you think you could just tell a story and everything would be right?" she asks Mr. Big (245). Realizing that things can't go on the way they have but despairing of escape, she finally begs him to "make it right" (246), handing Mr. Big the gun with which he shoots her to death.

As if dissatisfied with the bald alternatives—kill the abusive father or be destroyed by him—Pollock took one more look at the situation with the overtly autobiographical *Doc.* [11] Returning to the memory form, Pollock has her adult protagonist Catherine revisit her father's house after the elderly doctor has had a heart attack, and flash back to her childhood when she was called Katie. Like Arlene and Arlie in *Getting Out*, Catherine and Katie are played by different actresses. But unlike Norman's split female subject, Pollock's can communicate across the memory frame throughout the play, including to their mother, Bob, a strong capable woman who degenerated into alcoholism and eventually suicide. Was this the result of Doc's neglect? The dramatized memories seem clearly to answer yes. Arguing that his medical practice is more important than his family, but at the same time, like Mr. Borden with Lizzie, refusing to allow Bob to work, Doc drives his wife to despair, even forcing her into an unnecessary hysterectomy.

Doc's abuse is directed entirely at his wife, not at his daughter. But Catherine/Katie, fearing that she too might be suicidal, identifies with Bob and with her paternal grandmother who may also have killed herself:

> **KATIE.** ...Sometimes I look...
> **CATHERINE.** ...in the mirror, I look in the mirror...
> **KATIE.** ...and I see Mummy and I see...
> **CATHERINE.** ...Gramma, and Mummy and me... (108)

At the same time she despises her mother for her weakness and identifies with her powerful father: "I'm like you Daddy. I just gotta win" (124). (Even more than Jean and Cam in *Play Memory*, Catherine/Katie and Doc are doubles.) [12] But unlike Doc Katie feels partly responsible for her mother's death. The scene haunts her. Screaming "I hate you and I wish that you were dead!" (118), she stops her ears and refuses to call for help as Bob's offstage voice nightmarishly repeats, "Katie!" (120). Catherine has carried that guilt into adulthood. When she asks Doc about Bob's death, and he sarcastically responds, "It was all my fault, go on, say it, I know what you think," Catherine answers, "It was my fault" (32).

So although revisiting her past provides sufficient evidence to convict the abusive father/husband, Catherine, much like Jean, chooses to de-emphasize the most damning evidence and let her father off the hook. She has to, so implicated does she feel herself to be in her father's crime. For Catherine, whose dysfunctional personal life is classically characteristic of the adult survivor of childhood abuse, remembering the past is literally a re/membering: a healing process of piecing together the chaotic fragments of her life reflected in the fragmented, non-chronological structure of the play, itself analogous to the abuse survivor's reflexive coping strategy of "multiplicity." [13] Catherine must finally forgive her father so that she might forgive herself, and in the play's last scenes she embraces and accepts Katie—the child Katie within her. Katie always took the blame for her parents' marital problems, deciding that they reluctantly married because Bob was pregnant with her, and that "they didn't want to have me" (50). But when she asks Catherine, "Would you want to have me?" her older self replies unhesitatingly, "Yes, yes I would" (121). And near the end when Doc cries "Katie, Katie," it is Catherine who answers, "I'm here" (124). What I find uncomfortable about this silencing of the dead mother (and grandmother, whose unopened letter, apparently blaming Doc for *her* suicide, Catherine burns), is that the daughter pays too high a price for her own peace. Perhaps even more unsettling is the satisfaction Catherine seems to find in this resolution of the oedipal triangle—lit by "*the dying flame*" from the grandmother's burning letter (126), she and Doc share a smile of complicity in her being, at the end daddy's only girl.

To save their own lives, Sharon Pollock's daughters must either kill the abusive father or forgive him. Betty Lambert's daughters can do neither. In *Jennie's Story*, set in 1930s Alberta, Jennie takes her own life when she finds out that she will never be able to have children because she has been unwittingly sterilized at the behest of the local priest with her mother's collusion. Unlike the punning title of Lambert's earlier sex comedy *Sqrieux-de-Dieu*, the screwing in *Jennie's Story* is done not by God but by the priest, Father Edward, who had sex with the teenage Jennie while she was housekeeping for him. Unable to resist Jennie, the good Father arranged her sterilization in the hope that "it would stop the occasion of my sin," though it did not (102). Jennie's mother makes clear the surrogate family structure of this incestuous triangle when she explains to her daughter, "I couldn't do for the Father…So I sent you in my stead" (64).

Jennie's Story has no memory frame. Its form is naturalistic melodrama. But the incest play's split self emerges in the character of Molly, the young girl who comes to work for Jennie and her husband, Harry, and who shares Jennie's sixth sense. Unmarried and pregnant, Molly both is and carries the child within that Jennie will never have. Just before her confrontation with the priest, and her suicide, Jennie ceremoniously presents Molly to her mother as her mother's "reborn" daughter, and to Harry as his rightful new wife (100). After Jennie's death Molly has her child and marries Harry in a very upbeat ending.

Jennie kills herself by swallowing lye. In an interview Betty Lambert pointed out the pun: how, in killing herself, Jennie is "swallowing the lie" that what happened to her was somehow her own fault (Worthington 63). But at the same time, the ending of the play, with its emphasis on futurity and the flourishing Molly, suggests the positive effects of confronting and exorcising the abuse. "I wanted a female tragic form," Lambert said. "Women know something that maybe men don't know. We know that after the death, somebody cooks bacon and eggs. And that suicide is not an answer, because life bloody goes on" (Worthington 64–65).

Those realities cut to the heart of Lambert's next play, *Under the Skin.* "Life goes on and on, and it has no business going on," cries Maggie, the anguished single mother whose twelve-year-old daughter Emma has gone missing (Lambert 136). Over the six-month span of the play, Maggie, a university professor, finds some comfort in the friendship of her blue-collar neighbours John and Renee. Not until the end do we and Maggie learn that her daughter has been held captive the whole time by John in a secret room underneath his garage. John's wife Renee reveals the horrible truth; her growing awareness is one of this play's most powerful elements.

Under the Skin is the only one of these plays that does not directly dramatize the abused daughter as an onstage character. She remains offstage (under the skin of the set) and unseen. But Renee is her onstage double, as well as the double of Maggie, ostensibly her social and intellectual opposite. Together they comprise another polyphonic split female subject. Just as he has presumably done to the daughter, John abuses his wife in every way—slaps her around, calls her "whore" and "cunt," and forces sex on her. Typical of so many battered wives and abused daughters, Renee takes it all, afraid for her own safety and security and for her children (John's stepchildren, whom he despises). She infantilizes herself, putting on for John what Maggie calls her "cringing whelp act" (148). She plays, to a tee, daddy's girl. At the same time Renee is the surrogate-mother complicit in the surrogate-father's abuse of Emma. (Though Maggie is Emma's birth-mother, within the structure of the play John, Renee and Emma constitute the incestuous family triangle.) Renee doesn't allow herself to be fully aware that John has Emma in that secret room until long after she has suspected it, and then does nothing about it for longer still. The play graphically illustrates Judith Herman's contention that "even by patriarchal standards, the mother in the incestuous family is unusually oppressed....Maternal collusion in incest, when it occurs, is a measure of maternal powerlessness" (49). By conflating the figure of the offstage daughter with that of the onstage wife and mother, the play projects a terrible continuity of abuse within the patriarchal family.

Under the Skin is presented as both Maggie's and Renee's nightmare—every mother's nightmare. But perhaps even worse than the terrible fate of this one particular daughter is the play's implication that no security is to be found anywhere. Danger lurks even within the family, or in the man next door. John justifies himself by arguing, "I'm really like everyone else" (Lambert 176). He cites biblical authority, patiently explaining to Renee that "even Moses said you should rape young girls" (179). We hear much in the play about Anne Frank's diary, too, Emma's favourite book. Its resonances are bitterly ironic. Anne's secret room provided her only the illusion of sanctuary from the violence of the Fatherland; the surrogate father's secret room becomes Emma's torture chamber. "In my father's house are many rooms," reads the gospel according to another John (14:2). But none of them, in the dramatic imagination of Canadian women playwrights, is a safe place for a daughter.

This is the implicit message of all these plays: that ultimately no woman can feel secure as long as any man might abuse any little girl, even his neighbour's—or his own. "Perhaps," Andrea Dworkin writes, "incestuous rape is becoming a central paradigm for intercourse in our time" (Dworkin 194). These plays suggest that incest may be a paradigm for the very nature of the father-daughter relationship itself within the patriarchal family. But they also suggest that, for the wounded daughter, finding the courage to heal is the first step in a revolution from within. The split self may paradoxically provide daddy's girl with the opportunity to reconstitute herself as autonomous subject in a drama of her own making.

(1995)

Notes

1 For the first instance of what might be called Canadian "backlash drama," see Wendy Lill's *All Fall Down*, a *Crucible*-like play (with a feminist twist) about unfounded allegations of child sexual abuse against a female daycare worker.

2 Morrisey's *Dora: A Case of Hysteria* dramatizes Freud's famous case history of a female patient abused by her father's male friend—a case that has become a locus of feminist psychoanalytical revisionism.

3 E. Sue Blume points out that therapists have in recent years evolved a new, broader, working definition of incest that need not involve either blood relations or sexual intercourse *per se*: "the imposition of sexually inappropriate acts, or acts with sexual overtones, by—or any use of a minor child to meet the sexual/emotions needs of—one or more persons who derive authority through ongoing emotional bonding with that child" (4). Russell employs a somewhat more restrictive definition of "incestuous abuse" in her study: "any kind of exploitive sexual contact or attempted contact that occurred between relatives, no matter how distant the relationship, before the victim turned eighteen years old" (41).

4 Janice Williamson distinguishes Elly Danica's memoir from those of Fraser and Allen "in [Danica's] refusal of compensatory narratives involving family or father," her radical refusal of forgiveness, and her creation of a dissociated, split self "not named or personified as character...[and] unmediated by a comfortable framing narrative..." (137–39).

5 The authors of a study by Vancouver's Women's Research Centre on women survivors of childhood sexual abuse explain that they chose the title *Recollecting Our Lives* because "it sums up what adult survivors of child sexual abuse struggle to do, how they collect the pieces of their experience, reflect on them, try to fit the pieces together and come to an understanding of their lives" (Women's Research Centre 23).

6 An unpublished stage version of Fraser's *My Father's House*, adapted by Brian Morton and Bruce Vavrina, splits the autobiographical narrator into three characters, each played by a different actress: the adult writer who discovers the repressed truth about her childhood abuse, her teenage self, and the abused child. One actress also doubles as the mother. The father is dramatized only as an offstage voice (see Crossland 13). For a review of the 1995 Toronto production, see Wagner.

7 Blume catalogs the characteristics common to both adult children of alcoholics and incest survivors (18).

8 In a discussion of Glass's play *Canadian Gothic*, Anne Nothof comments on how the young protagonist (also named Jean) "has assumed the responsibilities of a wife to her Father," and how Glass's novel *Women Wanted* "suggests that the roles of daughter and mother are congruent, and that the male-female dynamics of family are incestuous..." (63).

9 For a bibliography of Pollock criticism, see Wasserman 365–67.

10 Pollock significantly alters Lizzie Borden's historical circumstances by having her and Emma remain in the family home ten years after the murders. In fact shortly after Lizzie's acquittal they bought and moved to a big house on the hill that Lizzie dreams about in the play ("I dreamt that my name was Lisbeth...and I lived up on the hill in a corner house..." [28]). Elizabeth Borden changed her name to Lizbeth and lived there until her death in 1927. See Jones 248.

11 Pollock describes her early home life in detail in Hofsess 44, 48–52.

[12] Even with no suggestions of sexual abuse, two recent love-hate biographies of Canadian actors written by their daughters make a fascinating adjunct to the incest literature and drama under discussion here. See Drainie (esp. 270–71 for parallels with *Play Memory*) and Harron, who opens her memoir, "I wrote Don Harron a hate letter on my twenty-first birthday" (11); see also 85, 304 *et passim* for echoes of *Doc.*

[13] The therapist of one incest survivor explains how repressed memories of abuse may come flooding back: "Memories can come as feelings, in fragments, physical sensations, pictures or slices of pictures." She describes the "multiplicity" of fragmentations and splits as "a spontaneous way our minds grow to cope with an intolerable reality, a way to store unspeakable information until it can be spoken and believed" (qtd. in Steed 181).

Works Cited

Ackerman, Robert J. *Perfect Daughters of Alcoholics.* Deerfield Beach: Health Communications, 1989.

Allen, Charlotte Vale. *Daddy's Girl.* Toronto: McClelland, 1980.

Ashby-Rolls, Trysh. *Triumph: A Journey of Healing from Incest.* Toronto: McGraw-Hill, 1991.

Bass, Ellen, and Laura Davis. *The Courage to Heal: A Guide for Women Survivors of Child Sexual Abuse.* New York: Harper, 1988.

Blume, E. Sue. *Secret Survivors: Uncovering Incest and Its Aftereffects in Women.* New York: Ballantine, 1990.

Case, Sue-Ellen. "From Split Subject to Split Britches." *The New Women Playwrights.* Ed. Enoch Brater. New York: Oxford UP, 1989. 126–45.

Cixous, Hélène. "Aller á la mer." Trans. Barbara Kerslake. *Modern Drama* 27 (1984): 546–48.

Crossland, Jackie. *Collateral Damage: The Tragedy of Medea.* Vancouver: Press Gang, 1992.

Danica, Elly. *Don't: A Woman's Word.* Charlottetown: Gynergy, 1988.

Daniels, Sarah. *Beside Herself.* London: Methuen, 1990.

DeSalvo, Louise. *Virginia Woolf: The Impact of Childhood Sexual Abuse on Her Life and Work.* Boston: Beacon, 1989.

Drainie, Bronwyn. *Living the Part: John Drainie and the Dilemma of Canadian Stardom.* Toronto: Macmillan, 1988.

Dworkin, Andrea. *Intercourse.* London: Secker, 1987.

Fraser, Sylvia. *My Father's House: A Memoir of Incest and Healing.* Toronto: Collins, 1987.

Freud, Sigmund. *New Introductory Lectures on Psychoanalysis* (1933). Trans. and ed. James Strachey. New York: Norton, 1965.

Gault, Connie. *Sky.* Winnipeg: Blizzard, 1989.

Gilbert, Sandra M. "Life's Empty Pack: Notes toward a Literary Daughteronomy." *Daughters and Fathers.* Ed. Lynda E. Boose and Betty S. Flowers. Baltimore: Johns Hopkins UP, 1989. 256–77.

Glass, Joanna M. *Play Memory. NeWest Plays by Women.* Ed. Diane Bessai and Don Kerr. Edmonton: NeWest, 1987. 1–61.

Greer, Germaine. *Daddy, We Hardly Knew You.* London: Hamish Hamilton, 1989.

Griffiths, Linda. *The Darling Family.* Winnipeg: Blizzard, 1991.

Harron, Martha. *Don Harron: A Parent Contradiction.* Toronto: Collins, 1988.

Herman, Judith. *Father-Daughter Incest.* Cambridge: Harvard UP, 1981.

Hofsess, John. "Families [Sharon Pollock]." *Homemaker's* 15 (March 1980): 41–60.

Jones, Ann. *Women Who Kill.* New York: Fawcett Crest, 1981.

Keyssar, Helene. "Drama and the Dialogic Imagination: *The Heidi Chronicles and Fefu and Her Friends.*" *Modern Drama* 34 (1991): 90–106.

———. *Feminist Theatre.* New York: Grove, 1985.

Lambert, Betty. *Jennie's Story & Under the Skin.* Toronto: Playwrights Canada, 1987.

Lill, Wendy. *All Fall Down.* Vancouver: Talonbooks, 1994.

Masson, Jeffrey M. *The Assault on Truth: Freud's Suppression of the Seduction Theory.* New York: Farrar, 1984.

Morrisey, Kim. *Dora: A Case of Hysteria. Canadian Theatre Review* 65 (1990): 31–45.

Norman, Marsha. *Getting Out.* New York: Avon, 1978.

Nothof, Anne. "'Groping Inside the Flesh': The Prairie Gothic of Joanna Glass, Connie Massing and Connie Gault." *Canadian Journal of Drama and Theatre* 1.2 (1991): 59–69.

Pollock, Sharon. *Blood Relations and Other Plays.* Edmonton: NeWest, 1981.

———. *Doc.* Toronto: Playwrights Canada, 1984.

———. *Whiskey Six Cadenza. NeWest Plays by Women.* Ed. Diana Bessai and Don Kerr. Edmonton: NeWest, 1987. 137–347.

Russell, Diana E.H. *The Secret Trauma: Incest in the Lives of Girls and Women.* New York: Basic, 1986.

Schroeder, Patricia L. "Locked Behind the Proscenium: Feminist Strategies in *Getting Out* and *My Sister in This House.*" *Modern Drama* 32 (1989): 104–14.

Steed, Judy. *Our Little Secret: Confronting Child Sexual Abuse in Canada.* Toronto: Random House, 1994.

Thompson, Judith. *The Other Side of the Dark: Four Plays by Judith Thompson.* Toronto: Coach House, 1989.

Wagner, Vit. "Memoir Best Left in Book Form." *Toronto Star* 20 February 1995: B4

Wasserman, Jerry, ed. *Modern Canadian Plays, Volume Two.* 3rd ed. Vancouver: Talonbooks, 1994.

Williamson, Janice. "'I Peel Myself out of My Own Skin': Reading *Don't: A Woman's Word.*" *Essays on Life Writing: From Genre to Critical Practice.* Ed. Marlene Kadar. Toronto: U of Toronto P, 192. 133–51.

Women's Research Centre. *Recollecting Our Lives: Women's Experience of Childhood Sexual Abuse.* Vancouver: Press Gang, 1989.

Worthington, Bonnie. "Battling Aristotle: A Conversation with Betty Lambert." *Room of One's Own* 8 (1983): 54–66.

Borderline Crossings in Sharon Pollock's Out-Law Genres: *Blood Relations* and *Doc*

by Rosalind Kerr

> Out-law genres renegotiate the relationship between personal identity and the world, between personal and social history. (Kaplan 130)
>
> I see political scenes and class oppression in a personal way. Yet as I look at my own plays, I can see them moving closer and closer to looking at very personal things as well as an exterior political scene. (Pollock in Dunn 2)

Sharon Pollock's renegade play texts, *Blood Relations* and *Doc*, qualify as deviant enough from traditional realistic drama to earn Kaplan's label "out-law genres." The presumption that both these plays could be considered to have auto/biographical elements—at least in the extended meaning that feminists are applying to women's and other minorities' texts—can be substantiated by Pollock's own increasingly self-reflexive remarks about her work. Interviews with her which extend back into the early 1970s indicate a gradual but growing consciousness of her own conflicted gender construction, as well as an admission that certain feminist auto/biographical concerns were informing her creation of both *Blood Relations* and *Doc.* In an important 1976 interview with Margo Dunn, she referred to *My Name is Lisbeth,* an earlier version of *Blood Relations*, as "the most personal of [my] plays to date" in its exploration of "the purity of emotion and motivation in any kind of extreme action, which gives you insight into very clouded things of your own, emotions you feel but can't handle. You gain insight because someone else has gone the whole way" (4). In *Doc*, which she temporarily retitled *Family Trappings.*[1] Pollock acted on her own suggestion and turned her attentions to seek for "insight[s] into very clouded things of [her] own." As an article written at its premiere in Fredericton reported: *Doc* was "a painfully honest confession, for the doctor is Pollock's own father, Dr. Everett Chalmers" (Fraser D11).

Following what Derrida calls the "law of genre" ("Law" 203–04), traditional genres, including classical realist drama, have reproduced and consolidated the Rousseauean notion of the universal human self as white, male, bourgeois, heterosexual. As Sidonie Smith sums it up, "'[H]is' life story becomes recognizable, legitimate and culturally real…[with the result that] the life stories of many people whose history differs….because of race, class and gender identifications go unwritten, or if written, misread or unread" (393–94). Thus, classical realist drama, which frequently represents a narrative focused on the auto/biography of a central character, usually invites audience members to identify with a strong male subject position in order to arrive at the desired understanding of events. Typically these strong male subject positions have been defined in opposition to those occupied by female characters who often exist only as the fragmented and fetishized objects of a male gaze. However, as Derrida suggests, this "law of genre" is always already undermined by the "counterlaw" ("Law" 203–04) on which it is based, and hence, genres can easily spill out of their boundaries. Certainly, some postmodern and feminist materialist playwrights have found the way to "invaginate"("Living" 97)[2] the margins of modern classical realistic dramatic conventions, in order to challenge the control of the narrative by the universalized male subject and to permit the female's "entry into the symbolic [as] the condition of her survival, without which she condemns herself to marginality, to the outside" (Feral 10).

Pollock first owned her feminist agenda with *Blood Relations*—a truly "counterlaw" or "out-law" production in both its form and content—which fits into Caren Kaplan's definition in "Resisting Autobiography: Out-Law Genres and Transnational Feminist Subjects" as mixing "two conventionally 'unmixable' elements" (119). The unmixable elements, collaborative discursive practices which expose the myth that a text has been individually authored, are very much in evidence in *Blood Relations* where Pollock frames the play by having Lizzie get the actress to reenact her story while she coaches her from the side. In the following example, the Actress/Lizzie character pointedly asks Miss Lizzie/Bridget for help in understanding how to react to Dr. Patrick's house call:

> **MISS LIZZIE/BRIDGET.** They're saying if you live on Second Street and you need a house call, and you don't mind the Irish, call Dr. Patrick. Dr. Patrick is very prompt with his Second Street house calls.
>
> **ACTRESS/LIZZIE.** Do they really say that? (31)

Kaplan stresses the critical accountability of the emerging out-law genres that she identifies as "requir[ing] more collaborative procedures that are more closely attuned to the power differences among participants in the process of producing a text." What results is that "instead of a discourse of individual authorship, we find a discourse of situation; a 'politics of location'" (119), just as Miss Lizzie/Bridget manages to locate herself gesturally in relation to Dr. Patrick so that the Actress/Lizzie character can play out the scene which follows.

> **MISS LIZZIE/BRIDGET.** Well—he's hoping to see someone who lives on Second Street—someone who's yanking up her skirt and showing her ankle—so she can take a decent-sized step—and forgetting everything she was ever taught in Miss Cornelia's School for Girls, and talking to the Irish as if she never heard of the Pope! Oh yes, he's very prompt getting to Second Street … getting away is something else.… (31)

Although Kaplan is referring to nondramatic texts, it is possible to identify the two Pollock plays with some of the autobiographical "out-law" genres that she isolates. Indeed, adding in the element of performance only enhances the intertextuality by extending the application to other sets of sign systems specific to the stage. Thus, *Blood Relations* could be read as "biomythography," "a writing down of our meanings of identity ... with the materials of our lives" (129), since Lizzie constantly feeds this private information into the actress's psyche to inform and comment on the larger than life-size myth which has grown up around her. Correspondingly, *Doc* might be approached as "cultural autobiography" in its remembering of experiences which are "nonsynchronous with [the] dominant culture" (130). *Doc*'s reliance on recording the fragments of remembered conversations with the lost and despised mother and grandmother also qualifies it as a *crossover genre* in its "blur[ring of] the boundaries between orality and writing" (Davies 7, emphasis in original).[3] When Bob talks about herself as if telling a story about someone who no longer exists, we get caught up in her folklore:

> **BOB.** Eloise Roberts, and they called me Bob, and I could run faster and play harder and do better than any boy I ever met! And my hair? It was all the way down to there! And when I asked my Mama – Mama? – She said, we have been here since the Seventeen Hundreds, Eloise, and in your blood runs the blood of Red Roberts! Do you know who he is? A pirate, with flamin' red hair and a flamin' red beard who harboured off a cove in P.E.I.! (62)

Having staked my claim to read *Blood Relations* and *Doc* as "out-law genres" that resist hegemonic patriarchal structures, I must offer the caution that the feminists whose work on women's autobiography I have referred to above, are committed to avoid

> privileging the oppression of gender over and above other oppressions [since this] effectively erases the complex and often contradictory positionings of the subject [by ignoring the fact that] the axes of the subject's identifications and experiences are multiple, because locations in gender, class, race, ethnicity and sexuality complicate one another and are not merely additive. (Watson xiv)

My concentration in this paper is necessarily focused on a white middle-class Canadian woman's perspective of gender oppression which sustains the "Oedipalized" bourgeois family structure of the Western world. Fortunately, Pollock's careful attention to the specific historical circumstances affecting her oppressed female subjects mitigates against this universalizing tendency and facilitates her inclusion of different class, community, ethnic and sexual identifications. Turning now to the texts, I hope to show how, even though we are only working across one obvious national boundary line, Pollock's plays call upon feminists to participate in creating the "transnational feminisms" which could help us to break down the "law of genre," resist our pasts, and revolutionize our futures (Kaplan 136).

Superficially at least, Pollock's turning to a notorious American female outlaw for her first feminist play can be interpreted as an act intended to foreground the doubly colonized status of being both Canadian and female (Dunn 6).[4] Such plays as *Walsh* and *The Komagata Maru Incident* challenged Canadians by exposing forgotten public figures who participated in shameful events which Pollock discovered to have been whitewashed in the interests of maintaining the fiction that we are "nicer" than our American cousins (Hofsess 52). When *My Name is Lizbeth* was first produced in 1976, it marked an abrupt departure from the string of earlier plays which Pollock had written to force Canadian audiences to recognize the dominant ideologies underlying official government policies (104–11). Crossing the border to find her first central female character, and selecting an infamous murderess at that, could be read at some level as a message that mythic Canadian female subjects were even less easy to find than their male counterparts. In *Blood Relations*, she teases contemporary Canadian audiences's aural memories, reminding us of our obsession with "more interesting" American legends by including the words of the children's skipping rhyme:

> Lizzie Borden took an axe
> Gave her mother forty whacks,
> When the job was nicely done,
> She gave her father forty-one. (16)

As the actress tortures Lizzie by reciting it, its familiarity reverberates in most spectators' ears—proof of how thoroughly our cultural identity has been permeated by our more aggressive neighbour. If Pollock were still attempting to demonstrate, as she claimed to be with her earlier plays, to teach Canadians that "to know where we are going, we must know what we have come from" (Programme Notes, *The Komagatu Maru Incident*, qtd. in Page 107), the implications of her choice of subject matter are staggering. In more than one interview she claims her attraction to Lizzie was to "use... history to make a comment on contemporary women" (McKinley 36). I might posit that her very choice of Lizzie[5] is intended to draw attention to women's absence in official culture, and to confront us with the truth that only women whose transgressions in the private realm have condemned them to public exposure can gain entry, and then, only as reviled outsiders who have been pushed beyond the borders of civilization. Reclaiming women's lives by locating them historically is both a crucial and thankless task as Pollock shows by exposing how limited Lizzie's choices are, despite her relative wealth and privilege:

> **MR. BORDEN.** Just listen to me, Lizzie....I'm choosing my words, and I want you to listen. Now...in most circumstances...a woman of your age would be married, eh? have children, be running her own house, that's the natural thing, eh? *Pause.* Eh, Lizzie? (37)

Through Lizzie, Pollock explores the annihilation which awaits the bourgeois daughter as she is forced to enter into an "Oedipalization" process which can only reduce her to the objectified and exchangeable "Other." Setting up the play within the play whereby Lizzie consents to let her inquisitive same-sex lover mirror her earlier self at the time of the murders ten years before, Pollock draws attention to the traditional dramatic structure of the Oedipal narrative while at the same time revealing that the daughter will be forced to discover that she has been doubly displaced and cannot ever make a successful entry into representation. Sue Ellen Case has noted how Pollock's brilliant deployment of the metatheatrical device of splitting the subject between Lizzie and the Actress reflects the Lacanian split-subject position which the child experiences at the moment of recognizing that he is forever separated from both himself and from the object of his desire (130). She argues that Pollock has captured the further split which female children suffer when they discover that there is no way for them to enter the male symbolic by representing the actress's recreation of Lizzie's role as a repeat of Lizzie's earlier traumatic discovery that she had no chance of establishing a separate social existence. The Lacanian baby who looks in the mirror and sees "the structure of a whole self [and] ... enters the system of representation ... in this unified form" can only be gendered male in a discourse controlled by the Law of the Father (Case 130). Hence a female child will have to identify herself as male if she wishes to believe that she is included in the mirror, although she will always be conscious at some level that she is also having to deny her own biological sex in order to do so. The brash, rebellious, younger Lizzie as played by the actress, Case proposes, is still unaware that she cannot access male privilege. The play charts her coming to awareness of her exclusion and ends up with her wielding the axe. The older Lizzie, who has endured the trial and the social isolation which follows it, has been chastened by it and now recognizes what the traps are. It is she who knows, as all women do at some level, that she is in the shadows of the mirror reflections:

> **LIZZIE.** I'm supposed to be a mirror. I'm supposed to reflect whatever they want to see, and everyone wants something different. If nobody looks in the mirror, I'm not even there. I don't exist. (39)

Lizzie's scream at her defectiveness represents the moment when she discovers that individuation for a woman equals cultural death. Lizzie's guilt-ridden confession in which she accuses herself of "killing her mother" revisits the moment of the female child's tragic "Oedipalization," when she, too, has to abandon her first love and choose to compete with her for her father's affections:

> **MISS LIZZIE/BRIDGET.** I can remember distinctly ... that moment I was undressing for bed, and I looked at my knees—and there were no scabs! At last! I thought I'm the nice little girl Emma wants me to be! ... But it wasn't that at all. I was just growing up. I didn't fall down so often.... *She smiles.* Do you suppose ... do you suppose there's a formula, a magic formula for being "a woman"? Do you suppose every girl baby receives it at birth, it's the last thing that happens just before birth, the magic formula is stamped indelibly on the brain—KaThud!! Her mood of amusement changes and ... through some terrible oversight.... perhaps the death of my mother ... I didn't get that... Ka Thud!! I was born ... defective.... *She looks at the ACTRESS.* (36)

The girl child's passage into culture, which requires that she remain permanently alienated from her own disempowered gender, culminates in Lizzie's discovery that she has no "blood" relations since her father plans to sign off the farm to his wife's male relative. When even her own sister refuses to stand by her, she finds herself closer in kin to her more oppressed non-blood sister, the maid Bridget.

Case believes that *Blood Relations* belongs to the works of the first rebellious feminist playwrights who foregrounded the struggle of women trying to move into subject positions free from patriarchal controls; however, she also sees the play as caught at the stage where the female characters who take subject positions are still worried about whether they have the right to take them. I would suggest that Pollock has gone further in her metatheatricalizing of subject positions and has split "Lizzie's" story across multiple subject positions which proliferate different "sites" occupied by other identities than her own. Her lesbian actress lover, the Irish maid Bridget, her scheming stepmother, her passive sister cannot be reduced to one unified "woman." So, too, her bird-killing Papa, and her flirtatious Irish doctor, also participate in producing diverse gendered sites. As such, Pollock's axe-wielding message addresses multiple oppressions that implicate contemporary audience members in the need to destroy the patriarchal script, and, therefore, can be considered to have moved beyond merely questioning women's newly found rights. Even if, at the traditional narrative plot level, the actress-lover must experience the same fury as the Lizzie character by moving through the same chronological stages that Lizzie did ten years earlier, the progression is frequently halted by the shared moments of delight when the actress finds herself able to mirror Lizzie back to herself. The characters may be frozen again by the end, but symbolic representation has been shattered by glimpses of a symbolic order which sites the presence of the female. So too, the synchronic counter-narrative where an older, wiser Lizzie acknowledges her closer mirror reflection in Bridget, as the character she chooses to split into on stage, has also been put into motion even from the beginning.

A few years later when Pollock came to reveal her own scandalous, unmentionable personal life story in *Doc*, she imported the model of the legendary outlawed murderous daughter across the border to her own small New Brunswick home town in the form of Catherine, the alienated Daddy's girl, who returns home to revisit the primal scene. If the sensational murder trial had forever exposed the intimate details of Lizzie's menstrual madness to the public eye,[6] Pollock's own "shedipal" tragedy could have been kept a secret permanently. In retelling the life of a successful and adulated small town doctor and benefactor—the official biography of her father Everett Chalmers (Hofsess 44–48)—[7] Pollock need never have mentioned the absent, silent, and dead women who had removed themselves from his controlling presence. For in this case, Catherine has come home to "murder" her father's reputation, as the real murders—the violent suicides of both her mother and grandmother—have been dismissed as either accidental or inevitable. Thus, the indelible gestic image in *Blood Relations* of the actress/Lizzie poised over her sleeping father with the axe in her upraised arms has its corresponding never-ending moment in *Doc,* with Ev sitting hunched in his chair holding the unopened suicide note written to him by his mother, tormented by the accusatory voice of his dead wife Bob.

While *Blood Relations* replays the male-identified daughter's shattering discovery of her exclusion from public existence, *Doc* takes another daddy's girl back to rediscover the personal deathly disempowerment which the culturally inscribed rejection of the mother had required from her. Reversing the Electra figure, this daughter puts the father on trial for his misuse of patriarchal privilege and destroys the illusion of the uniqueness of his life story, showing how interwoven it was with the lives of those he had sacrificed to get there. In an 1987 interview, Pollock called it "a detective story [about] the daughter's attempt to understand the relationship between her mother and her father and herself and what it was that caused her mother's death" (qtd. in Deakin 29).

Instead of building up a glowing tribute in recognition of Ev's great accomplishments, *Doc*'s narrative flow is always already interrupted by playback memory scenes offering snippets of private family moments which can no longer be repressed. As Catherine observes to Ev, "And it all comes down to you sitting up here alone with Gramma's letter" (32). The play's halting movement back and forth from one remembered incident to another destroys the linearity of the traditionally ordered life of respectable auto/biography. Other recurrent patterns appear—moments when life-altering gender inscriptions were made. By positioning Catherine as the chief investigator who has the power to withhold her validation of Doc's life, Pollock has found the staging metaphor which recognizes that "woman is the locus of the process/trial of the subject's entry into culture" (Feral 10); the "Other" on whom male identification depends. To undo her male-identification, the character of Catherine has to re-enact her past by meeting up with her younger split-self, the little girl Katie. Together they must re-interpret their role in murdering the mother figures. The adult-child Catherine needs to know the process whereby she chose to participate in her mother's death in order to relieve her own self-hatred:

> **CATHERINE.** What about Mummy?
> **EV.** You blame me for that.
> **CATHERINE.** No.
> **EV.** It was all my fault, go on, say it, I know what you think.
> **CATHERINE.** It was my fault. (32)

Crucial scenes where Katie becomes her mother's punisher are replayed at strategic narrative moments; in the beginning, a disassociated Catherine narrates as Katie enacts the scene in which she poured out some of her mother's alcohol and then was driven to assault Bob physically (8–9). What both of them discover is how Katie learns to enter culture as the keeper of the law of the father, the watchdog who guards him against the despised mother/wife. In scene after scene, Katie announces her hatred for Bob, while a distanced Catherine observes and continues to reject her mother's pleas for understanding. Slowly, Catherine is able to enter into Katie's emotional battles as they watch Bob's progressive deterioration re-played. But, as an adult, Catherine can no longer pretend, as Katie did, that she has not glimpsed her reflection in her hated mother and grandmother:

> **KATIE.** I wonder ... do you know what I wonder? I wonder, did she take the pills to sleep like she sometimes does, or did she...
> **CATHERINE.** It was
> **KATIE.** An accident? ...Sometimes I look...
> **CATHERINE.** ...in the mirror, I look in the mirror...
> **KATIE.** ...and I see Mummy and I see...
> **CATHERINE.** ...Gramma, and Mummy and me...
> **KATIE.** ...I don't want to be like them. (108)

Only when they have symbolically united, after Catherine has re-experienced how she learned "not to cry" (115) and Katie finds the grownup label for Bob's alcoholism (119), can they participate in the re-creation of the shameful moment when Katie, in abandoning Bob to her death, also destroys a part of herself. Along with a few tentative moments when Catherine comes close to responding directly to her mother's drunken stories, we hear the disembodied offstage voice of Bob calling out for her daughter. When it becomes frantic and incessant, Katie deliberately shuts out her cries, comforting herself with the nursery rhymes of her lost childhood:[8]

> **BOB.** *(on mike, offstage)* Katie!
> **KATIE.** *(chants louder)* Fire on the mountain/ break your heart/Years to come—kiss and run/bitter bark—break your heart *(KATIE slowly takes her hands from her ears. There is silence. Pause)* I don't hear you! *(pause)* I don't hear you! *(pause)* I don't! (120)

Although they could never meet in the flesh in this patriarchal world, Catherine has let herself hear enough of her Mother's stories to enable her to reconstruct her lost life. Bob, "outlawed" for her failure to succeed as a doctor's wife, is pushed out into the public sphere, where her reputation as a notorious drunk—bad enough to be banned from the local liquor store—makes her the butt of town gossip. However, it is as a facet of this outlawed public status that she is made credible to us as a woman whose career ambitions were thwarted:

> **EV.** Look, you're not just an R.N. anymore.
> **BOB.** No.
> **EV.** You're not Eloise Roberts, you're not Bob any more.
> **BOB.** Who am I?
> **EV.** My wife. (57)

Bob's rampant alcoholism *speaks* to us of her despair at having her hard-won nursing degree dismissed as a convenient stepping stone to marriage, even by her own mother who had charred to send her daughter to school (71). These stories, so easily forgotten in the wake of Bob's ugly downward slide, bring to life a Bob who found her attempt at a professional career cut short by pregnancy (55), whose status isolates her from the maids she fires and from the mother-in-law who despises her for "trapping" her son. We discover that it is this same isolation—the condition experienced by women who come to believe that their only value is derived from the success of the men in their lives—that drives Ev's mother to walk out in front of the night train (98–99). In giving voice to the unrecorded, unrecognized, devalued lives of the women in her past, Pollock's alter-egos, Katie and Catherine find the way to shatter the master narrative of Ev's great achievements. Ev's complacent excuses that he sacrificed his family in the medical interest of relieving the poverty he had come from only underlines his unexamined male privilege:

> **EV.** Supposin' it were, her death my fault, put a figure on it, eh? Her death my fault on one side—and the other any old figure, thousand lives the figure—was that worth it? (123)

What he fails to take into account, and we now know, is that Bob's similar heroic efforts to have a meaningful career had been swept aside because of her *inferior* gender position.[9]

Although Catherine's split-self supposedly heals, in that she sends Katie away before the final moments of reconciliation with Ev, the final heavily charged gestic moment when she takes the burden of guilt away from her father by burning her grandmother's unread suicide letter only serves to remind us that the traces of women's lives in official auto/biographical accounts of their famous men tend to be paper thin and barely decipherable. In *Doc,* Pollock has gone back to retrieve them from the margins and it is here that Catherine is able to find her female relatives' faint reflections in a new cultural mirror. They too, like their notorious American cousin, Lizzie Borden, have crossed the borderlines to enter into theatrical representation. It is no longer the official auto/biographical accounts which interest us in either *Blood Relations* or *Doc,* but the women's untold stories that have been rescued. We no longer care to look for the simple answer to *whether* Lizzie, Bob or Gramma "did it"; now we are interested in *why* and *how* they (might) (could) (would) (should) have chosen to cross over those borderlines. No longer bound by the master narratives, Pollock's plays have given us a glimpse of a new transnational feminist sharing, of a revolutionary literary future where we will feel safe enough to bring our outlaws home.

(1996)

Notes

1 Matthew Fraser reports that Pollock regretted that she had "caved into pressures from Theatre New Brunswick artistic director Janet Amos and changed the play's title to *Family Trappings. Doc,* it was felt would lead audiences to expect a heroic portrait of a great man, while *Family Trappings* will ready them for something less cheerful." He went on to reveal that "[t]he mother in the play, Bob, commits suicide,

as did Pollock's own mother when she was eighteen. And the play's daughter, like Pollock, is a writer. Except for her own character, she hasn't even changed the names."

2 "Invagination is the inward refolding of *la gaine* (sheath, girdle), the inverted reapplication of the outer edge to the inside of a form where the outside then opens a pocket. Such an invagination is possible from the first trace on. That is why there is no first trace" (Derrida, "Living" 97).

3 Carole Boyce Davies defines the *crossover genre* as one which "challenges the oral/written separations and unites these forms as they maintain their distinct textualities" in order to give voice to unheard women's stories (7).

4 Pollock's closing words in the interview stress her decision to write about Canadian content, "What I write is quite Canadian-oriented. I couldn't live in the States. I couldn't work for the States either. I really believe that the artist has a *job*, a responsibility not just to her/himself but to the society s/he comes from. I represent the kinds of questions some Canadians are asking, and my responsibility is here" (6).

5 My generic use of the name Lizzie will be differentiated from the specific roles that she plays. It is sometimes difficult not to mix up her historic persona with her various stage characters.

6 Evidence at the trial included references to Lizzie's monthly cycle and offered an explanation for the removal of bloodied linen. Angela Carter, "The Fall River Axe Murders" (103–04), refers to Lizzie's menstruation in her fictionalized version of the event.

7 For other articles that relate Pollock's real life story to the play see Ashley, Brennan and Sweet.

8 Pollock's description of her mother's funeral as "hysterically *embarrassing*" (emphasis in original) to her at eighteen, fails to mask what must have been a very traumatic event. She explained that her mother had tried to commit suicide so many times that when she told the doctors that she had swallowed a mercury compound, none of them believed her. "It took her a week and a half to die …; it was a terribly unpleasant way to die" (Hofsess 52).

9 Pollock revealed that she had come to understand her mother's self-destruction better as she grew up. "I see now what a difficult position she was in. She came from a very large and very poor family in New Brunswick. She was the only one to get an education. No sooner did she become a nurse than she married my father, who was chief surgeon, and her career was terminated. Her whole personality was geared to striving—that's how she escaped whatever forces pulled everybody else in her family into an unending cycle of menial jobs and poverty. Yet suddenly she was expected to retire and play the role of a doctor's wife—gracious, idle, nothing much to do" (Hofsess 48).

Works Cited

Ashley, Audrey M. "Sharon Pollock …from the inside." *Ottawa Citizen* 16 November 1984: D12.

Brennan, Brain. "Pollock play confirms art follows life." *Calgary Herald* 1 April 84: F1.

Carter, Angela. "The Fall River Axe Murders." *Black Venus.* London: Picador, 1985. 103–21.

Case, Sue Ellen. "From Split Subject to Split Britches." *Feminine Focus: The New Women Playwrights.* Ed. Enoch Brater. New York and Oxford: Oxford UP, 1989. 126–46.

Davies, Carole Boyce. "Collaboration and the Ordering Imperative in Life Story Production." Smith and Watson 3–19.

Deakin, Basil. "*Doc* changed treatment with author Pollock." *Halifax Chronicle-Herald* 5 February 1987: 29.

Derrida, Jacques. "The Law of Genre." Trans. Avital Ronell. *Glyph* 7 (1980): 201–30.

———. "Living on. Border Lines." Trans Avital Ronell. *Deconstruction and Criticism.* New York: Seabury P, 1979. 75–176.

Dunn, Margo. "Sharon Pollock: In the Centre Ring." *Makara* (August–September 1976): 2–6.

Féral, Josette. "Antigone or the Irony of the Tribe." Trans. Alice Jardine and Tom Gora. *Diacritics* 8 (1978): 2–14.

Fraser, Matthew. "*Doc* may be a tough pill for New Brunswick." *The Globe and Mail* [Toronto] 7 March 1986: D11.

Hofsess, John. "Families Sticking Together." *Homemaker's Magazine* March 1980: 41–60.

Kaplan, Caren. "Resisting Autobiography: Out-Law Genres and Transnational Feminist Subjects." Smith and Watson 132–35.

McKinley, Marilyn. "Sharon Pollock's bloody relations." *Alberta Report* 28 February 1983: 36.

Nunn, Robert C. "Sharon Pollock's Plays: A Review Article." *Theatre History in Canada* 5 (1984): 72–83.

Page, Malcolm. "Sharon Pollock: Committed Playwright." *Canadian Drama/L'Art Dramatique Canadien* 5.2 (1979): 104–11.

Pollock, Sharon. *Blood Relations and other plays.* Edmonton: NeWest Press, 1981.

———. *Doc.* Toronto: Playwrights Canada, 1984.

Smith, Sidonie. "Who's Talking/Who's Talking Back? The Subject of Personal Narrative." *Signs* 18 (1993): 393–94.

———, and Julie Watson, eds. *Decolonizing the Subject: The Politics of Gender in Women's Autobiography*. Minneapolis: U of Minneapolis P, 1992.

Sweet, Louise. "Playwright's life provided the tools of her trade," *Toronto Star* 3 March 1984: D1.

———. "Writer explores mother's suicide," *Winnipeg Free Press* 4 February 1987: 35.

Watson, Julia and Sidonie Smith. "De/Colonization and the Politics of Discourse in Women's Autobiographical Practices." Smith and Watson xiii–xxxi.

"Painting the Background": Metadrama and the Fabric of History in Sharon Pollock's *Blood Relations*

by Herb Wyile

If, as Jean-François Lyotard argues, one of the notable features of the postmodern condition is an "incredulity toward metanarratives" (xxiv), the self-conscious treatments of historical figures and events with which Canadian writers have increasingly occupied themselves in recent decades are positioned on two related fronts of this resistance: they question the picture of history as an objectively describable sequence of events, and they disrupt the notion of literature as "simple mirror to or window onto the world outside" (Hutcheon, *Canadian Postmodern* 2). In postmodern historiographical metafiction and metadrama, these two impulses intersect, and the result in such works, for instance, as Timothy Findley's *Famous Last Words*, Susan Swan's *The Biggest Modern Woman of the World* and Sharon Pollock's *Blood Relations* is a complex and profound disturbance of epistemological and ontological certainties, both about the past and the present.

Sharon Pollock, on the basis of *Walsh*, *The Komagata Maru Incident*, *Doc* and other plays, has gained a place as one of Canada's most significant playwrights, particularly because of the postmodern, postcolonial and feminist elements of her work. Pollock's most challenging play, however, is the metadramatic *Blood Relations*, based on the legend of Lizzie Borden, who was acquitted of the 1892 murders of her father and stepmother in Fall River, Massachusetts. The Lizzie Borden story has received numerous theatrical, film and musical treatments, but Pollock's version, by presenting the story of Lizzie Borden as a play within a play, departs from the tendency of previous productions to either indict Lizzie or defend her. While much attention has been given to the metadramatic characteristics of the play, to its self-conscious presentation of a notorious episode in 19th century New England, little attention has been given to its historiographical character: while on one level the play presents an alternative version of that historical episode, at the same time it troubles our understanding of what history is and of how history is represented. Most commentaries have concentrated on the play as a relatively autonomous text, as an imaginative representation of historical material, without substantially taking into account the historical material being transformed. The notoriety of the Borden murder case—as embodied in the familiar children's rhyme with which the play opens[1] —seems to be taken as a given, while at the same time there seems to be little recognition of the details of Lizzie Borden's history beyond its representation in *Blood Relations*. This seems a bit surprising, given that the Borden case is one of the most infamous and puzzling murders in American history, though it is primarily the skipping rhyme that has survived to the present.[2] To appreciate the complexity of the issues *Blood Relations* raises, it is useful to look at the play against the background of the legend of Lizzie Borden, not so much to assess the "truth" of Pollock's version (that is, its compatability with the case as it has been documented), as to bring those fragments out of which we construct history, and to which Pollock is responding in constructing her play, into view in order to get a better sense of how, and for what purposes, Pollock has imaginatively transformed that material in *Blood Relations.* Pollock's play provides some interesting insights into the way that postmodern historiographic literary texts underline the complexity of—and overlap between—historiography and literature as discourses and disrupt our notions of what is real—both in the past and in the present.

In describing the play within the play as one form of metadrama, Richard Hornby notes that the characters of the outer play must acknowledge the inner play and "acknowledge it as performance" (35). While this is true of *Blood Relations,* the play's fulfillment of these qualifications is complex, and the role of the play within the play in *Blood Relations* is much more extensive than usual, taking up most of the play and substantially affecting interpretation of it. Whereas the precursor to *Blood Relations, My Name is Lisbeth* (a 1976 student production), provided a naturalistic representation of the events in the Borden household leading up to the murder (109), in *Blood Relations* the same events are staged as a game involving Lizzie and an actress friend; the Actress's role is strengthened through the metadramatic structure "to the point at which it dominates the play" (Stone-Blackburn 172). Pollock sets the action in the Borden home in Fall River in 1902, ten years after Lizzie Borden has been acquitted of the murders of her father and her stepmother, with Miss Lizzie entertaining her friend (and, it is suggested, her lover), who is generically titled the Actress. In response to her friend's persistent curiosity about Miss Lizzie's guilt/innocence, Miss Lizzie proposes a game in which the Actress will play Lizzie and Miss Lizzie will play Bridget O'Sullivan, the Bordens' maid at the time of the murders. One of the innovative but also challenging features of the "dream thesis," as Pollock calls it (*Blood Relations* 13), is the way in which the game is filled out by the imaginary characters of Andrew and Abbie Borden, Lizzie's sister Emma, Abbie's brother Harry, and Lizzie's married suitor Dr. Patrick. The technique thus allows Pollock to provide a representation of the events in the Borden household leading up to the murders, but it also puts the Actress's performance on an ambiguous footing.

At the time of her trial, Lizzie Borden was very much a *cause célèbre* for a nascent feminist movement in America, and both Lizzie's situation at home prior to the murders and her treatment by the public, the press, and the legal system provide telling insights into the patriarchal mindset of late 19th century New England.[3] The Actress's portrait of Lizzie certainly highlights the feminist possibilities of Lizzie's story. Resentful of her stepmother's influence on her miserly father, and disenchanted with her role in the Borden household and in Fall River society, the Actress/Lizzie reacts with concern to the news of Harry's visit, which signals the imminent transfer to Abbie of a farm that rightfully belongs to the Actress/Lizzie and Emma. As a thirty-two-year-old spinster unattracted to marriage, denied the opportunity to work in her father's business, and discouraged particularly through the intervention of her stepmother from pursuing a more freewheeling and luxurious social life, the Actress/Lizzie's options are seriously constrained. Combined with criticism of her resistance to Victorian feminine propriety, this conspiracy to wrest the farm from the sisters' control compels the Actress/Lizzie to be increasingly desperate and confrontational, and after Emma departs to visit friends and avoid the imminent confrontation, the circle rapidly closes in on her, reducing her options to suicide or murder, ultimately driving her to the latter. These events, however, are the product of the game and are not intended as an objective representation of history. Instead, the metadramatic structure allows Pollock to maintain a critical distance from her historical material and to avoid taking a stand on what continues to be a nagging and controversial case. It also, as most critics have noted, produces a much more complex and interesting theatrical performance.

Because the source of the "dream thesis" is somewhat ambiguous, one of the issues the play raises is the degree to which Miss Lizzie's presence serves as a guarantee of the authenticity of the Actress's interpretation. While most critics are cognizant of the influence of the metadramatic structure of the play, there are significant differences of opinion on its implications for the play as a representation of history. The "game" is initiated in the opening 1902 scene, as the Actress, hoping to prompt Miss Lizzie to tell the truth about her guilt or innocence, offers her opinion that Miss Lizzie is "aware there is a certain fascination in the ambiguity.... You always paint the background but leave the rest to my imagination. Did Lizzie Borden take an axe? ...If you didn't I should be disappointed... and if you did I should be horrified" (20). Then, in response to the Actress's request for her to "paint the background again" (20), Miss Lizzie proposes the game, in which she will play Bridget and the Actress will play her. In this role, of course, the Actress is driven to commit the murders, freezing at the end of the game with the hatchet raised above Andrew's head, which is taken as suggesting that Miss Lizzie "did it." Some critics argue (e.g., Nunn 78, Gilbert 117), particularly because of the way the game is set up, that Miss Lizzie is in control of the Actress's interpretation, that she establishes the background and provides in her role as Bridget the cues that determine the Actress's interpretation. Other critics (e.g., Stone-Blackburn 173, Bessai 100) take a more qualified approach in arguing that the Actress is not so much following Lizzie's lead as she is responding in a similar fashion to the circumstances which are recreated through the game. This is an important distinction, as the first reading of the game minimizes the role of the play within the play, whereas the second grants the Actress a little more autonomy in her performance as Lizzie.

Given that metadrama "occurs whenever the subject of a play turns out to be, in some sense, drama itself" (Hornby 31), it is characteristically metadramatic that a central concern in the "dream thesis" should be the relationship between director and actor, the degree to which Miss Lizzie "directs" the game and the Actress follows her directions. Examination of a few scenes from the play reveals the importance of the relationship between inner and outer plays, but also, ultimately, the ambiguity of that relationship. At the beginning of the game, Miss Lizzie clearly provides directorial assistance when the Actress makes her entry as Lizzie, following an exchange between Bridget and Harry:

> **HARRY.** Miss Lizzie loves kittens and cats and horses and dogs. What Miss Lizzie doesn't love is people.
> **BRIDGET.** *Some* people. *(She looks past HARRY to THE ACTRESS/ LIZZIE. HARRY turns to follow BRIDGET's gaze. BRIDGET speaks, encouraging an invitation for THE ACTRESS to join her.)* Good mornin' Lizzie.
> **THE ACTRESS.** *(She is a trifle tentative in the role of LIZZIE.)* Is the coffee on?
> **BRIDGET.** Yes ma'am.
> **LIZZIE.** I'll have some then.
> **BRIDGET.** Yes ma'am. *(She makes no move to get it, but watches as LIZZIE stares at HARRY.)*
> **HARRY.** Well … I think … maybe I'll … just split a bit of that kindling out back. *(He exits. LIZZIE turns to BRIDGET.)*
> **LIZZIE.** Silly ass.
> **BRIDGET.** Oh Lizzie. *(She laughs. She enjoys THE ACTRESS/LIZZIE's comments as she guides her into her role by "painting the background.")* (23–4)

As the Actress and Miss Lizzie warm up to their roles, indications of Miss Lizzie's influence on the Actress's interpretation disappear, and their dialogue is introduced with the single names LIZZIE and BRIDGET. However, on occasion, the split designations reappear, usually in order to set up a scene which the Actress will subsequently take over.

At a couple of key points in the play, these reversions seem to be very revealing of Miss Lizzie's "true" character, such as in the first act when Bridget advises Lizzie to be less uncompromising, since her options are limited:

> **BRIDGET.** You dream, Lizzie … you dream dreams … Work. Be sensible. What could you do?
> **LIZZIE.** I could
> **MISS LIZZIE/BRIDGET.** No.
> **LIZZIE.** I could
> **MISS LIZZIE/BRIDGET.** No.
> **LIZZIE.** I could
> **MISS LIZZIE/BRIDGET.** No!
> **LIZZIE.** I … dream.
> **MISS LIZZIE/BRIDGET.** You dream … of a carousel … you see a carousel … you see lights that go on and go off … you see yourself on a carousel horse, a red-painted horse with its head in the air, and green staring eyes, and a white flowing mane, it looks wild! … (43)

Miss Lizzie/Bridget proceeds to provide an ambiguous and surreal image of herself (and, implicitly, of the Actress/Lizzie) as the carousel slows down, removing the mask from the horse and discovering no eyes, "[j]ust black holes in a white mask" (44)—a subconscious representation of Miss Lizzie's desire to break out of her oppressive position. At the end of the scene, in her directorial role, she draws attention to Andrew and Harry conspiring together, and the Actress once again picks up the role of Lizzie as she moves over to eavesdrop. The scene provides a good illustration of Miss Lizzie's ambiguously split role, as she is simultaneously Bridget guiding Lizzie, Miss Lizzie guiding the Actress, and the acquitted Miss Lizzie revealing in her expressionistic dream a suggestive degree of psychological instability. A similarly explicit directorial moment occurs at the opening of the second act, when Miss Lizzie/Bridget tells the Actress/Lizzie (by this time clearly shaken by the experience of playing Lizzie) the story of the sick puppy "[o]n the farm, Papa's farm, Harry's farm, when I was little and thought it was my farm and I loved it" (49). Here Miss Lizzie is clearly not speaking as Bridget, and the lesson she draws from the drowning of the sick puppy underlines the dangers of her situation:

> .... That's what you do on a farm with things that are different.
> **ACTRESS/LIZZIE.** Am I different?
> **MISS LIZZIE/BRIDGET.** You kill them. (49)

Miss Lizzie's sense of difference and the vulnerability and social isolation which that difference entails, furthermore, are intensified through the suggestion at certain points in the play that she is a lesbian: the sexual nature of her liaison with the Actress is implied by various references in the 1902 sequences, such as Emma's comment that the Actress's presence in their house is "disgraceful" (69), and also through the Actress/Lizzie's reflections on her "difference" in the 1892 sequences. At this point, at any rate, Miss Lizzie seems to be speaking as herself as she provides insight into her past (and, by implication, her present) situation.

The ending, of course, is the most important consideration in assessing the significance of the Actress's interpretation and the extent of its validity. As the Actress is poised to strike Andrew, having already, it is clearly implied, disposed of Abbie, there is a blackout, and Miss Lizzie re-enters and takes the hatchet from the Actress's hand as the two drop their respective roles and the action returns to 1902. The Actress, having reached the conclusion, dramatically speaking, that Miss Lizzie committed the murders, backs away from the now-armed Miss Lizzie, which suggests that she has learned to be afraid of her. At this point, the "real" Emma, who is present in the house in the frame of the play, descends, and a confrontation with Miss Lizzie ensues in which Miss Lizzie implicates Emma in her own actions: "Did you never stop and think that if I did, then you were guilty too?" (69). As various critics have argued (see Stone-Blackburn 172, Miner 20, Gilbert 117), the ending subverts the demonizing of Lizzie Borden by opening up the question of culpability and foregrounding the social forces constructing the situation in which the Actress/Lizzie is pushed to murder. As the Actress approaches the arguing sisters, Miss Lizzie extends culpability for the crime beyond Emma:

> **EMMA.** You didn't ... did you?
> **MISS LIZZIE.** Poor ... Emma.
> **THE ACTRESS.** Lizzie. *(She takes the hatchet from MISS LIZZIE.)* Lizzie, you did.
> **MISS LIZZIE.** I didn't. *(THE ACTRESS looks to the hatchet—then to the audience.)* You did. (70)

As Reid Gilbert notes, the confrontation with Emma, the recognition that the game has been the Actress's interpretation, and Miss Lizzie's final line, render the question of guilt provocatively open:

> The pronoun is completely ambiguous: is it 'you' the Actress who, as Lizzie, swung the axe? Or the Actress as herself, capable of the murder? Or Emma, the sister? Or the audience, who represents a society which represses individuals? Or the legend itself, which we have collectively created to exorcise our own guilt at the frightening potential of our natural will to live? (117)

Blood Relations, as Gilbert effectively illustrates, thus widens the notion of complicity and undermines the traditional construction of Lizzie Borden as a monster.

The question of guilt aside, there is little doubt that Lizzie Borden, as represented by both Miss Lizzie and the Actress, is presented in a sympathetic light; most critics read the "dream thesis" as portraying an oppressed heroine struggling to break out of a suffocating patriarchal system. Whether or not one maintains that Lizzie's directorial hand is firmly on the Actress throughout the play, what *Blood Relations* stresses are the limited options of a woman like Lizzie Borden and the extremities to which such an oppressive society could drive any woman; as Ann Saddlemyer puts it, "[t]he question has been translated: 'did she or didn't she?' has become 'would you or wouldn't you?'" (228). Thus the play gives a contemporary feminist slant to a notorious Victorian episode.

However, the debate about directorial control tends to assume a certain dramatic and ontological stability on the part of the "dream thesis"—that it is a fixed backdrop against which Miss Lizzie and the Actress "produce" their play. That is, because Miss Lizzie "paints the background," the circumstances to which the Actress reacts in her interpretation of the role of Lizzie are taken as given in the dramatic economy of "the dream thesis," and that it is only the conclusion which the Actress reaches—that Lizzie "did it"—that is really debatable. The play within the play thus becomes primarily a vehicle for creating in the Actress (and by extension, the audience) "an emotional understanding of the dilemma with which the heroine was confronted" (Loiselle 97). Rather than solving the Borden murders, in other words, "Pollock explores the circumstances that *might* have led her to commit them" (Bessai 99). But to assume that stability is to sell short the metadramatic qualities of the play and to give insufficient credit to the way in which Pollock writes (of) history.

Indeed, if the aim of the "dream thesis" is empathy, it is a failure, at least within the play. Pollock herself sees the game as "an effort on Miss Lizzy's [sic] part to bring the Actress closer to her. And what I felt was the tragedy of it was that, in fact, it didn't bring the Actress closer to her. It made her draw away once she had that information" (Pollock, Interview 124). Pollock's description suggests that the Actress's performance is a process of learning, of coming to (yet failing to) understand Miss Lizzie's past and her present dilemma as a perpetual suspect. However, by looking at *Blood Relations* as historiographical as well as metadramatic it can be argued that that process is much more complex than it seems. If the dominant tendency in post-modernist texts, as Brian McHale argues about postmodernist fiction (10), is to raise ontological questions, including questions about the stability of the literary work, postmodern historiography raises similar questions about history as an objective account of the past. "Post-modern historiography," Richard Paul Knowles argues, "recognizes that the past, insofar as it is external and objective, can only exist as fragments, 'facts' and documents that are, in their own cultural terms, impenetrable. Historiography, then, becomes the ongoing process of *re*making history, of 'making it new,' as fiction and myth" (228). This view of history as the product of story-making rather than a narrative record of objectively substantiated facts is increasingly reflected in contemporary Canadian literary treatments of historical subjects, though, as Knowles argues, Canadian dramatists' "use of self-reflexive, metadramatic forms to highlight the instability both of history and of dramatic texts" (228) have significant and often overlooked implications. By focusing on the historiographical qualities of the play we can see that the instability of the game extends back much further than its violent conclusion and that the relationship between Miss Lizzie and the Actress involves much more than directorial authority. In her chapter on historiographic metafiction in *The Canadian Postmodern*, Linda Hutcheon, drawing on Michel Foucault and Fredric Jameson, argues

> that in a very real sense history, while it had a real "referent" once upon a time, is accessible to us now only in textualized form, that is, through documents. Therefore postmodern historiographic metafictionists, who also deal with "events already constituted", but who self-consciously signal this textual nature within their novels, are perhaps in an even more complex position than the historian: they are constrained by the demands of narrative fiction as much as by those of historical events. (67–8)

Hutcheon's observation underlines the importance of looking beyond a reading of *Blood Relations* as a feminist historical drama with a self-conscious twist to preserve the ambiguity over Lizzie Borden's guilt, in order to recognize how the play dramatizes that history itself is unstable, already textualized, already constituted, as well as the need to be attentive to the interplay between literary imperatives and the complex story-making which is historiography.

One of the most important features of postmodern metafiction and metadrama is the dissolving of the barrier between reader and text, often accomplished through the inscription of the figure of the reader/audience in the text, and in this regard it is important to recognize that though Miss Lizzie obviously influences the "dream thesis," and is presumably the Actress's main "source," the Actress is far from disposed to be passively situated in the "background" which Miss Lizzie paints. First of all, prior to the game she is already familiar with the legend of Lizzie Borden (she comments to Lizzie early in the play that "[t]he reports of the day said you were definitely jowly" [17]), is far from convinced of Miss Lizzie's innocence (she prevents children from harming a cat but does not intervene when she hears them chanting the infamous rhyme about Lizzie [17])—and it seems perilous to assume that she is merely responding to life in the Borden household and not constructing it. That is, the dynamics of the "dream thesis," and thus the degree of responsibility for the interpretation, are ambiguous throughout the play, up to and including Miss Lizzie's apparent disclaimer at the end. Furthermore, while the self-conscious structure of *Blood Relations* is typically metadramatic, it is also historiographical, a *looking back* from 1902 to 1892. Given that the Actress has formed her opinions on the case at least in part by reading about it, her putting together the pieces of Miss Lizzie's story is a gesture which very much mirrors Pollock's historiographical approach to the legend of Lizzie Borden. Indeed, by looking in more detail at the way Pollock has shaped historical and more recent accounts of the murders and the Borden household, we can see that the Actress's interpretation is not necessarily a faithful one, but all through is a "remaking of history" which dramatizes how constructed and unstable it ultimately is. The Actress's role destabilizes the play as revisionist historical drama—as an alternative, contestatory, but nonetheless conventionally cohesive version of history—and foregrounds history as discursive, constructed, relative and ideological.

As Hayden White argues, the writing of history is a (re)construction which involves the selection, arrangement, interpretation and narrativizing of detail, and a closer look at Pollock's use of historical material shows how complex (yet far from authoritative) her representation of that history is. The play, for instance, presents the atmosphere of the household as fairly poisonous, a conclusion drawn by most commentators arguing for Lizzie Borden's guilt and which in *Blood Relations* allows for a sense of claustrophobia to heighten the Actress/Lizzie's position as beleaguered heroine. The Actress/Lizzie's hostility towards her stepmother is clearly a key factor in the play, as it is Abbie through her henpecking of a somewhat reluctant Andrew who enforces the Victorian code of feminine docility and subservience on Lizzie. However, this domestic rancour is an example of the selectivity historiographical representation involves, underlining that what the Actress presents is—like all histories—one interpretation of a complex, irrecoverable, and much debated cluster of events. During and after the trial of Lizzie Borden, Emma Borden testified that she was less warm than Lizzie towards her stepmother, and opinions differ on the degree of hostility within the family, with at least some commentators (Brown and Kent, for example) arguing along with the defence that there was no friction in the Borden household such as the play depicts. The Actress/Lizzie's emphatic denial in the play of a blood relationship with Abbie—"She is *not* my *mother*!" (39)—was a comment made by Lizzie Borden in a conversation with a police officer shortly after the murders and was similarly construed as hostile and defiant by the Fall River police during the investigation, though Lizzie Borden argued that the observation was made in a more neutral tone

(Kent, *Forty Whacks* 53). The Actress' version of the family dynamics thus demonstrates the point increasingly being made in contemporary historiography that "there are many stories, not only different stories about different events, but even different stories about the same events" (Mink 140), as it is woven out of scraps such as Lizzie's repudiation of Abbie that can be interpreted and textualized in various ways. "History as narrative account," as Hutcheon observes, "is unavoidably figurative, allegorical, fictive; it is always already textualized, always already interpreted" ("History" 170).

If history is a narrative account, a weaving of interpreted and textualized scraps, Pollock's intention is not to provide a rigorous and seamless dramatic reading of the case; there are certainly places in which dramatic concerns override historiographical credibility—in which, in short, to those familiar with the case, Pollock's stitches show. One striking innovation on Pollock's part, for instance, is the scene of Miss Lizzie giving testimony at her trial—striking because indeed Lizzie Borden did not actually testify at her trial. Miss Lizzie's replies to the defence are based on testimony Lizzie Borden gave at an inquest into the murder, to which her lawyer was denied access (hence there was no "defence" present to ask her such questions). Though Lizzie Borden's comments were originally directed to a district attorney at the inquest, they are presented, like Bridget's lines, as replies to questions from the defence at the trial. For obvious reasons of dramatic convenience, Pollock reworks Lizzie Borden's testimony and collapses it with Bridget's as part of "painting the background" of the case. The most prominent departure from established details of the Borden case, however, involves the character of Harry, Abbie's brother, who gives a little more substance to the conspiracy between Abbie and Andrew to consolidate Andrew's wealth and property in Abbie's hands in the event of Andrew's death, and thus to the oppressiveness of the Actress/Lizzie's situation, as she faces being under the thumb of her despised stepmother. While Abbie Borden had no brother Harry, John Morse, the brother of Lizzie Borden's biological mother, was present at the time of the murder. Accounts differ about his allegiances to members of the Borden family, but as the brother of the first Mrs. Borden rather than of the second, he seems an unlikely candidate for a conspiracy with Abbie, and his role in the family (as opposed to, say, that of Andrew himself, who was almost universally recognized as a miser) obviously did not make such a dramatic contribution to Lizzie's position as an independent woman stifled by Victorian mores.[4] The existence of a more shadowy figure in the Borden case, Andrew Borden's brother-in-law Hiram Harrington, who claimed to have visited Emma and Lizzie on the eve of the murders (Brown 118), suggests the possibility that Pollock's "Harry" is something of a composite, a departure from the established details of the historical case but nonetheless influenced by figures associated with the family and not, in that sense, a complete and convenient fabrication on her part. In contrast, it is harder to identify the historical precedent(s) for the character of Dr. Patrick, though rumours of suitors abounded both before and after the trial of Lizzie Borden. Such conspicuous liberties point to Pollock's desire to reflect in the Actress's interpretation how stifled is Lizzie's life in the Borden household, but they also highlight the intertextual, synthetic and creative nature of historiographical representation, which, as Hayden White puts it, "is thus necessarily a mixture of adequately and inadequately explained events, a congeries of established and inferred facts, at once a representation that is an interpretation and an interpretation that passes for an explanation of the whole process mirrored in the narrative" (*Tropics* 51).

Pollock's construction of the character of Harry and her use of material from transcripts of the inquest and trial, however, are only the most conspicuous examples of her manipulation of historical detail for dramatic purposes. Various other elements of the play demonstrate the way in which the play is not simply attempting to hold up a mirror to history but is a complex mesh of already textualized reflections on the Borden household, the murders, the trial, and Lizzie Borden's life after her acquittal. For instance, Pollock takes what seems to have been a fairly inconsequential episode in the Bordens' history, the killing of Lizzie's pigeons by her father,[5] places it immediately before the murders, and makes it a crucial turning point in the Actress's portrait of Lizzie—clearly foreshadowing the violence to which she will resort at the end of the play. Another interesting detail is that the Actress/Lizzie's observation, as she follows Abbie up the stairs prior to murdering her, that "[w]hen a person dies, retained on her eye is the image of the last thing she saw" (64), was one of many theories passed on to the Fall River police by members of the public eager to solve the enigmatic murders (Kent, *Forty Whacks* 85). Thus the play illustrates Hutcheon's point that in historiographical literary texts fidelity to historical detail is in constant play with literary imperatives.

That Pollock's manipulation of historical material goes beyond taking dramatic licence with a historical episode is illustrated by the most interesting and overlooked intersection between historical detail and dramatic concerns in *Blood Relations*: her use of the Actress as a vehicle to metadramatically represent events in the Borden household. Though the Actress is given a significantly generic title, which allows her (as somebody whose profession it is to represent) to serve as a proxy for both writer and reader/audience, she is clearly modelled on Nance O'Neill, a noted actress in Boston with whom Lizzie Borden struck up a friendship after her acquittal. Emma's sense of outrage over their liaison in the play is a refracted version of a split between Emma and Lizzie Borden over Lizzie's entertainment of people from the theatre. *The Boston Sunday Herald* reported on 3 June 1905 that Emma Borden moved out of the house she had been sharing with Lizzie in Fall River (not, as in the play, the same house in which the murders were committed) and cited various reasons, including "Miss Lizzie's recent infatuation for stage folk and dramatic matters," noting also that "gossips" attempted to tie Lizzie's friendship with Nance O'Neill to the quarrel (Kent, *Sourcebook* 329). Even more interesting is that the article on Emma's departure mentions a "rumor that Miss Borden is to write a play and that Miss O'Neil [sic] is to act it," though no "hint is given as to what the new play will be based on" (Kent, *Sourcebook* 329). Thus historical accounts suggest the degree to which Pollock's approach to the story of Lizzie Borden and even the metadramatic structure of the play are grounded in historical detail. On the subject of Lizzie's homosexuality, however, though other commentators on the Borden case are more explicit in maintaining that Lizzie was a lesbian (e.g., Samuels 8–9), Pollock is somewhat cagy, implying rather than asserting the possibility: "Anything I've ever read has also gone to great pains to deny [their relationship] had even the slightest hint of homosexuality about it, which, given the edition date [of] the books I read and the background of the people who have written them, is a perfectly natural response" (Pollock, Interview 124). Her comment is interesting, though, because of the way in which Pollock, rather than taking a firm stand herself, foregrounds the underlying assumptions of other accounts—an eminently postmodern historiographical gesture. The way in which Pollock mixes material from historical sources on the Borden case, therefore, raises what Brian McHale sees as crucial postmodernist questions: "What happens when different kinds of worlds are placed in confrontation, or when boundaries between worlds are violated?" (10).

Pollock's weaving of elements gleaned from documentation of the Borden case into the dramatization of Lizzie as socially ostracized heroine underlines the importance of resisting the conclusion that the Actress's "recreation" has Pollock's *imprimatur*, that the Actress simply presents the playwright's reading of the case. The Actress, in presenting Lizzie Borden, is like anybody else trying to give an account of the case, is putting a certain spin on the characterization—and, given her profession, it is not surprising that the results are dramatic; she provides a theatrical example of White's central insight into historiography, that there is "an elective affinity between the act of prefiguration of the historical field and the explanatory strategies used by the historian in a given work" (427). The Actress's depiction of Lizzie in numerous places comes across as somewhat histrionic, particularly when she throws a tantrum (complete with smashed plates) after being teased by Abbie over her dependency on Andrew; Bridget's comment, "you outdid yourself that time" (42), is thus an instance of the "seeing double" which Richard Hornby argues "is the true source of the significance of metadrama" (32), as it is a reflection not just on the extremity of Lizzie's tantrum but on the dramatic qualities of the Actress's performance. A similar consciousness of the Actress's performance as performance is raised when she pursues Abbie in a sinister, somewhat psychopathic fashion prior to killing her and when she reminisces with Andrew in the tender scene just before he is to be dispatched:

> **LIZZIE.** You've got on my ring.... Do you remember when I gave you that? ...When I left Miss Cornelia's—it was in a little blue velvet box, you hid it behind your back, and you said, "guess which hand, Lizzie!" And I guessed. And you gave it to me and you said, "it's real gold, Lizzie, it's for you because you are very precious to me." Do you remember, Papa? *Mr. Borden nods.* And I took it out of the little blue velvet box, and I took your hand, and I put my ring on your finger and I said "thank you, Papa, I love you." ... You've never taken it off ... see how it bites into the flesh of your finger. She presses his hand to her face. I forgive you, Papa, I forgive you for killing my birds.... (67)

It's not that the sentimentality of the latter scene or the suspense of the former rings false (indeed, the gift of the ring was a key detail during the trial in establishing Lizzie Borden's affection for her father), rather that they emphasize that what we are seeing is indeed a dramatic interpretation, an opaque, layered theatricality: Pollock the playwright is writing scenes for an actress playing an Actress playing Lizzie Borden. Hornby notes of modern metadrama that "[i]n the twentieth century we find the same characters moving between inner and outer play, the boundaries between inner and outer play becoming blurred and sometimes disappearing …" (47), and it can be said of *Blood Relations* that just as there is a blurring of the boundary between inner and outer plays, there is a blurring of the boundary between the dramatic and historiographical inclinations of the Actress and the dramatic and historiographical inclinations of the playwright.

Sharon Pollock was obviously cognizant of the complexities of the evidence in the Borden murders and also of conflicting accounts of Lizzie Borden's personality and her relationship with the rest of her family, and as a result she walks a fine line in *Blood Relations.* On the one hand, the play provides a representation of Lizzie Borden and what happened on those two days in August, 1892—important particularly since familiarity with the case on the part of the audience could not be assumed. On the other hand, the metadramatic structure and historiographical elements of the play radically qualify what might otherwise be a revisionist feminist historical drama, particularly through the rooting of that representation in the perspective of someone (the Actress, that is) responding to the legend of Lizzie Borden. The Actress/Lizzie's complaint in the play about her submissive role can be taken as a trope for the social construction of feminine identity in a repressive, patriarchal Victorian society: "I'm supposed to be a mirror. I'm supposed to reflect what you want to see, but everyone wants something different. If no one looks in the mirror, I'm not even there, I don't exist!" (39). But it can also be taken as a trope for the kind of historiographical approach Pollock takes in the play, as it speaks to the legend of Lizzie Borden as a pastiche of conflicting and often heavily overdetermined interpretations. That is, rather than letting a realistic, revisionist version of the Lizzie Borden story stand unchallenged, Pollock, through her modulation between fidelity to historical detail and a more intertextual stitching together of and elaboration on material from various sources, and through her situating of that historiographical representation in the subjective, interested, dramatic perspective of the Actress, underlines history not as a neat, transparent mimesis of the past but as an assembling of (already constituted, already semiotized) fragments that always involves our perspective, our desire for narrative, and our desire for drama. The way in which postmodern historiographical literary texts like *Blood Relations* play with historical material, then, goes beyond simply taking poetic or dramatic licence; they remind us that taking licence is not the exclusive preserve of the literary but is a condition of all discourse, including historiography. While it might be argued that literary texts and historiographical texts make different truth-claims and that the rules of engagement for taking license are different for each, the relationship between them is far from a binary opposition between the "fictional" and the "non-fictional" or "true." Postmodern historiographical literary texts illustrate the dangers of drawing such discursive boundaries (already muddied in the often sensationalistic scholarship on the Borden case) by simultaneously deconstructing the illusion of objectivity of historiographical discourse and the representational conventions of mimetic literature, "teasing us with the existence of the past as real, [but] also suggest[ing] that there is no direct access to that real which would be unmediated by the structures of our various discourses about it" (Hutcheon, "History" 173).

The success of such a strategy is certainly a central issue in *Blood Relations*, as not only is Pollock's manipulation of historical sources likely to be lost on a good part of her theatrical audience, but also the argument can be made that the power of the Actress's presentation of Lizzie eclipses the metadramatic aspects of the play (Stone-Blackburn 175). Pollock clearly intends the Actress's performance to have such power and to produce an empathetic response, yet the metadramatic conclusion runs the risk of neutralizing that power by distancing Miss Lizzie from the Actress's representation and by questioning the Actress's dramatic "solution" to Miss Lizzie's dilemma. This tension is fairly characteristic of the postmodern ambivalence towards conventions of representation, which are at once both exploited and questioned, but the play may also demonstrate the shortcomings of this ambivalence—that in some cases, such strategies are too clever by half. These reservations, I would argue, may be justified in considering the impact of the play on a theatre audience, for whom the momentum of the dream thesis may well overwhelm Miss Lizzie's explicitly metadramatic response at the end, but it is still possible, whether reading the play or seeing it, to absorb the implications of Miss Lizzie's resistance to the Actress's interpretation (i.e., that the Actress's solution is not necessarily accurate and may be flawed, and that the character of Miss Lizzie remains ambiguous)[6] without the impact of the critique of patriarchy that the play within the play provides being undermined. While its ontological stability is questioned, the dream thesis nonetheless effectively shifts the emphasis from Lizzie Borden to the larger patriarchal "background" to her story.

Moreover, the self-conscious historiographical elements of *Blood Relations* help to make it extremely durable, rich and intriguing as a dramatic text—like its historical source, an interesting study in motivation, evidence and (pardon the pun) execution. Going beyond a revisionist realistic presentation in this fashion allows Pollock to give a complex case its due—to dramatically recognize the difficulties of rendering a verdict on Lizzie Borden—but also to underline the implications of those difficulties. If *Blood Relations* inscribes concerns about the power and authority of theatrical representation (which, as various critics have noted, has serious implications for the position of women in particular), it also does the same for historiographical discourse. "To write either history or historical fiction is equally to raise the question of power and control: it is the story of the victors that usually gets told," observes Linda Hutcheon; while the dream thesis provides a formally coherent version of the Lizzie Borden story that challenges those of "the victors" (in which Lizzie must be either innocent or monstrous), underlying *Blood Relations* is a consciousness that the "creator or discerner of that formal coherence is in a position of power too—power over facts, clearly, but also power over readers" (Hutcheon, *Canadian Postmodern* 72), and Pollock's resistance to closure at the end of the play is an attempt to return at least some of that power back to her audience.

While *Blood Relations* does not problematize the writing of history as openly and effectively as, say, Findley's *Famous Last Words*, it nonetheless exhibits similar concerns through its self-conscious historiographical intertextuality and its metadramatic questioning of the recreation of history. Marie Lovrod argues in "The Rise of Metadrama and the Fall of the Omniscient Observer" that metadrama lends itself to the expression of multiple perspectives and thus to subversive political possibilities (507), and a work like *Blood Relations* extends such a recognition to historiographical discourse, dramatizing the dangers of historiographical omniscience, of pretending to "tell it like it was." Postmodernist writers have continually challenged "the reality effect" in part because literary realism reaffirms positivist conceptions of reality as objective, knowable and describable, and such a challenge is equally important when extended to the writing of history. If history is the preserve of the victorious, postmodern historiography—and by extension postmodern historiographical literary texts like *Blood Relations*—shows us how active, attentive and skeptical we need to be both in writing history and in reading it. If, as Hayden White argues, "it is possible to view historical consciousness as a specifically Western prejudice by which the presumed superiority of modern, industrial society can be retroactively substantiated" (2), it is necessary to contest the exercising of that hegemony not on the same terms, by rewriting history within similar assumptions about representing the past (thus implicitly validating those assumptions), but rather by exploring the process of writing history itself, the complex relationship between historiographical discourse and the material out of which it constructs historical narratives. What makes *Blood Relations* such an intriguing and complex play, then, is the way in which it inscribes such a perspective on historiography, providing the opportunity to (re)view Lizzie Borden and the patriarchal "background" from which her story cannot be detached, but within a metadramatic framework which interrogates the legend of Lizzie Borden and the multiple, conflicting, contestatory perspectives through which that legend—as part of the larger narrative we call history—has been constructed.

(1997)

Notes

1 As any Lizzie Borden aficionado will testify, the rhyme is based on a series of misconceptions about the timing of the murders, the number of blows, and the relationship between Lizzie and Abbie Borden, who was not her mother (Brown 12).

2 It is hard, writing in the mid-1990s, not to draw comparisons between the Borden case and the so-called "Crime of the Century," the murder case involving football star and celebrity O.J. Simpson. The Borden case, like the Simpson case (though

somewhat less hyperbolically), drew substantial media attention, involved notable figures, polarized popular opinion, raised doubts about the competence and integrity of the police, was marred by dubious legal procedures, and resulted in a controversial acquittal. As in the Simpson case, the Borden trial was intriguing because of contradictory testimony, the timing and logistics of the murders, and debates over motivation, and the murders are still unsolved and continue to puzzle. The Borden case has produced, like the assassination of John F. Kennedy and the Simpson trial (though not to the same degree), a great deal of commentary and a host of aficionados with their own theories about the murders, as well as inspiring various fictionalized versions.

3 See the chapters on Lizzie Borden in Ann Jones' *Women Who Kill*, 209–37, for such a reading of the case.

4 Morse's actions and testimony at the trial made him an object of suspicion from the moment of the murders on, despite his having a tight alibi; indeed, the day after the murders, he was rescued by police from a certain lynching at the hands of an angry mob.

5 The fate of her pigeons was acknowledged matter-of-factly by Lizzie Borden at the inquest, in response to a question about the presence of blood on a hatchet and an axe in the cellar of the house. She noted that her father "killed some pigeons in the barn last May or June" but thought they might have had their necks wrung (Brown 366).

6 Sharon Stone-Blackburn argues (172) that the metadramatic structure, because it leaves ambiguous whether Miss Lizzie has taken a stand by committing the murders, somewhat deflates her potential as a feminist heroine, whereas Madonne Miner reads the play as quite intentionally revealing the contradictions of liberal feminism's reliance on an ostensibly liberatory conception of the essential self (20).

Works Cited

Bessai, Diane. "Women Dramatists: Sharon Pollock and Judith Thompson." *Post Colonial English Drama: Commonwealth Drama Since 1960*. Ed. Bruce King. New York: St. Martin's, 1992. 97–117.

Brown, Arnold. *Lizzie Borden: The Legend, the Truth, the Final Chapter*. Nashville: Rutledge, 1991.

Findley, Timothy. *Famous Last Words*. Toronto: Clarke, 1981.

Gilbert, Reid. "Sharon Pollock." *Profiles in Canadian Literature* 6. Ed. Jeffrey M. Heath. Toronto: Dundern, 1986. 113–20.

Hornby, Richard. *Drama, Metadrama, and Perception.* London: Associated UP, 1986.

Hutcheon, Linda. *The Canadian Postmodern: A Study of Contemporary English-Canadian Fiction.* Toronto: Oxford UP, 1988.

———. "History and/as Intertext." *Future Indicative: Literary Theory and Canadian Literature.* Ed. John Moss. Reappraisals: Can. Writ. 13. Ottawa: U of Ottawa P, 1987. 169–84.

Jones, Ann. *Women Who Kill.* New York: Holt, 1980.

Kent, David. *Forty Whacks: New Evidence in the Life and Legend of Lizzie Borden.* Emmaus, Penn: Yankee, 1992.

———, ed. and comp. *The Lizzie Borden Sourcebook.* Boston: Branden, 1992.

Knowles, Richard Paul. "Replaying History: Canadian Historiographic Metadrama." *Dalhousie Review* 67.2/3 (1987): 228–43.

"Lizzie Borden Left By Sister." *The Boston Sunday Herald* 3 June 1905. Kent, *The Lizzie Borden Sourcebook* 329–30.

Loiselle, André. "Paradigms of 1980s Québécois and Canadian Drama: Normand Chaurette's *Provincetown Playhouse, juillet 1919, j'avais 19 ans* and Sharon Pollock's *Blood Relations.*" *Québec Studies* 14 (1992): 93–104.

Lovrod, Marie. "The Rise of Metadrama and the Fall of the Omniscient Observer." *Modern Drama* 37.3 (1994): 497–508.

Lyotard, Jean-François. *The Postmodern Condition: A Report on Knowledge.* Trans. Geoff Bennington and Brian Massumi. Theory of History and Lit. 10. Minneapolis: U of Minnesota P, 1984.

McHale, Brian. *Postmodernist Fiction.* New York: Methuen, 1987.

Miner, Madonne. "'Lizzie Borden Took an Axe': Enacting *Blood Relations.*" *Literature in Performance* 2.6 (1986): 10–21.

Mink, Louis O. "Narrative Form as a Cognitive Instrument." *The Writing of History: Literary Form and Historical Understanding.* Eds. Robert H. Canary and Henry Kozicki. Madison: U of Wisconsin P, 1978. 129–49.

Nunn, Robert C. "Sharon Pollock's Plays: A Review Article." *Theatre History in Canada* 5.1 (1984): 72–83.

Page, Malcolm. "Sharon Pollock: Committed Playwright." *Canadian Drama/L'Art dramatique canadien* 5.2 (1979): 104–11.

Pollock, Sharon. *Blood Relations and Other Plays.* Ed. Diane Bessai. Prairie Plays IV. Edmonton: NeWest, 1981. 10–70.

———. *Doc.* Toronto: Playwrights, 1986.

———. Interview. *The Work: Conversations with English-Canadian Playwrights.* Ed. Robert Wallace and Cynthia Zimmerman. Toronto: Coach House, 1982. 114–26.

———. *The Komagata Maru Incident.* Toronto: Playwrights, 1978.

———. *Walsh.* Vancouver: Talonbooks, 1973.

Saddlemyer, Ann. "Crime in Literature: Canadian Drama." *Rough Justice: Essays on Crime in Literature.* Ed. M.L. Friedland. Toronto: U of Toronto P, 1991. 215–30.

Samuels, Charles and Louise. *The Girl in the House of Hate.* Mattituck, NY: Aeonian, 1953.

Stone-Blackburn, Susan. "Feminism and Metadrama: Role-playing in *Blood Relations.*" *Canadian Drama/L'Art dramatique canadien* 15.2 (1989): 169–78.

Swan, Susan. *The Biggest Modern Woman of the World.* Toronto: Lester, 1983.

White, Hayden. *Metahistory: The Historical Imagination in Nineteenth-Century Europe.* Baltimore: Johns Hopkins UP, 1973.

———. *Tropics of Discourse: Essays in Cultural Criticism.* Baltimore: Johns Hopkins UP, 1978.

"Women and Madness": Sharon Pollock's Plays of the Late 1980s and Early 1990s

by Craig S. Walker

In a 1982 interview, Sharon Pollock speculated on the direction of her work to come, declaring:

> I think that the plays that I'll write in the future will be more about women. I know there's a play that follows *Blood Relations* about what happens to a woman who is unable to kill either her father or her mother or, indeed, even herself. Obviously it's about women and madness. (Wallace and Zimmerman 118)

Pollock's subsequent plays do indeed vaguely answer this description, exploring various configurations of "women and madness" in domestic, political and psychological contexts. In *Whiskey Six Cadenza* (1983), for example, Leah feels helplessly trapped by her perverse relations with her foster parents (including Mama George's conniving at the situation), and ends up having Mr. Big kill her. In *Doc* (1984), we see a daughter haunted by the spectre of her mother and grandmother's self-destruction, and by the overwhelming figure of her father, though in the end, the play embraces the possibility of positively reconciling parental-daughter tensions. Later, in *Fair Liberty's Call* (1993), Pollock construed madness as the vision of a mother traumatized by war; and in *Saucy Jack* (also 1993) the distinction between madness and sanity was shown to be contingent upon accurate memory. But between *Doc* and *Fair Liberty's Call*, Pollock essayed the theme of "women and madness" even more directly in *Egg*, a play that was never produced in its original form, although from the large-cast *Egg* was eventually hatched the one-woman drama *Getting it Straight* (1989).

Given that *Egg* survives only in a relatively early draft, we cannot reasonably expect it to be comparable in quality to any of Pollock's produced and published work, and it is difficult to say what the play might have become had she finished it in its original form. However, even in its inchoate state, for those with an interest in Pollock's work, the play is worth considering, not the least because in style it is quite unlike the work for which Pollock is best known. In some ways *Egg* suggests the kind of grotesque irony associated with George F. Walker's early plays. Among Pollock's works, it is closer to the absurdist satire that characterizes her two early produced but unpublished plays, *And Out Goes You?* and *A Compulsory Option*, than it is to any of the more subtle, psychologically-based drama she had been writing in the intervening years.

However, *Egg* is far more complex and grotesque than either of those early works. There are three interrelated spheres of action in *Egg*, arising from an attempt to show how multinational corporations, military syndicates and ordinary human beings affect one another. The central character is Martha, an escaped mental patient who is the forerunner of Eme in *Getting it Straight*. It becomes apparent that Martha's "mental illness" is a result of her inability to live with the condition of the nuclear bomb-threatened world created by patriarchal, corporate and militaristic interests. Her husband, George, is a General engaged in a promotional campaign intended, as he explains:

> to get people round the world behind the concept of war as a means to peace. There are worse things than turning the globe into a cinder falling through space, but it isn't an easy proposition to sell. (24)

Consequently, when Martha escapes, the doctors decide not to "impose on the General at this time a lot of hullabaloo concerning a looney tunes wife he was basically warehousing at our institution" (24). Instead, instinctively seeking a subterfuge, they announce preposterously that she has been infected with a "deadly, eighteen-hour" virus.

Meanwhile, at the offices of Universal Inc., the military's partner in the "Whole Earth Nuclear" campaign, we see two contrasting groups. In one room, three women—a television producer, a financial officer and a secretary—unpack eggs from a carton and calmly discuss the problems of sexism in their homes. In another, the male CEO of the company, R.D. Farkerson, rants erratically and paranoically to a male subordinate about his distrust of the women who seem to be infesting his company:

> We are surrounded by women. Have you noticed that? They're everywhere. It's frightening. Everyplace you look. Women. I'm starting to notice their faces. I catch myself, every once in a while, looking right into their faces… We need some statistics on their numbers. Because I think there's more of them. And I'll tell you something else. There's got to be a reason the Chinese kept leaving them out on river banks because the Chinese are a very smart people. (42)

As it turns out, Farkerson's fearful misogyny has some basis in the emergent circumstances, for, led by Martha, a massive international coalition of women (along with Beggs, the General's male assistant, who renounces his manhood and dons drag so that he can join [51]), decides to overthrow the absurdly violent patriarchy and set up a peaceable matriarchal civilization in its place.

The approaching showdown between the male and female forces appears at times almost apocalyptic, though at others, a much smaller, localized revolt. Meanwhile, Martha rallies her followers with a series of strange inspirational speeches augmented with poetic passages from a disembodied "voice":

MARTHA. We are living inside an egg, sisters, and the egg is blue, and if you screench up your eyes just a little, open your mind just a little, and try to listen a little…

VOICE. …The unseen world is no longer a dream
It's floating just within grasp
A shimmering radiant heavenly orb
I know the way
To move, yes move towards that.

MARTHA. …We can stop the spread of war, we can give the word to the women of the world, that word's Unite. No more war. It's started, sisters. Listen. [*She holds the hand containing eggshells up. There is a murmuring of women's voices in a number of languages.*] All you have to do is believe, sisters. We take control. We talk to the world of women. We deliver a culture shock to the world of men via satellite link-up! We blast their dislocated minds into meaning.
We tell them loud and clear
We do not believe your promises!
We will not follow your commands! (50–52)

The women capture Farkerson, and having done so, force-feed him a giant, boiled egg, including the shell. Farkerson regresses to a child-like mindset, and tells the story of how, at his birth, he was mistakenly named "R.D." by a nurse who did not understand that his mother was calling him "Artie" (60).

It appears Pollock had not quite decided how to end the play when she abandoned it. The other men are still determined to fight, as they declare by singing:

For fatherland, motherland, homeland
We have the right to die
We love our land, we'll make a stand
Nation is all
The state will not fall
Let women wail
Men will prevail. (79)

But, as the forces outside besiege them, Martha speaks to Farkerson:

> Did you know, Arthur, that we are living inside an egg? And the egg is blue. It's a royal blue that's been lightened up with buttermilk. The egg opens up, like … a thousand suns … and the egg … says … stare ugliness in the face, don't … don't turn away from the pain and suffering … no … maybe you can just do a little bit … but if a great many do a little bit … then a lot will get done… (95)

And here the play ends, with a hint of personal responsibility, but with the plot largely unresolved.

Because *Egg* was never finished to a production-ready state (a hand-written note to director Guy Sprung on the typescript makes it evident that the draft was written well before any production had been scheduled), there are a number of outstanding questions that make it difficult to interpret the play with any great confidence. For example, it is tempting, with the hindsight bestowed by *Getting it Straight*, to consider the action as a projection from Martha's mind: a "psychomachia" drama. However, apart from the play beginning and ending with Martha's monologues, and a few non-realistic elements, there is not enough to support such a reading in the draft as it stands.

The non-realistic elements in the play would be at least equally compatible with the sort of fabulist, satiric propaganda that can be found in, say, Brecht's *Good Woman of Setzuan*. The puppets and songs, and the montages of advertising and radio announcements that punctuate the action, would neatly support an ongoing ironic commentary were that Pollock's intention; although, as it stands, the propaganda is rather underdeveloped.

At any rate, the political implications are better integrated in *Getting it Straight* (1989), the main difference being that everything in this play is set unequivocally within the frame of a genuinely mentally distressed woman who is attempting to work out a sane understanding of an irrational world. Whereas in *Egg* the grotesque distortions sometimes detract from the political criticism, here the seamless transitions from legitimate fear and anger into paranoid terror and hostility not only make for a persuasive psychological portrait, but also create a compelling, passionate argument for a sane and coherent world-view.

In *Getting It Straight*, as Eme says at one point, "real and unreal [are] shuffled like a deck of cards" (89). This doubtful ontology puts heavy demands upon the spectator or reader; but the difficulty of discriminating between sane analysis and insane distortion supports a main theme of the play: the idea that sometimes insanity is the most rational response to a disordered world. Or, as Eme herself puts it, "they say I'm mad / I say enola gay little boy fat man!" (89). She is referring to the bomber plane, Enola Gay, and its cargo of atomic bombs which were dropped on Hiroshima and Nagasaki in 1945; "little boy" and "fat man" were the respective code names for the smaller and larger prototypes developed through the Manhattan Project.

The plot of *Getting it Straight* is fairly straightforward, though it takes some close attention to pick it out of the text. Eme (short for Emily), a mentally disturbed middle-aged woman, has been taken on a group outing to a rodeo and has left the group on the pretext of going to the washroom and is hiding beneath the grandstand. Less clear is the background story to which Eme continually but elliptically alludes. Most of Eme's allusions are in the nature of personal memories of her immediate family. We hear, for example, of her affection for her grandfather, and also of minor, seemingly arbitrary details about her father and brother. Yet, however trivial some of these memories may appear, it would be imprudent to lightly dismiss any of them, for perhaps the most important theme running through Pollock's work as a whole is that of memory besieged by social forces. For Pollock, the authentic recollection of the past is the chief means of establishing integrated personal identity, so most references to characters' personal memories are in some respect crucial to the central themes of her plays.

One such personal recollection in *Getting It Straight* is a passage lifted almost verbatim from *Egg*. It concerns Eme's father's name, transcribed by a nurse at his birth as "R.D.," though his mother had been calling him "Artie." The joke is not a rich one, so at first glance this seems an odd detail to preserve intact for transference from *Egg* into the new script. But, in a play dealing with mental illness, it is likely that Pollock is nudging our attention in the direction of history's most famous "R.D.": R.D. Laing. The idea is supported by Eme's mention of a "layman's guide to schizophrenia" (89): a reasonably accurate description of R.D. Laing's controversial, bestselling 1960 study of schizophrenia, *The Divided Self*. There Laing tried to invert established preconceptions about insanity by arguing that labelling some individuals as "crazy" is merely an expedient mutual agreement used in dysfunctional circumstances where one person does not fit what has been determined to be the norm. Applied to Eme's situation, the theory implicitly asks whether it is not the "social norm" (which, in the Cold War, included the terrifying logic of maintaining nuclear overkill capacity to deter war) that should be regarded as insane. Thus, buried in the homonym "R.D./Artie" is the question: who is really mad?

Another at first seemingly insignificant detail is Eme's recollection that, in childhood, the "only way bubu [i.e., her brother, now a wealthy and powerful man of forty-two] could win a board game was by divine intervention." Her parents told her "games aren't that important let bubu win tonight" (101). This is a common parental request of an older sibling, but in the context of Eme's anxieties about global power, it may be a microcosm for passive acceptance of the geo-political "boys' game" of nuclear deterrence. More recent among Eme's scattered ruminations are her references to Myrna, ostensibly a fellow patient, and Freida, a patient who apparently jumped or fell to a concrete surface (107). It is difficult to tell whether this latter image is a fantasy or if it actually occurred at the rodeo Eme has just fled, repelled by the violence inherent in the sport.

However, most striking among these ambiguous images are Eme's references to her husband's briefcase. To the extent to which these allusions can be made coherent, it seems that Eme once secretly opened the briefcase she had been forbidden to touch (there are shades here of Bluebeard's wife or various folktales, such as "Sleeping Beauty," in which the heroine inevitably violates a taboo by opening a forbidden door), and found inside it documents pertaining to nuclear warfare. She fears that, in a state of horror, she may have then murdered her husband (125). But this notion is dubious even to Eme:

> maybe I dreamt it
> myrna says they say I dreamt it
> I say no
> no
> I say strike out strike down this is a lesser

> crime I am guilty of that I accept that I hope I
> have killed him, to have known and done
> nothing? that is the crime of that I am not guilty
> not guilty of that. (125–26)

Much as Laing questioned the validity of judgments about the madness of some people living in alienating and destructive circumstances, Eme questions the immorality of murder in a situation where to be peaceful is to connive at plans involving the possible obliteration of the human race.

Set against these "memories" is Eme's vision for the future, which is chiefly drawn from *Egg*. Indeed, Eme often uses egg imagery in passages taken almost verbatim from the earlier play:

> we are living
> inside an egg and I
> I see that it's blue
> and the egg opens up
> and a bright light
> like a thousand suns and if I can open my eyes
> just a little open my mind just a little try to
> listen a little [...]
> the visible world   is no longer real
> it's shattered   and turned into glass
> a mirror   of ugliness   agony   shame
> you know the way   you know the way to change
> to change all of that the unseen word
> is no longer a dream   it's   floating   just within
> grasp a   shimmering radiant   heavenly   orb you   know the way
>   to move yes move... (123–24)

The egg image is appropriate in several ways: an egg encloses potential for future life, yet is sealed off from the outside world, and the life within cannot emerge without effort; the fragility of an egg suggests the vulnerability of the earth, which can be destroyed through recklessness; the egg's surface is continuous, without beginning or end, like the vast unity Eme dreams of; the egg is associated with nurturing by females. As did Martha in *Egg*, Eme ends *Getting It Straight* with a "call for action" to "all members a the female sex" (126). She envisions them spinning:

> ...a gossamer net of women's hands and rapunzel's
> hair and that net will encircle the globe and if a
> person stood on the far left star of the utmost
> edge of cassiopeia's chair that net would twinkle
> in the inky cosmos like fairy lights on a christmas
> tree—and what would it spell? (126)

Earlier, when Eme recalls giving the same speech to Myrna, Eme's answer had been "love." Myrna had laughed, so Eme furiously tried to smash Myrna's face into the floor

(122). The irony of Eme's violent response perhaps indicates Pollock's skepticism, her awareness of the difficulties in realizing such a transfiguration of the world into a place of universal co-operation.

Still, Eme's interweaving of mythical figures and cosmic imagery to create a vision of universal harmony is undoubtedly pleasing. Her allusions to Cassiopeia (who aroused the wrath of the patriarchal Olympian, Poseidon, by boasting of her daughter's beauty), and to Rapunzel (locked away because of her beauty), raise again the question of whether it might not be that she has incurred entrapment because her thinking is too beautiful and good for the world, rather than too flawed. As usual, Pollock prefers the ambiguity of the open question to definite answers. Perhaps the biggest open question is inherent in the grandstand shadows that are cast across the space Eme occupies, suggesting, says Pollock in her opening stage directions, "what may be bars [or] ribs." Is Eme's condition necessarily one of imprisonment within the bars of insanity? Or is she, like Jonah within the ribs of the whale, trapped only temporarily in her despair, paused in what is only one stage in a journey whose ultimate objective is universal enlightenment?

Pollock returned to historical subjects for her next several plays.[1] *Fair Liberty's Call* (1993) recalls several aspects of Pollock's earlier work. As well as returning to a historical setting comparable with the early history plays (in this case a 1785 Loyalist community in New Brunswick), *Fair Liberty's Call* also returns to the family-based themes Pollock had explored in the eighties. However, there are significant differences in the treatment of these circumstances in *Fair Liberty's Call*, most of which arise from the concerns Pollock had been addressing in the intervening years.

For example, Joan, the matriarch of the Roberts family, is thematically related to Martha from *Egg* and Eme from *Getting It Straight*: a middle-aged woman who, through grief and despair, has become mentally disordered, unable to reason effectively and often uncertain of her location or the identity of others. As we might expect from Pollock's previous work, Joan's mental state stands as a touchstone for the disordered world of the play as a whole. Her mental crisis indicates a dysfunctional environment as surely as Hamlet's malaise suggests that something is rotten in the state of Denmark. And, as we also may have expected, the environmental dysfunction here has something to do with unreconciled relations with the past. In this case, however, the dramatic issue is not focused upon one individual cultivating a healthy perspective on history; rather, it is the concern of a whole community. Rather than being secluded with her own thoughts like Eme, Joan remains matriarch of and among the fractious and confused family who have not yet foresworn the violent outlook that has caused her mental breakdown in the first place. As such, she seems to combine the circumstances and force of personality of Clytemnestra with the helpless distress of Cassandra.

Joan's husband, George, is a former Bostonian loyalist who fought against the American Rebels, a violently-minded man who is still angry at the Rebels and embittered about being beholden in his adopted country to the plutocratic Committee of Fifty-five Families. Joan and George lost both sons, Richard and

Edward, to the War of Independence, but they still have two daughters, Annie and Eddie. The latter was born Emily, but has been dressing and living as a man since she took her dead brother's name and place as a soldier at sixteen. An honorary member of the Roberts family is Daniel Wilson, Annie's fiancé and an ex-corporal in the loyalist Legion. The other two loyalist characters are Major Abijah Williams, representative of the local establishment, and Black Wullie, an ex-slave and scout for the Legion, and Eddie's loyal companion. Finally, there is Major John Anderson, who eventually reveals himself to be a vengeful Rebel.

All of the characters are highly conscious of the need to establish correct relations with the past, and yet they are by no means in agreement about how these are to be constituted. The play begins with the Roberts family directing a series of interlaced speeches about the past towards the audience and one another. Pollock says of this scene:

> They have a compelling need to tell; to tell before someone else tells; to correct a former mistelling; to tell before they're unable to tell, or prevented from telling. (17)

Despite this competitiveness to establish their own narratives, they are sensible of the need to arrive at some kind of joint account of the past. To this end, the loyalists of the Roberts household have devised a "Remembrance Ritual" (not unlike the ceremony Pollock had devised twenty years earlier for *And Out Goes You*, in which Goose's family commemorate the Dominion Day riot of 1935). "Totems, souvenirs and trophies of war" (36) are dragged out to serve as properties in a ritual invoking the honourable struggles that gave the Roberts family its essential identity. "Gotta fill the place up with things that speak of the past," says Daniel. To which the Major responds: "Else how's a man to know who he is" (37).

The impulse to affirm identity in this way appears to stem from a demand tacitly made by the land. The chorally shared first line of the play is: "You want to know where to put your eye so you can hear the heartbeat of the country comin' into bein'" (19–20). But by then Pollock has already introduced the idea in her description of the initial setting:

> A bare stage, the floor of which radiates in a dark-hued swirl of colour, represents the "virgin" land. Although this space appears empty and uncorrupted, it projects an aura of foreboding, a sense of the unseen. A subtle sound fills the space as if the air itself is vibrating just below the level of conscious hearing. (19)

This sense of place is related to that described by Douglas LePan in "A Country Without a Mythology." The difficulty, as in LePan's poem, is not that there is not any history or mythology, but rather that its true nature is not disclosed to the observer. The sense of incipient power effectively demands that its past be divulged truthfully, that the menacing emptiness of place be dispelled by the proper attention to the collective history.

As with all tribal recollections of primordial struggles, the problem is that there is a selective bias at work in the memories of the participants; and even then their several notions of which elements of the past should be remembered are not always in concert. An exchange between Annie and Anderson sums it up: "I notice you've got a powerful recollection of some things, and none at all for others." "An accident of war" (43). Even among supposed allies there is no guarantee of agreement. While the ritual is underway, the exasperated Major yells at Daniel, "You're not rememberin' right!" (53): that is, through the appropriate haze of veneration.

But the paramount source of dissent in the Remembrance Ritual arrives in the person of Major Anderson, the former Rebel who brings into this house his indictment of the Loyalists' merciless slaughter of the Rebels at the battle of Waxhaws. While Eddie is prepared to acknowledge the disgrace of this bloody Loyalist victory (albeit weighing it against the subsequent slaughter of Loyalist troops at the hands of the Rebels in the battle of King's Mountain), Major Williams refuses to see in it anything but a glorious conquest, and Daniel refuses to hear about it at all. Anderson, however, is relentless:

> ...when it was over, well over, some of you went from one pile of bodies to another, pullin' off the dead and killin' the wounded and the livin'. And one of the livin' was a fourteen-year-old boy who had time to cry "quarter" 'fore the sabre came down. Do you remember that boy? ...None of you remembers that boy?
>
> **DANIEL.** We don't want to remember. We spend time forgettin'.
>
> **ANDERSON.** Well I can't forget, nor do I want to. (62)

The boy, it turns out, was Anderson's brother. Anderson's plan is to hold the others hostage until the murderer of his brother is surrendered for execution.

In some respects, Anderson's function within *Fair Liberty's Call* is similar to that of the Inspector in J.B. Priestley's *An Inspector Calls*, or even the ghostly gunfighter in the Clint Eastwood western, *High Plains Drifter*: a stranger, like an avenging angel heralding Judgement Day, arrives in an arrogant, corrupt and hypocritical environment to forcibly polarize differences and galvanize the search for truth among the inhabitants. Anderson's siege quickly shows that the pieties regularly invoked by the Loyalists throughout the play are hollow shams. The vaunted commitment to courage and honour crumbles into craven self-preservation as each man tries, by turns, to shift the blame onto the shoulders of another or to offer reasons why the value of his person suggests that his life particularly should be spared. Or, more precisely: each of the white men reveals such despicable weakness. Pollock is careful to preserve the dignity of the one black man, Wullie, and Eddie, whose transvestism keeps her among the men (indeed, she proves the most "manful" of the lot).

What is behind Pollock's effort to discriminate between the behaviour of those who are white men and those who are not is, I suggest, less a matter of insisting upon essentialist differences in race or sex than of her being interested in finding out fresh ground upon which less violent and adversarial cultural alternatives might take root.

Surely a new world is conceivable in which people would see the incongruity in the very idea of a "due process" in condemning a man to death? And since those dominant in the established culture are male and white, the founders of Pollock's alternative culture are not.

In pursuing this optimistic notion of a new society, *Fair Liberty's Call* at times drifts closer to the conventions of romance than those associated with the history play. Reconciling these two genres poses no little difficulty. For where the ethic of the history play (at least in Pollock's hands) is founded upon the paramount value of truthful remembrance, the ethic of romance is based in the hope of redemption, optimistic values having more to do with faith than with a ruthless scrutiny driving the search for historical truth. Where, after all, in examining the past, *does* one put one's "eye to hear the heartbeat of the country coming into being?" One is looking for "the substance of things hoped for, the evidence of things not seen" (Hebrews 11:1).

Pollock's solution is to delicately juggle her depiction of the known facts of history so as to place them within conventions of romance that can accommodate real moral concerns. For example, taking her cue from the reciprocal moral transgression attached to both sides of the War of Independence, Pollock uses a version of the mirror-plotting common to many romances in order to lift the siege in this play. Anderson's single-minded determination to avenge his brother's death is dissolved when he finds himself faced with Annie's admission that she betrayed a Loyalist spy into the hands of the Rebels to avenge her own brother's death. Realistically, that this would suddenly end the hostility is no more "natural" than that the "natural perspective" embodied by Viola and Sebastian at the end of *Twelfth Night* should bring that play to a happy conclusion. Both devices are sleights of hand, using fortune's symmetries to distract our attention from the past, and turn it to new beginnings. Thus, Major Williams is a sort of vanquished *alazon* figure, leaving the Roberts home with a final threatening speech like Malvolio's, thereby clearing the way for the inauguration of a new world. Joan, in a moment reminiscent of Hermione's resurrection and her reunion with her lost daughter at the end of *The Winter's Tale*, begins to recover her life in the present, to see that Eddie is indeed her daughter, Emily. "It's a new world, Mama," says Eddie, "you gotta look up close" (78).

Finally, pursuing the hope for a better world Pollock hinted at when she preserved Eddie and Wullie from degradation, the freed slave and emancipated woman declare they will remain together to start a new family. Meanwhile, Joan envisages a blessing from another alternative to patriarchal authority:

> I feel my feet pressin' flat 'gainst the surface of the soil now. I kneel readin' the contours of the skull and listenin' to the words spoke by the man with the missin' jawbone, and the caps of my knees make a small indentation in the dirt. [...] And the red woman with the baby on her back steps out from under the glade of trees and she holds out a bowl, she offers a bowl of earth. [...] Eat, she says, swallow. And I do. (79–80)

The new world being made here is meant to transcend the antinomies and violence of the old, to begin new lives, having acknowledged and atoned for the errors of history.

To be sure, Pollock could be charged with indulging in a biased mythologizing of the past not much different from that she condemns the Loyalists for perpetuating, of succumbing to the temptation of wishfully revising the past by putting something as improbable as Eddie's transvestism and union with Wullie into her play. But by this point in her career, Pollock had grown less interested in precisely reconstructing history than in exploring ways of reconciling her sense of the mistakes of the past with her project of encouraging ethical constructions for the future.

Pollock's most recent play, *Saucy Jack* (1993), was certainly approached in such a frame of mind. *Saucy Jack* treats a subject that has fascinated many writers, the mystery of the most famous serial killer in history, Jack the Ripper. Yet, where most treatments of Jack the Ripper focus on the questions of who he was and why he committed the murders, Pollock argues that such questions are irrelevant. For her, the nub of the issue is that:

> the women are killed because they can be killed with relative or complete impunity. It is done because it can be done. That reason is sufficient for those who undertake such actions. (5)

To be sure, that may be a thin theory of human nature, and it disregards the obvious fact that Jack the Ripper differed from the vast majority of the population living in London in 1888, who, notwithstanding the opportunity, did *not* choose to become serial murderers and indeed were horrified by the crimes. After all, that is precisely why Jack the Ripper became so notorious. Still, the comment is a focused declaration of the political premises underlying this play. The character Kate might speak for Pollock when she sings, ostensibly as a warning to Montague:

> There's no time to tell you how
> He came to be a killer
> But you should know as time will tell
> That he's society's pillar
> For he is not a butcher
> Nor yet a foreign skipper
> He is your own light-hearted friend
> Yours truly, Jack the Ripper. (28)

In short, social implications, not the personal details of the man known as Jack the Ripper, are the issue here. Accordingly, notwithstanding any similarities between *Saucy Jack* and Pollock's treatment of the late nineteenth-century's next most legendary murderer in *Blood Relations*, there are significant differences in the approach to characterization and conflict in these two plays.

In *Saucy Jack*, Pollock's political thesis demands that Jack should not be a lone, monstrous figure, but someone who operates with the assistance, or at least, the connivance, of others; because the whole point is that the murders should not be seen as social transgressions but, on the contrary, as acts which enjoy social support. Hence, it is left unclear just who was directly responsible for the actual murders, Eddy (Prince Albert Victor, grandson to Queen Victoria and heir to the throne) or Jem (James Stephen, friend and former tutor to the Prince, and the more forceful personality). Responsibility is thereby spread; and a further blurring of the guilt will follow. Jem's plan is to displace suspicion for the murders onto their mutual acquaintance, Montague, by murdering him and planting evidence upon the body. The only other character in the play is Kate, a "music hall entertainer and actor" whom Jem has hired to enact each of the murdered prostitutes.

Jem's motive for having the murders re-enacted is also left unclear, despite a comment of Pollock's to which I will come in a moment. In part, the uncertainty arises because Jem has received a head injury some time in the past, which makes him frequently speak and behave in very peculiar ways. The play begins with a long, frighteningly irrational monologue, which Jem delivers in the presence of Kate. Apart from its arousal of our anxiety for Kate's safety, the effect of the speech is to discourage us from expecting Jem's subsequent behaviour to have logical reasons attached to it. So, although Jem says that his object in having the murders re-enacted is to "save Eddy," it is not at first apparent how this could be so, especially given that Jem is at least equally suspect. The element of sadistic nostalgia that prompts psychopaths to preserve souvenirs of their murders perhaps also figures to some extent, yet neither does this satisfy as a final explanation of Jem's motivation, because there is no sign of the salacious glee we would expect in such a case.

Pollock raises this issue in her introductory note, saying:

> The end or objective or motivation for the re-enactment of the women's deaths in the play is not to achieve the death of the women, but to achieve some other end or objective that relates to the relationship between the men. Love, loyalty and friendship are words the men use, but the actions through which such noble sentiments manifest themselves are the ones of betrayal, duplicity and murder. (5)

To be sure, they could hardly be out to "achieve the death of the women," because the women are already dead. Yet Pollock's point about the "objective that relates to the relationship between the men," remains somewhat cryptic. The men are indeed utterly despicable, regardless of what they say, but this is little help. In what sense does their discreditable partnership motivate the re-enactment? The point is clarified a little further on, when Pollock declares:

> I am less interested in whether Jem, or Eddy, or some combination of them and possibly others, are indeed guilty of the murders than I am interested in the whys and ways Jem attempts to bind Eddy to him as well as to confirm or negate his fearful suspicions regarding his own role in the Ripper events. He's caught in a terrible dilemma. If he is indeed guilty of the crimes, he is "sane" for his clouded recall is founded on

> reality. If he is innocent of the crimes, his memory and mind are serving up false data and he's "insane." (5–6)

Thus, the key to sanity, in Pollock's formulation here, is not whether one's *behaviour* is rational or psychotic, but whether one *remembers* accurately or not. This would be a rather remarkable assertion, were it not that we have been prepared for it by the decisive role played by memory in virtually all of Pollock's previous plays. Where Ibsen showed how the past could determine a character's destiny, Pollock shows how the *retelling* of the past determines one's destiny and, hence, sanity. Jem wants the murders re-enacted because he seeks validation for a certain version of the past. To be sure, at one level, he hopes Eddy can tell him who was actually responsible for these murders; but the main emphasis leans upon the question of whether Jem and Eddy (and, in his own way, poor foolish Montague) will remain partners in the act of recollection.

Further light is shed by the style of the re-enactments. It is quickly apparent that the vignettes are not meant to be realistic – neither in the sense of capturing what the murdered women might have actually said in the street, nor in the sense of being likely versions of what might be devised by two murderous aristocrats and a music hall performer. For one thing, the writing is too poetical to be commensurate with either such project. For example, here is Kate as Polly:

> Call me Polly. Can I help you? Is there anything I might have you might want? I was a good girl once but me old man ran off with me best friend who acted as a midwife when Sarah was born—Oh he come back. They always come back. I wish to God he'd stay away.
> [*sings*] Oh hear me cry Almighty Host
> I quite forgot the quail on toast
> Let your kindly heart be stirred
> And stuff some oysters in that bird.
> So he comes back and I have another one—the little boy who lives with me father now—and the old man kicks me out because a me drunken habits. [...]
> Up and out and in, with the cry a slaughtered horses ringin' in me ears, and the press a Buck Row bricks markin' me back—But hold—look—look at the sky, it's glowin', yes it's ... there's a wonderful fire down on the docks and it's lightin' up the heavens, oh I wish I could be there, see the flames feedin' on the wood, reachin' up over the water, the water and fire and wood, wish I could be up close, right in the middle, surrounded by flames burnin' in hell and floatin' to heaven on a spire a golden smoke. (26)

Essentially, the speech is a stylized, poetic condensation of Polly's whole character: the combination of stream-of-consciousness, catchphrases, fragments of autobiography and mental imagery quickly, deftly adumbrate a whole life, a soul. The contrast between this and the coroner-like forensic inventory initiated by Jem, which immediately follows, could not be starker. For, in Kate's speeches, the important meanings lie not with mimetic, but with symbolic and thematic concerns.

Plainly, then, the re-enactments in *Saucy Jack* have quite a different function from the re-enactment in *Blood Relations.* In the earlier play, the Actress enters into the terms of a reality prescribed by Miss Lizzie so as to work through the sense of Lizzie's situation, to sympathetically speculate on the motives for Lizzie's real or imagined behaviour. Miss Lizzie already knows what happened in the past; the re-enactment is intended to achieve understanding in the Actress (and of course, the audience).

The actress in *Saucy Jack* is far more autonomous. Because Jem does not himself know the extent of his and Eddy's role in the murders, he could not be much of a coach to Kate; and at any rate, he certainly has nothing of Lizzie's interest in teaching the actress. Indeed, it is pointedly established that the prior contact between Jem and Kate has been minimal (one is reminded of a magician's introduction of a "volunteer"). The others never address Kate by name, so it may be that her name and occupation is known only to us. Except when performing, she remains a silent, anonymous figure, seeming to occupy a different level of reality from that of the men.

The significance of maintaining Kate's dramatic autonomy and of providing her with such evocative, stylistic renderings of the murdered women seems to be this: Kate is engaged in a sort of mortal competition with the men for the control of the past. I call the contest mortal not in reference to anyone's actual life being at stake (although, to be sure, Montague's is certainly endangered, and Kate's may be). Dramatically speaking, what is most potently at stake is the inner lives of the murdered women, and by inference, the inner lives of all women, their possession of their own souls, and it is in this sense that the contest is mortal. The matter is related to Pollock's recurrent theme of the role of memory in protecting individual integrity against deterministic forces. Jem seeks validation for his dubious memories even at the risk of conclusively establishing his own and Eddy's guilt. In Pollock's dramatic world, the power of recollection bestows not only sanity but validity; for, those whose memories prevail set the terms of sanity, determining (here again we recall R.D. Laing) who shall be considered sane or insane, and thus, in essence, which truth claims are valid.

Hence, Jem passionately wants to "re…member," as he frequently puts it, to reestablish the validity of his (and his class's) vision of the world by reassembling, or re-membering, the dismembered fragments, as if with the dismemberment of the women's bodies had occurred a fundamental disintegration of objective truth itself. But Pollock intends that Jem should find no such validation. Accordingly, far from re-establishing themselves as arbiters of truth, the men are made pathetic and impotent by their imperfect attempt to remember. In contrast, Kate grows stronger and more powerful through her vivid re-enactments of the souls of these murdered women. Pollock writes that through her performances Kate evolves "from a silent, unknown, nameless figure […] to the only vital or potent figure or force in the play when the final blackout occurs. Her exploitation has not victimized her; it has empowered her. She is larger than herself at the end. […] She lives. They die" (6).

It is irrelevant to object that, realistically, Kate would not be allowed to escape with her life were the men really the ruthless murderers they are meant to be. Pollock has created a confrontation between two versions of the past to pose the question of which is more valid. And, because this trial takes place within the dramatic imagination, the authority which determines the outcome of the confrontation is not that of social class, or brute force, or even political office, but an authority of the imagination, invoked in response to the questions: which is more convincing, which more compelling, which more truly vital? There is little doubt that, in such terms of the spirit, Jem and his cohorts and all those like them are quite, quite dead.

(2000)

Notes

[1] I do not have room to fully discuss two published shorter plays that were written during this period, but because they are thematically linked to the larger works, I would like to at least briefly mention these short works. In *The Making of Warriors*, a 1991 radio play, Pollock interweaves the stories of Sarah Moore Grimké, a nineteenth-century American abolitionist, and Anna Mae Pictou Aquash, whose unsolved murder occurred during the confrontation between the FBI and the American Indian Movement in the mid-seventies. In 1994, Pollock published *"It's all make believe, isn't it?" —Marilyn Monroe*, a short play set in the last moments of Monroe's life. This latter play is loosely related to *Getting It Straight* (as well as *Fair Liberty's Call* and *Saucy Jack*), in that it depicts Monroe—referred to only as "She"—losing her grip on her sanity as an alliance of criminal and political forces, including the Mob, the Kennedys and the CIA, converge upon her.

Works Cited

Laing, R.D. *The Divided Self.* 1960. London: Penguin, 1965.

Pollock, Sharon. *Egg.* Typescript. University of Guelph Archives, n.d.

———. *Fair Liberty's Call.* Toronto: Coach House, 1995.

———. *Getting it Straight. Heroines: Three Plays.* Ed. Joyce Doolittle. Red Deer, Alta.: Red Deer Press, 1992.

———. *"It's all make believe, isn't it?" —Marilyn Monroe* in *Instant Applause: 26 Very Short Complete Plays.* Winnipeg: Blizzard, 1994. 91–95.

———. *The Making of Warriors* in *Airborne: Radio Plays by Women.* Ed. Ann Jansen. Winnipeg: Blizzard, 1991. 99–132.

———. *Saucy Jack.* Winnipeg: Blizzard, 1994.

Wallace, Robert and Cynthia Zimmerman, eds. *The Work: Conversations with English Canadian Playwrights.* Toronto: Coach House, 1982.

Sharon Pollock: Transfiguring the Maternal

by Cynthia Zimmerman

Every writer knows that his or her own biography is an important resource. Personal experiences and lived memories exist like photographs, ever ready to become the site where imaginative fiction can begin. In the programme note to her most overtly biographical play, *Doc*, Sharon Pollock commented on her approach to personal or documentary sources: "My father is Ev but Ev [the character] is not my father... [These characters] aren't really the people I know any more. They started out that way but now have grown past them" (Zimmerman, "Sharon Pollock" 84). The story and the characters develop beyond the strictly personal or the documentary. As Pollock said, "If it was just my story, I would have put it in a letter and sent it to my family" (84). Moreover, the writing of fiction deeply rooted in biography can yield discoveries for the artist too. According to Pollock "Self discovery is why plays are written" (Zimmerman, "Towards" 38). In *Doc*, Pollock bravely raised ghosts from her own past—once summoned, they brought with them new challenges.

In an interview in 1991, I asked Sharon Pollock if there was anything left unfinished when she completed *Doc* (1984). She replied that there was, that the tragic figure of the mother, Bob, had overshadowed the main character, Catherine: "Central to the play is Catherine's journey, the discovery which allows her to accept the responsibility that belongs to her and to lay the rest aside without guilt. It frees her from the past" ("Towards" 38). Yet Catherine's story seems less compelling because Bob's presence is so haunting. According to Pollock, "because Bob is more present, more active even though she is acted upon, I don't think the audience sufficiently realizes what has happened to Catherine. Catherine is the figure that has learned from the tragedy" ("Towards" 38). Bob dominates the play even though it is named for her husband, the doctor, and even though Pollock intended the focus to be on Catherine. The truth of this is apparent when one finds that the critics also emphasize the fate of the mother, a point I will return to. However, the spirit of Bob has not been easily put to rest by the playwright either. This paper argues that the spectre of Bob inhabits all of Pollock's mother figures, and most especially those created after *Doc* (1984): Eme, the protagonist of *Getting it Straight* (1988), and Joan, the mother in *Fair Liberty's Call* (1993). These women are related. The portrait of the maternal figure evolves through the course of these plays and, as it is altered, Pollock reconfigures not only the image of the maternal, but also that of the other participants in the family plot: father and daughter.

Pollock's semi-autobiographical play *Doc* makes it clear how close to home many of her earlier plays are, not always in the details of theme or exposition, but in the force which drives the work. For example, Pollock herself has spoken of having trouble with authority (Zimmerman, "Sharon Pollock" 93). A troubled relationship with authority has provided the central critical conflict in numerous plays. The struggle takes a critical turn in *Blood Relations* (1980), a play Diane Bessai calls a "turning point." The first play with an "entirely feminine point of view," *Blood Relations* is also the first to have the locus of its political and social issues completely in the family home (qtd. in Zimmerman, "Sharon Pollock" 73). The daughter's trouble with her father, the undisputed authority, leads to murder. It is not surprising that the father is not only dominating and unyielding, but also charismatic—or that his daughter, who challenges his authority, is deeply attached to him. His inspirational source is clearest in *Doc*, Pollock's most intensely personal play to date.

Sharon Pollock's father was Doctor George Everett Chalmers, a vibrant personality who, like Ev, was a tireless and dedicated family doctor. He pioneered polio treatment in the province, was an active member of the provincial legislature, and in 1974 had a hospital named in his honour. In his book *Gentlemen, Players, and Politicians*, Dalton Camp describes Everett Chalmers as "impressive on sight, exuding confidence [...] . Clothed in an impeccable white suit, he looked [...] like Clark Gable" (71). More importantly, Camp comments on Chalmers's "commanding presence, his terrible candour, and [his] personal authority and prestige" (72). He was a man, says Camp, "worshipped by legions of patients" and "celebrated for his compassion," a "remarkably fearless [and] combative man" (75). He was, in fact, "the ablest practitioner in New Brunswick" and "[h]e looked it" (84). Chalmers's mother did commit suicide and he did marry a nurse named Eloise Roberts (nicknamed Bob) who became an alcoholic and committed suicide in 1954, when their daughter was a teenager.[1]

The handsome and commanding Doctor Everett Chalmers provides a blueprint for Pollock's authoritarian males, a figure at once idealizable and infuriating. One could argue that a number of Pollock's plays map a kind of working-through of this complicated connection. Young Katie suggests as much when she speaks of how she "figure[s] things out" (*Doc* 49) and, when looking at her notebook, she says "I write it all down. And when I grow up, I'll have it all here" (*Doc* 83). When Catherine, now a writer in her thirties who no longer uses the name Katie, returns to the family home, her father Ev is no longer as formidable. Although still angry and combative, he has mellowed, having just suffered a heart attack.

Doc is a watershed play not only because of its complicated bending of time and space, its inwardness, and its use of highly personal material, but also because it presents a kind of closure on what has been a central preoccupation to this point: the struggle with authority. At this juncture the adult daughter is not beholden; the aging patriarch is simply her father. So, at the end of the play, to mark the change in his character, Ev is able to give his daughter the unqualified support he was unable to give his wife, and Andrew Borden in *Blood Relations* was unable to give his daughter. Recalling a photograph of her mother, Catherine says:

> **CATHERINE.** [...] she looked as if she was waiting. Just waiting. [...] whatever it was [she was waiting for], she couldn't grab it.
> **EV**. Do you know what you want?
> **CATHERINE.** ...Yes... Yes, I do.
> **EV.** Then you grab it. (125)

Father and daughter then burn the unopened letter from Ev's mother which they assume is an accusing one. There is a sense that they have both come to an understanding about the limits of responsibility and the limits on choice. Extinguishing the accusation becomes a pact to stop assigning blame. Perhaps now they can forgive themselves and each other. As the stage lights go down on the dying flames from the letter, "CATHERINE looks at EV and smiles" (126).

Some critics have found this reconciliation scene disturbing because it seems to diminish the mother's tragedy:

> [...I]n accepting the sacrifice and silencing of the dead mother [...] the daughter pays too high a price for her own peace. Perhaps even more unsettling is the satisfaction Catherine seems to find in this resolution of the oedipal triangle [...] she and Doc share a smile of complicity in her being, at the end, daddy's only girl. (Wasserman 32–33)

Wasserman says Catherine "lets her father off the hook" because she feels herself implicated in her mother's death. She "must [...] forgive her father so that she might forgive herself" (32).

The problem, I think, is that Wasserman forgets the child Katie in this story, as does Rosalind Kerr in her excellent article. By focusing on the mother as victim, they marginalize and minimize the daughter's traumatic experience, which leads me back to Pollock's important comment: "I don't think the audience sufficiently realize what has happened to Catherine" (Zimmerman, "Towards" 38). And so it is that in *Doc* Sharon Pollock reaches closure on one front (the struggle with the authoritarian father), and reveals unresolved conflicts on another (the maternal connection). The mother in *Doc* is a haunting presence; her spectre remains long after the lights on her go out.

In *Doc* young Katie is adamant that she does not want to be like her mother or her grandmother (83). "I'm not like them," she claims, "I'm like you, Daddy" (124). She even changes her name from Katie to Catherine so as not to have the same name as her gramma.[2] In Katie's eyes, her mother and grandmother are losers and victims because they surrendered. Her mother's situation especially infuriates her: "You all say she's sick, she isn't sick," she yells at her father. "She's a drunk and that's what we should say!" (119). This is extremely important because to young Katie "not sick" means her mother has a choice. To her, being an alcoholic is a wilful indulgence. So, when her mother complains, the adult Catherine asks the logical question, "why couldn't you leave?" (94). Katie knows that Oscar's mother "had the good sense to get out" (35). She also knows that Oscar is in love with *her* mother and would help Bob leave her marriage, if that was what Bob wanted. Catherine will herself get out. So, why is Katie so enraged? Why does the mature Catherine have difficulty summoning sympathy? It is not only the wish to identify with the idealized achieving father; it is also because this child was abandoned, neglected by both of her narcissistic parents. And this is my point: both put their own needs before their daughter's. Her father's neglect amounts to his never being home and being oblivious to the fact that he is leaving her alone with a suicidal, alcoholic mother. The non-nurturing unempathic and totally self-absorbed mother is even worse. She isn't there for her daughter either; she leaves the scene by entering an alcoholic haze and then calls on her little girl for help. Bob fails Katie completely. Still seeking the approval of a husband who is no longer paying attention to her, she does not take care of her children. Ev says "she'd let the kids starve to death if it weren't for the maid!" (106). "I hate you and I wish that you were dead!" (118) Katie screams. The rage is not simply Katie's inability to empathize with the one who succumbs; it is also that she believes she was, and remains, an unwanted child (121).

So, the adult Catherine comes home as chief investigator and it is as if Ev is placed on trial. Was his success worth it? Whose fault is Bob's alcoholism and suicide? Whose fault is it if a "strong, capable woman degenerates into alcoholism," as Wasserman describes her (32)? It is too easy to read her simply as the neglected wife. She had been an achiever like Ev, but now she tells Katie: "There is nothing I can do" (97). She is talking about her own lack of resources. As in the photograph that Catherine recalls, the one Oscar took of Bob "looking up at the camera" where "she looked as if she was waiting. Just waiting" (125), Bob waits for rescue. It is Katie who will prove resourceful, who will do it by herself (84). Now, as Pollock puts it, the daughter must "take control of her life in a positive way" (Zimmerman, "Sharon Pollock" 93). After the writing of *Doc*, Pollock moves away from such surrenders and suicides, from figures as trapped as Bob.

Pollock's plays, then, have consistently presented a preoccupation not only with authority but also with the spirited protagonist who struggles against it. The main theme is not the oppressive situation, but the protagonist's considered reaction to it. This is true whether one is referring to *Walsh*, or *Whiskey Six Cadenza*, or *Doc*. And Bob does not struggle sufficiently; she does not fight back like Pollock's other protagonists. She relinquishes significant choice. That is hard for her daughter to forgive; her daughter will become the self-reliant fighter.

The mother figures in Pollock's earlier plays bear a striking resemblance to Bob; they, too, have failed their daughters utterly. In *Blood Relations*, Lizzie has three mothers and they all abandon, desert, or betray her. Her birth mother dies when she is born; her stepmother is totally merged with the patriarchy and resents Lizzie's spirit; her surrogate mother, her sister Emma, opts out when the going gets tough. Complicit in the incestuous exploitation of Leah by Big Daddy, the adoptive mother in *Whiskey Six Cadenza* is even worse. All these mothers fail to nurture and protect their daughters; they are not mothering.

I have spent some time on Bob's culpability and her failure to resist because I want to turn to the transfiguring of the maternal. By that I mean how the image is reconstructed so that it becomes a more desirable one—to the daughter. Bob reappears in *Getting it Straight* and in *Fair Liberty's Call* but her worst faults—those traits most damning to a child—have been conspicuously modified. In *Getting it Straight* Pollock returns to the trapped woman. Bob was angry, and in that sense mad. In *Doc* we witness her surrender to alcoholism and forgetfulness. We hear of her suicide attempts. The play does not develop the delusional aspect of her behaviour that Ev refers to when he says, "Every statutory holiday your mother's killin' herself or seein' things crawlin' on the walls or some goddam thing or other"(16). Bob could not get out of her situation. In contrast Eme, the protagonist of *Getting it Straight*, has escaped the asylum. She is the solitary occupant of the stage. There is no one to hear her. But she is not "shut up" in either sense of the word. Pollock had anticipated this creation: "I know there's a play that follows *Blood Relations* about what happens to the woman who is unable to kill either her father or her mother or, indeed, even herself. Obviously it's about women and madness" (Zimmerman, "Sharon Pollock" 90). Eme, like Katie before her, is trying to "figure it out," to "get it straight" (*Doc* 91). She has escaped during a group outing and is now hiding under the bleachers of a rodeo arena. This location, like the title, is metaphoric. The game is over; the crowd has gone; Eme has been left behind. She is out of the game. She has broken the rules (*Getting it Straight* 115). She does come out from under but she is not free from what haunts her: in her associative ramblings she tries to piece together meaning. Her monologue is a swirl of fragmented memories and stories, unconnected fears and paranoid feelings, snatches of news and media horrors, all communicated in the frantic voice of one close to the edge. She is guilty of an undisclosed crime for there is a red stain on her skirt and she says repeatedly "I'm afraid for the children." Did she harm the attendant or murder her husband? Like Lizzie in *Blood Relations* and Catherine in *Doc* she may be guilty; she *says* she is (117). But she proclaims proudly, as did those daughters,

> ... to have known and done
> nothing? that is the crime of that I am not guilty
> not guilty of that! (126)

Hers is the poetry and pain of one who does not shut down her feelings, or restrain them; she does not repress them as young Katie had to do so that she would not cry (115, 116); nor does she lose herself in Bob's alcoholic haze. Rather, like Lizzie Borden, she refuses passivity; she fights back. "I am not mad," Eme says, "I am/ getting it straight" (119) and "I blame him" (118).

Pollock has explained that in *Getting it Straight* the "discovery was that, for her, it is better to be open to the pain of the world and lose [her] mind, in some respects" (Zimmerman, "Towards" 38). Eme also embodies the Laingian idea that the one deemed mad may be the one who feels most keenly; that, in a world which denies the inner life, the one in touch with it becomes the outsider. In the reconfiguring of the maternal blueprint offered by Bob, Eme is a mother who breaks out of the strait-jacket, who fights for her truth even if it costs her everything.

Problematically, however, the maternal figure is separated from her children and more marginalized than ever. Eme gets out; she has not complied nor surrendered. But she is totally alone and, regardless of the power of her truth, no one listens. It is Joan, the mother in the historical play *Fair Liberty's Call*, who speaks openly and is heard. She is the one who has gotten it straight; her values are clear. She does not have Bob's sense of injured merit. Cherished and protected by her daughters, she is an empathic and nurturing maternal presence. Bob, the unavailable mother, is replaced by Joan, the one who puts home and family first. Joan's identity is mother, not wife.

Fair Liberty's Call takes place in a New Brunswick forest in October 1785. The family of merchant George Roberts is hosting a Loyalist Legion reunion to commemorate the final battle of the American Revolution. Burned out of Boston, the once prosperous Roberts family has been devastated. They have lost everything, including their two sons who fought on opposing sides. Their daughter Emily cropped her hair, changed her name to Eddie, and put on battle dress to fight in her twin brother's place. The mother, Joan, is half-crazed by grief and the other daughter, Annie, is haunted by ghosts of her own. To make matters worse, what they have met in New Brunswick is a more insidious form of tyranny than anything the Americans rebelled against; it is the "fiefdom of a few."

The play opens with the women entering the clearing first—Joan, Annie and Eddie, followed by the men. Joan has the first speech. Speaking in fragments, she voices her disorientation, the strangeness she feels: [this is] "like nothing I know," "This wasn't home, isn't home" (20). Her next words are of family: "Four Children, Father, Mother, Richard, Annie, Emily, Edward, Home!" (21). Home for Joan *is* family; her family decimated, she is in mourning, maddened by grief.

"Open to the pain," her thoughts often confused and obsessional, Joan shares some symptoms of madness with Bob and Eme. But unlike them, she is also something of a seer, a mystic. She intuits what is unspoken, she notices what no one else does, she senses danger in the stranger, and she will be the one who can connect to the land and to the Indian woman, "the red woman with the baby on her back" (79). Unafraid, perhaps protected by her madness, she accuses her husband. She "blames him" as did Bob and Eme before her. Joan accuses George of destroying their family, of driving out his own son, of being totally unyielding. "I begged," she says, "and he wouldn't" (25). "And when Edward died, [he made] Em'ly go! … Three of them gone! Murderer!" (25).

In this play the men retain the real political and economic power (as historically they did), but they are of diminished stature. Though George was clearly an authoritarian—and perhaps charismatic—patriarch in Boston, the equivalent to Mr Borden in *Blood Relations* or Ev in *Doc*, in *Fair Liberty's Call* George is not an idealizable father figure. Furthermore, to show the change in his character, much like she did with Ev at the close of *Doc*, Pollock has George break down. When the stranger demands that one of them volunteer to be executed, George says, "Choose me! … I left my life in Boston and I turned my back … on my oldest son … I turned my back on Richard … and Edward, I … Choose me" (73). In this breakthrough, just as the dawn light is growing, George poignantly confirms the values Joan espoused all along.

In *Fair Liberty's Call* it is the women who provide the play's emotional centre. The three of them determine all the important events. They begin the play, and they conclude it. This is fitting since the play's real subject is not the past battles, which preoccupy the men, but how to create a "place" here, a home. Significantly, it is Joan who has the first word, as well as the last. She tells us that the red woman came out from under the trees and offered her a bowl full of earth. "Eat, she says. Swallow." "And I do" (80). Uttering the marriage vow, "I do," ingesting the earth, Joan marries this new country, this new land. She is home.

One can see that Bob's ghost has undergone a sea change. Unlike Bob, Joan has tenacity and hopefulness, compassion and courage, and her children are her first priority. These features can all be seen as correctives to Bob's tragic deficiencies as a mother. In *Fair Liberty's Call* the family plot concludes with the father humbled, the mother revered, and the daughters empowered. Pollock brings us to an end which suggests a return, a new beginning. One could even say that, by transfiguring the maternal, she effects a reconciliation with the rejected part of self.

• • •

The plays produced since *Fair Liberty's Call* in 1993, *Saucy Jack* (1993), *Moving Pictures* (1999), *End Dream* (2000) and *Angel's Trumpet* (2001), do not include a figure whose role as mother is important to the plot. However, it is interesting that in *End Dream*, the striking image from *Doc* returns: the beautiful unhappy woman in an elegant dressing gown who always has a glass in her hand or a cigarette. An alcoholic or drug addict, she is an incompetent mother. Doris is fully aware of her husband's illegal drug smuggling and unconflicted about her involvement in the exploitation of her young employee. Keeping the family secret, a central plot device in many of Pollock's plays, will necessitate sacrifice. The significant difference is that in *End Dream* the young woman, Janet, feels no special rage at the maternal figure. Hired to be nursemaid for baby Rosemary, she has no expectations of Doris. Of course, Doris is not her mother or her stepmother but, more significantly, Doris is depicted as totally trapped by her circumstances. She is powerless. Janet, another young female protagonist who "acquires knowledge by listening and observing" (Pollock, *Saucy Jack* 6) just as Katie does in *Doc*, will understand that completely. Young Katie could not. Janet does not survive, but she is a fighter and concludes the play empowered. Echoing the struggle in *Doc*, Janet is "[a]ble to [l]eave" as Pollock puts it (5). Janet is a surrogate daughter of Bob, another Katie/Catherine who would defiantly say, "I'm not like her! I would never do that!" (*Doc* 42).

(2001)

Notes

[1] The play does include alterations to suit dramatic ends: for example, Dr. Chalmers remarried in 1956; Pollock's grandmother's death came after her mother's; Katie is a young girl, rather than a teenager; Bob is in her mid-twenties to mid-thirties, and so on. Making Katie and Bob younger increases their vulnerability and the play's pathos.

[2] The concern over inherited character traits is not only Katie's. Ev, Oscar and Bob also refer to the impact of their respective parents on their personalities and on their lives. Ev mentions his disappointing father and his doting mother (52, 79). Oscar refers to his overbearing father who he likens to Ev (37). Several times in the play Oscar mentions "my mother in me" in reference to a side of himself both his father and Ev reject (35, 37, 40). It is interesting to note here that whether or not Oscar's mother is "soft," she still found the strength to leave her marriage (35). When Ev says Katie is like her mother, Catherine's quick reply is: "She always said I was just like you" (82). Fearful of her roots, Katie/Catherine is determined to be her own person.

Works Cited

Camp, Dalton. *Gentlemen, Players, and Politicians.* Toronto: McClelland and Stewart, 1970.

Kerr, Rosalind. "Borderline Crossings in Sharon Pollock's Out-law Genres." *Theatre Research in Canada/Recherches théâtrales au Canada* 17.2 (1996): 200–15.

Pollock, Sharon. *Angel's Trumpet. Sharon Pollock: Three Plays.* Toronto: Playwrights Canada, 2003. 165–224.

———. *Blood Relations. Blood Relations and Other Plays.* Ed. Diane Bessai and Don Kerr. Edmonton: NeWest, 1981.

———. *Doc.* Toronto: Playwrights Canada, 1986.

———. *End Dream. Sharon Pollock: Three Plays.* Toronto: Playwrights Canada, 2003. 97–163.

———. *Fair Liberty's Call.* Toronto: Coach House, 1995.

———. *Getting it Straight. Heroines: Three Plays.* Ed. Joyce Doolittle. Red Deer: Red Deer College Press, 1992. 85–126.

———. *Saucy Jack.* Winnipeg: Blizzard, 1994.

———. *Whiskey Six Cadenza. NeWest Plays by Women.* Ed. Diane Bessai and Don Kerr. Edmonton: NeWest Press, 1987. 137–251.

Wasserman, Jerry. "Daddy's Girls: Father-Daughter Incest and Canadian Plays by Women." *Essays in Theatre* 14.1 (November 1995): 25–36.

Zimmerman, Cynthia. "Sharon Pollock: The Making of Warriors." *Playwriting Women: Female Voices in English Canada.* Toronto: Simon & Pierre, 1994. 60–98.

———. "Towards a Better, Fairer World: An Interview with Sharon Pollock." *Canadian Theatre Review* 69 (1991): 34–38.

Staging the Intersections of Time in Sharon Pollock's *Doc, Moving Pictures* and *End Dream*

by Anne Nothof

Canadian playwright Sharon Pollock has frequently constructed theatrical environments that act out the intersections of past and present. The lives of her characters are staged on several levels or planes of time, meeting at common points. Past and present may be conflated, disrupting linearity of form, and of time and space to problematize assumptions of cause and effect. As Ric Knowles has observed of Foucault's principles in relation to "forms" of Canadian drama, authoritarianism and patriarchy are countered not by subdivision and pyramidal hierarchization, but by "proliferation, juxtaposition and disjunction"—by the multiple, different and fluid (Knowles 81). In many of Pollock's plays, "spacial structures of multiplication" conflate time and fragment character (Knowles 162). To quote Einstein, as quoted in Knowles's text, *The Theatre of Form and the Production of Meaning*, "time and space are modes by which we think and not conditions in which we live" (215).

In *Blood Relations*, the past is present in the role-playing, and in the process the "real" and the "imagined" are conflated. In the radio play, *Sweet Land of Liberty*, the protagonist experiences his past as present through flashbacks of memory; in *The Making of Warriors*, the lives of two women activists from two centuries are replayed within a contemporary social/political frame to show the ironic interaction of past and present and the interplay of historical "fact" and fictionalized event. In *Doc*, as Diane Bessai has observed:

> [T]he past occurs in a multidimensional refraction from the present with fragmented memory images arising associationally from the minds of the two present-day characters, Ev and Catherine, who are both remembering and commenting on the family past [...]. Here the years collapse into a swirl of dominant images of either word or actions. Dramatic progression is deliberately buried in the kaleidoscopic patternings of recurring character motifs within the scenes or fragments of scenes. This is facilitated by the presence of all the characters on stage throughout (the time montage ... controlled by lighting). (135)

In *Moving Pictures* character and time are fragmented into three stages of a woman's life, which interact and comment on each other, transforming life experience into fiction and fiction into life experience. Again, all the "characters" of the life drama are present on stage, created in terms of the memory of filmmaker Nell Shipman. In *End*

Dream events are collapsed into the final seconds of a woman's life, evoked through light and sound as lived nightmare. The theatrical space is envisioned as a limbo between reality and illusion, life and death.

Doc begins with the return of Catherine (a woman in her mid-30s) to the family home to visit her father (Ev) who has suffered a heart attack. As in *Moving Pictures* and *End Dream*, lives are re-experienced close to the moment of death. The confrontation of father and daughter resurrects ghosts from the past—Katie, or Catherine as a child, and her mother, Bob. A family friend, Oscar, functions as intermediary and commentator, observing and interacting with his friend and colleague, Doc Everett, as a younger man in his roles as a dedicated doctor and an insensitive husband and father. For Catherine, this visit is also inevitably an encounter with her dead mother, whose life with Ev was one of desperate loneliness and frustrated ambition, ending with suicide. Ev's own reliving of this relationship, however, provides a variorum to the text inscribed in Catherine's memory: the point of view in the play is effectively fractured. Her memories are not countered or rebutted, but are placed in juxtaposition to Doc's; the "truth" remains occluded.

Pollock points out in her "Author's Notes" on the play that

> [s]tructurally, shifts in time do not occur in a linear, chronological fashion, but in an unconscious and intuitive patterning of the past by Ev and Catherine [...] which are often, but not always, time shifts as well. In production, music has been used to underscore the pattern shifts [as is also the case in *End Dream*]; however, the characters' shifts from one pattern to another must be immediate. They do not "hold" for the music. The physical blocking must accommodate this immediacy and the stage setting facilitate it. (129)

In her "Author's Notes" Pollock also suggests that the play "is most effective when the set design is not a literal one, and when props and furniture are kept to a minimum. [She] think[s] of the setting as one which has the potential to explode time and space while simultaneously serving certain naturalistic demands of the play" (129).

In the production for *Doc* at the Studio Theatre, Edmonton, in November 1999, the stage design by Narda McCarroll demonstrated this fluidity of time, but also the distinct moments that embed themselves in the memory. The set was constructed on several levels: on the lowest level downstage Doc Everett occupied an armchair, his patriarchal family throne; from a trunk placed in front of him, he took the habiliments of the past. Catherine also inhabited the foreground. The tiered levels upstage were the domains of the dead—her mother, Bob, and her father's friend, Oscar—the furniture draped in dustcloths. As the young Katie, Catherine moved through these levels; as a woman she remained in a confrontational position with her father. Looming behind the levels of present and past place and time were four draped columns, suggesting ancestral ghosts, brooding elms, or Greek columns—evoking other times, other tragedies.

The Studio Theatre production began on a dark stage with insistent, overlapping whispers infiltrating the silence, anticipating "bits and pieces of dialogue heard later in the play" ("Author's Notes" 129). A child's rhyme, spoken by Katie, penetrated through the miasma of voices:

> Fire on the mountain, kiss and run
> On the mountain berries sweet
> Pick as much as you can eat
> By the berries' bitter bark
> Fire on the mountain break your heart
> Years to come—kiss and run
> Bitter bark—break your heart.

The rhyme anticipates the tragic family events and places the child's perspective in relation to the others. In effect, this rhyme provides a choric comment on her own history:

> Stand up straight
> Upon your feet
> Choose the one you love so sweet
> Now they're married wish them well
> First a girl, gee that's swell. (130)

The woman, Catherine, is congruent with the child, Katie, and lives out the implications of the rhyme. Pollock often uses child's verses or songs as echoes of the past, but also as ironic or tragic comments on the present. The "kaleidoscope of memory" (129) that constitutes the dialogue and action of the opening sequence is rotated throughout the play to reproduce different coloured patterns of pain and loss.

Pollock also uses aural imagery to signal intersections in time—the past impinging on the present. The sound of a train whistle punctuates the play, bridging the death of Ev's mother with the death of his wife, and warning his daughter of a possible future. As a young girl, she has denied affinities with Bob, but as a woman she has come to empathize more with her mother, and Ev suggests that she is much like her. In her reassessment of the past, then, Catherine is indirectly assessing her own capacity for self-destruction as well as destructive behaviour in relationships. In the mirror, Katie sees "Gramma, and Mummy and me … and she doesn't want to be like them (162).

The play ends with a reprise of Katie chanting the "Fire on the mountain" rhyme as her mother's inevitable death draws closer. She blocks out the sound of Bob's voice, and denies her a sympathetic audience, realizing too late that she never did hear her at all. As an adult, Catherine witnesses and re-experiences the anger, pain, and guilt of the child, Katie:

> **KATIE.** I don't hear you! *(pause)* I don't hear you! *(pause)* I don't! *(KATIE jumps up and whirls around to look over at where she last saw BOB. Pause. Softly.)* I don't hear you at all. (165)

Catherine finally burns the letter that has haunted the family, which was written by Ev's mother before she was killed by a train as she walked across a railway bridge. In effect this brings the "time" of the play back to the beginning when Ev pulled the letter from the trunk in which is stored the detritus of the past. Bob has insisted that this is a suicide note, in order to punish him with the responsibility for his mother's death, but the contents are never revealed. As the letter burns, Catherine smiles at her father, an enigmatic acknowledgement of a shared complicity, and a ritualistic purgation of the past.

Moving Pictures similarly interrogates the life of a woman in terms of a fragmented body, but in three stages of time. The Canadian producer of silent films, Nell Shipman (1892–1970) is played as "Helen," a young actress; as "Nell," a director and actress in middle age; and as "Shipman," an older woman near the end of her life. Shipman looks back at her younger, ambitious selves from a cynical perspective, questioning whether all the sacrifice was "worth it." In the process of replaying her life, however, and reuniting with her younger selves in a final Gilbert and Sullivan chorus, "Three Little Maids from School," she accepts and celebrates her past. As in *Doc*, the different stages of Nell's life interact, showing how the past informs the present, and the present informs the past. In a typically informative introductory note to the 1998 rehearsal draft of *Moving Pictures*, Pollock provides a context for the play:

> The woman plays for and against herself in the reconstruction of a life dedicated to the creation of play on stage, on screen, and in life. She creates fiction in order to experience being. She transforms her life experience into fiction in order to determine how well she lived, why she lived—in order to know she did live and that her life has meaning [;] the fiction reveals to her [w]hat the actual living of her life did not.
>
> *Moving Pictures* plays with: the reconstitution of past memories because of present experience; the employment of life stories from the past for present and active motivations in the now; and the subjective recall of shared or individual experience with multi-layers of time, space and performance. The style and structure of the play is [sic] intended to comment on, inform, encapsulate and expand all of Nell Shipman's "stories" which form the parts of the play. (2)

The men in Nell's life are played as projections of her memory process—characters in the film of her life. They are played by two actors: the first enacts Carl Laemmle, a German immigrant and founder of Universal Studios, and Ernie Shipman, a theatre and movie entrepreneur, and Nell's first husband; the second "Man" plays Bert van Tuyle, American independent movie producer, and Nell's lover and creative partner, and Sam Goldfeldt, Polish immigrant and founder of Goldwyn Pictures. As in *Doc* and *End Dream*, all the actors are present on stage throughout, observing, witnessing and commenting, although the two "Men" in their various configurations fade in and out of the action as their lives intersect with Nell's. Other people in her life are evoked through voices—her young son, for example, who is not sufficiently present in her life to have even a corporeal existence on stage. The voice of

Thomas Edison is also present as a "voice over" on tape. His definition of "moving pictures" functions as a choric comment on the nature of Nell's attempt to reshape life as illusion and to replay time: "The illusion of continuous movement through persistence of vision" (*Moving Pictures* 17).

Moving Pictures unfolds in one continuous act. In structure and style, it simulates the screening of a film, the images flickering across time, as is suggested by the stage directions at the beginning:

> *Black. A light picks out SHIPMAN sitting in a chair behind a desk. Less visible is NELL, who stands behind SHIPMAN, and HELEN who is holding a script and standing behind NELL [...]. NELL leans forward and whispers in SHIPMAN'S ear.*
>
> **NELL.** Play
>
> **SHIPMAN.** Can't.
>
> **NELL.** Can so. *(snaps her fingers, then the sound of the rhythmic click of film running through a projector)* Play!
>
> *Black and white film plays on the set and the bodies of the characters which provide the "screen." Elusive images flicker and flash, a strobe-like effect, illuminating SHIPMAN, NELL and HELEN. All are looking out as if watching a film they see playing on a distant screen, as the film plays on them.* (17)

Light and sound effects distort present reality and blur the distinctions between life and art, past and present. Once the image of the "three in one" breaks apart, Helen assumes her role as a young actress studying her lines as Lady Teazle, while Nell gazes out as if she were still seeing the film, and Shipman ponders Edison's words. The three personae are placed in their respective time and place before they begin interacting. Like Ev in *Doc*, Shipman is close to her death: she will "drop dead" in a month. Her reluctant engagement with the past is, then, an attempt to justify her life, and to understand her choices and her motivations, to "make something of it." Her first attempt to address her younger self as Nell receives no response, however. Nell is not listening; she is wholly absorbed in her own present visions. The past is not always receptive to present overtures; it also requires a "persistence of vision." The ensuing exchange between Nell and Shipman further underscores the distance between the younger woman's ambition and the older woman's doubts, but Nell asserts her conviction that something can be made of a life through the replaying and collapsing of linear time into a present moment: "The beginning, the middle, the bits in between, then the end, make something of it" (22). In the process they replay the pain they have inflicted on others and the consequent guilt; for example, Nell was too busy with her filmmaking to be with her father when he died and to spend time with her son, who was sent to a military school. Although she achieves some success with her "wilderness" films, she makes disastrous business decisions and alienates the men who have tried to support her personally and professionally. At the close of the play, which ends as it began with a flickering black and white film projected on set and characters, the vision that has driven a life is reasserted. Time is frozen, and "hot pools of light" focus on the three women. Nell refuses to let the lights go to black, and the three personae join hands and laugh. The present is reconciled with the past, and the young Helen reasserts her optimistic anticipation of a new beginning.

In the premiere production of *Moving Pictures* by Theatre Junction, Calgary, in March 1999, the set and lighting design by Terry Gunvordahl imaginatively reconstructed the levels of time, and the interplay of reality and illusion, life and art. A raised upstage level suggested the "illusion" of film and Nell's imaginative vision: stage right under a proscenium illuminated with marquee lights were double flats constructed of wooden boards on which was written, like a silent film text, "Grubstake Saloon." A 1920s movie camera was also placed in this "film" space. Film scenes of Shipman's "A Girl in the Wilderness" were projected on the flats. Stage left, also under the proscenium, the title of the piece being enacted was projected on a draped white curtain—the play or scene titles, or the names of plays and vaudeville routines. Centre stage was a rack for costumes, and stage left a wind machine and phonograph player located behind a second draped, opaque black curtain. In the foreground was a circular playing area on the same level as the audience, which constituted the present *reality* of Nell's life. In this space were located the props of her working life—a desk and telephone, a steamer trunk on which were placed the costumes assumed by the men in her life, and a drinks table. These could be rolled around the area to accommodate the different places and times.

As in *Doc* and *End Dream*, songs also relocate the action and the character in time, the words assuming levels of irony as they anticipate the ends in the beginnings. *Moving Pictures* is placed in time through the music of the vaudeville stage and silent film—ragtime mimed in the style of Charlie Chaplin. Towards the end of the play, the words of the songs or vaudeville routines are fragmented and spoken by all three ages of "Nell" as the memories coalesce in the present and provide a comment on the past:

> **HELEN, NELL & SHIPMAN.** I never had a dream so nice
> Thought I was in paradise
> Waking up makes me feel cheap— *(music stops)*
> […]
> **HELEN.** Am I to blame be
> **NELL.** cause flowers are dear
> **SHIPMAN.** in cold weather
> **NELL.** you should find
> **HELEN.** fault with the cli
> **SHIPMAN.** mate and not with
> **NELL.** me for my part
> **SHIPMAN.** wish it was
> **HELEN.** spring all year round and
> **NELL.** that roses grew
> **HELEN.** under one's feet
> *Sound effects for a pratfall, then music plays.*
> **HELEN, NELL & SHIPMAN.** Everything is a source of fun

> Nobody's safe for we care for none
> Life is a joke that's just begun. (87–88)

The story remains incomplete: it continues in time to speak to other audiences, playing out Nell's assertion that "[she has] never wanted complete" (63).

In Pollock's *End Dream*, which premiered at Theatre Junction in March 2000, time is collapsed into a purgatorial moment experienced by a young Scottish nanny at the instant of her death. The circumstances of her death—whether by murder or suicide—are complicated by the variant points of view, and by her own variant responses to the individuals for whom and with whom she works. The story is one which Pollock encountered in a second-hand bookstore in Ottawa, written by a professor from the University of British Columbia, and based on an actual case in British Columbia in 1924. Although murder charges were laid against a Chinese houseboy, the police were unable to conclusively prove a murder, and he was acquitted, despite the racist climate of the time. The *facts* suggested a cover-up to protect the nanny's well-connected employer, who may have been involved in a drug smuggling operation. However, Pollock was more interested in investigating how Jenny Smith died, than in who killed her (Clark C9). To do so, she internalizes the drama, but she also problematizes the focus of vision by playing out several possible scenarios. In the intersection of present and past events she shows how reality can be reconfigured: "Theatre can present a surrealistic irrational way of penetrating the truth of things and in so doing free the imagination" (Pollock, qtd. in Clark).

The play begins with an ending: the moment of death of a young woman, evoked through sound and light:

> *Black. In the blackness a long low exhalation of a flute, followed by an extremely loud resonant sound accompanied by a blinding flash that diminishes to an increasingly smaller point of light in the darkness. There is the acrid smell of gunpowder.*
>
> *As the flash is diminishing to a point of light, the faint sound of blood moving through chambers, through channels, the barely audible drum of a heartbeat, is heard. This sound continues under the dialogue.*
>
> *A voice speaks in Cantonese. The voice is low, but not a whisper. As the soft low voice pervades, permeates the space, the face of JANET Smith gradually grows visible, seemingly suspended in space in the light.* (*End Dream* 101)

The voice of the Chinese houseboy, Wong Foon Sing, speaking in Cantonese, appeals to Janet to speak to him. Janet's initial response is "No," but gradually as the other players become apparent, she begins to relive the events of the recent past. As in *Doc*, Pollock lights up particular places and characters, juxtaposing them in a collage of disrupted narrative and recollection. Doris, whose baby has been entrusted to Janet's care, summons up remembrance, but also brings closure in her detached comments on the baby's name and her crying:

> DORIS. She'll stop. A little comforting is all it takes. I don't think she's really awake. We call her Rosemary [...]. Rosemary, for remembrance. [...]
>
> *The baby's cries are fading and soon stop altogether.*
>
> There, you see. She's stopping now.... Yes, she's stopped. She was stopping and now she's stopped. (102)

Wong Sien, a Chinese interpreter with an identified connection to Doris's husband, Robert, comments on the consequences of the death of Janet—the abduction and beating of Foon Sing, and his trial. Robert comments on the unreliability of Janet's record of events, kept in a diary:

> **ROBERT.** But I wouldn't take her word for things [...]. Oh she may have said things, thought things, wrote things.
>
> **WONG SENG.** A diary?
>
> **ROBERT**. It won't reflect reality. (102)

As "light begins a slow invasion of the space," the silhouette of a young woman is disclosed, standing in front of a door. Pollock's description of her entrance into the room is highly evocative:

> *In the light we see her more clearly now; a young woman in coat and hat. The room is full of shadow. She looks as if she's been abandoned at the front door shortly after entering this house.*
>
> *The almost subliminal ba-boom of heartbeat and the sound of moving blood are still present. The sound seems more a stirring of the air than an actual sound. One feels it as opposed to hearing it.* (103)

This room is the antechamber to Janet's experience of death, and she hears again the voice of Foon Sing, asking if she is afraid. He is at this point an intermediary between life and death, past and present, and his words are ambiguous and suggestive. Wind chimes signal a shift in a spatial or temporal dimension, and Janet's experience shifts more into a present lived reality—recreating the time when she first came to the home of her employers. She is greeted by Doris, who poses a series of questions: Why is Wong Foon Sing's name a joke? Why does Rosemary cry in the night? What are the personal habits of Robert, her husband, and why did he hire Janet? In effect, the play poses many questions, and in doing so questions the nature of experiencing reality and of any perceived "truth." Reality is constructed as a process of remembering which never stops, even after death.

As in *Doc* and *Moving Pictures* all of the characters remain on stage for the two acts, standing on the periphery and observing the action when not directly involved. Songs again precipitate shifts in time, and facilitate ironic allusions, and again they are typically children's songs or mordent nursery rhymes like "My Bonnie lies of the ocean," in which the singer "dreams that [her] lover was dead." Doris invites Janet to sing this song with her and sings it faster and faster, in a frenetic display of frustration, jealousy and anger.

Janet's dream of dying is placed in "historical" time through a narrative frame spoken by the Chinese "court interpreter," Wong Sien, who is also probably implicated in her death. He recounts the details of the abduction and beating of the murder suspect, Foon Sing, and his subsequent trial. The play suggests, however, that Janet's dream comes closer to the *truth* than any legal investigation. In Act Two, Foon Sing is illuminated by the point of light, and the focus is directed more on his lived experience at the time of Janet's death. His memories intersect with hers, sometimes corroborating them, sometimes contradicting them. He is a witness to her life and death, but not a wholly reliable one, since his point of view and his motives are conditioned by his feelings for her. He is constantly watching Janet, almost like a predator observes its prey, and at one point, Janet screams at him to stop looking at her. But Janet also watches him and the others, as they replay the critical moments before her death.

The end replicates the beginning with some minor variations and additions: Wong Foon Sing repeats his final words to Janet (this time in English)—"I did not want this. I do care for you. *(He touches her face.)* Did you have feelings for me?" (163). Then all sounds stop before the blackout.

The set design for the March 2000 Theatre Junction production was highly evocative and symbolic—a timeless holding space or limbo which associated domestic space with violence. The large antechamber in which Janet relives her death was set on a raised thrust stage, the floor tiles suggesting a chessboard. In the centre of the "room" were four large upholstered red chairs, placed back-to-back, and each facing a different direction. The placement of the characters on these chairs, each one always partially obscured from the others, suggested different spatial and temporal configurations. Three tall, narrow windows with red glass constituted the back wall to this room, and two more red chairs were placed on the periphery of the room, suggesting a space out of current time. The chairs were initially covered with dustcloths that were taken off like shrouds as the evidence of Robert's illicit drug business was removed from the room.

Most of Pollock's plays work through series of disclosures—although rarely in terms of a linear temporal sequences. Incidents are played contrapuntally, each informing the other and contributing a rich texture of sound and imagery. Events and characters function like aural and visual imagery, juxtaposed, resonating, their present reality only an illusion. Time and space are reconfigured in order to stimulate variant ways of imagining the *truth.*

(2001)

Works Cited

Bessai, Diane. "Sharon Pollock's Women: a Study in Dramatic Process." *A Mazing Space: Writing Canadian Women Writing.* Ed. Shirley Neuman and Smaro Kamboureli. Edmonton: Longspoon/NeWest, 1986: 126–36.

Clark, Bob. "Playwright likes 'simple stories.'" *Calgary Herald* 10 March 2000: C9.

Knowles, Ric. *The Theatre of Form and the Production of Meaning: Contemporary Canadian Dramaturgies.* Toronto: ECW Press, 1999.

Pollock, Sharon. *Doc. Modern Canadian Plays.* Vol. 2. Ed. Jerry Wasserman. 3rd ed. Vancouver: Talonbooks, 1994. 129–67.

———. *Moving Pictures,* Rehearsal draft 12/98.

———. *Moving Pictures. Sharon Pollock Three Plays.* Toronto: Playwrights Canada, 2003. 14–96.

———. *End Dream. Sharon Pollock Three Plays.* Toronto: Playwrights Canada, 2003. 98–163.

Imagining Canada: Sharon Pollock's *Walsh* and *Fair Liberty's Call*

by Sherrill Grace

> As a Canadian, I feel that much of our history has been misrepresented and even hidden from us. Until we recognize our past we cannot change our future.
>
> (Sharon Pollock, Introduction 226)

> Theatre is at its most powerful when it is least literal.
>
> (Sharon Pollock, Nothof "Interview" 179)

I

History *and* theatre, even more than history *in* the theatre, are subjects fundamental to Sharon Pollock's oeuvre. She made the first of the remarks I have quoted above in the introduction to her 1976 play *The Komagata Maru Incident* and the second in a 1999 interview with Anne Nothof, but the two decades that fall between these comments only reinforce the importance of these two subjects—poles, I am tempted to say—in her thinking and her plays.[1] I take them as my signposts and starting points because, at the beginning of the 21st century I believe that Pollock's oeuvre is ready for a new reassessment and that, sadly, we live in a historical moment made urgent by the need to revisit and understand what Pollock has been telling us for more than twenty-five years. In the discussion that follows I will circle these two poles of history and theatre, as Pollock configures them, in an effort to reassess her alignment of each pole and to explore how and why some of her plays are so important to the imagining of Canada.

Since at least the early 1980s, Pollock's plays have attracted the attention of Canada's mainstages and its leading theatre scholars. The two plays I want to examine in detail, *Walsh* and *Fair Liberty's Call*, have both received Stratford productions (see Brady and Whittaker). Of the two plays I will consider more briefly, *The Komagata Maru Incident* (1978) has received professional productions, a television treatment, and publication, and *End Dream* (2000), which premiered at Calgary's Theatre Junction, will soon be available in print. These plays span her career to date and testify to some of her most persistent concerns over close to thirty years of writing. Early discussions of *Walsh* and *The Komagata Maru Incident* linked Pollock with a Canadian tradition of history-play writing and documentary drama (see Bessai, Nunn and Rubin), but scholars quickly moved to refine, problematize, and theorize these categories as they applied to Pollock's work (see Gilbert, Knowles and Salter). By the end of the 1980s Pollock seemed to have pushed her abiding interest in historical events and public figures, in careful research, and in documentary evidence into increasingly personal, autobiographical, metaphoric, and what I describe, in "Creating the Girl from God's Country" and "Sharon Pollock's Portraits," as *performative* directions. Her so-called family plays—*Generations, Blood Relations, Doc* and *Getting It Straight*—appeared to signal a move away from the public to a more personal sphere at the same time as she began to experiment with metadramatic forms (Knowles 239).

As others before me have always recognized, however, Pollock's staging of histories, whether national or autobiographical, never conformed to simple classifications of history play or docudrama; from the beginning, with *Walsh*, she was exploring the potential of performance and experimenting with the complex dynamics of performativity (by which I mean the dramatic *re*presentation of identity-scripts) as ways to interrogate the power and assumed stability of history and story.[2] From *Walsh* onward, if with varying degrees of success, Pollock has asked the large questions, questions about justice, morality, responsibility, and authority to be sure, but also about identity, about how we know who we are, how our identities are constituted, or interpellated, or, indeed, performed, and how theatre mirrors, or participates in, or, indeed, might intervene in the ontological process.

While I cannot examine here all of Pollock's major stage plays (ten have been published; three more will appear in print soon), the four I will consider—and especially *Walsh* and *Fair Liberty's Call*—illustrate some of the ways she has charted the journey between the pole of history and the pole of theatre and negotiated the tensions between their highly magnetic fields in order to dramatize foundational moments in Canadian history. Between *Walsh* and *Fair Liberty's Call*, with a brief pause for *The Komagata Maru Incident* and a glance forward to *End Dream*, it is possible to see how Pollock imagines the possible community called Canada and why she laments its failures to imagine itself. Today, we urgently need plays like these on our stages because, as we have so often been warned, those who forget history are doomed to repeat it, to which I would add that, in Pollock's plays, history is a script that can be performed and, in performance, changed.

II

Walsh and *Fair Liberty's Call* are obvious choices for my purposes, and I will explain why I pair them in a moment. *The Komagata Maru Incident* and *End Dream*, each less well known to history and to theatre, are narrower in their scope, more particular in the windows they open onto a Canadian community, but they do focus on disturbing moments that resonate with the subjects and the form of the two other plays. *The Komagata Maru Incident* explores a little-known event in British Columbia history when the Canadian government successfully denied entry to 376 East Indian immigrants who held British passports and had the legal right to enter the country.

During the hot summer of 1914 the Japanese ship *Komagata Maru* was detained in Vancouver's harbour while officials manoeuvred, strategized, stonewalled and starved the Sikh passengers into submission. Later that Fall the ship returned to India, but the incident left ugly racist scars on the body politic. Those in power wanted to keep Canada white, and they were deeply invested in the notion that non-White immigrants would shatter their ideal of a homogenous, peaceable kingdom.[3] In *End Dream* Pollock returns to questions of race, class and immigration in Vancouver, this time through the story of Janet Smith, a British nanny found dead by a Chinese houseboy in her wealthy white employers' home. The Janet Smith murder, as the case has been called, took place in 1924, and the Chinese houseboy was accused of her murder. As with the arrival of the *Komagata Maru*, this case aroused a furor of racist rhetoric in the press, amidst which it was easy to scapegoat an Asian servant and deflect all suspicion from the nanny's privileged employers.[4]

Every bit as important for my purposes as the historical subjects of these plays is their form, and it is their form that makes them effective theatre. Both plays are intensely metaphoric, albeit in different ways, and both use the facts, the historical record, to motivate deeply personalized performances of history. *The Komagata Maru Incident* can usefully be described as presentational in its technique because it stages history as a carnival or circus controlled by the barker/manipulator "T.S." *We*, as audience or readers, are constructed as his audience and the event we have paid to watch on his mainstage is that ship in Vancouver's harbour with its cargo of unwanted brown people. Within this dominant circus trope, which co-opts us, the performance of William Hopkinson, Inspector with the Department of Immigration, unfolds in a play-within-the-historical-play that is set in a brothel. I have discussed this play at length elsewhere (see Grace and Helms), so here I wish only to stress the layers of performance in this complex, yet economical, text. Everything about the events of that summer and fall of 1914 is recreated as sleight of hand, artifice, role-playing, and spectacle (or three-ring circus) in which we watch T.S. manipulating Hopkinson and Hopkinson manipulating the immigrants and everyone on shore jeering the ship and cheering the show. What Pollock insists we also watch is the spectacle of William Hopkinson being gradually destroyed by the roles he agrees to play (of spy, racist, person-of-colour masquerading as White, and traitor to his own heritage). Reality, Pollock suggests, like an individual's identity, is performed, and Hopkinson's failure is his inability to see history as theatre and to imagine another more honest and liberating role for himself to play. *The Komagata Maru Incident* stages this moment in Canadian history as a kind of national allegory or morality play and Hopkinson's individual dilemmas (his struggle with racial origins and present class ambition) as symbolic of the challenge we all face: to recognize the past so that we can change the future by performing new roles in a continually reimagined community.

End Dream, while also exploiting presentational elements and refusing the literal, is more expressionist psycho-drama than national allegory or morality play. Janet Smith and her story occupy the centre of this play in ways similar to Hopkinson and his story, but her story is framed and interrupted by the aftermath of her death; the governing metaphor of the play is a trial, and her story is part of the evidence. Time moves backwards in this play and the dramatic action locks on trauma instead of moving forward to any form of conclusion. How Janet Smith died is never answered because the forensic question of her death was never solved and because Sharon Pollock is more interested in the complex social pressures and interpersonal intrigues that transform the Clarke-Evans mansion into such an intolerable, maddening prison that even suicide becomes as plausible a cause of death as murder. Throughout the play, in both its premiere and its script, Pollock calls for a range of expressionist techniques to represent Janet's inner life of initial confusion, racist rejection of the houseboy, and rapidly developing suspicion, terror and desperation: hallucinatory lighting, sound effects (for example, of pounding blood, hammer blows, whispering voices), and a jarring montage of confrontational scenes contained by the Chinese interpreter's commentary and by the houseboy Wong Foon Sing's repeated phrases, were complemented in production by a stark set with a black and white chequered floor, four large, red, winged-back chairs, back-lit screens, and two rows of straight-backed chairs draped in red cloth and trussed.[5]

End Dream is a tour de force, proof, if we needed it, that Pollock is right when she insists that "theatre is at its most powerful when it is least literal." To compare it with *The Komagata Maru Incident* is to realize, on the one hand, how intensely Pollock pursues watershed moments in Canadian history and yet, on the other, how far she has moved from dramatizing conclusions or underscoring ethical lessons. Both these plays are *about* race, class and gender. Both explore the ways in which a white elite in Canada held on to political and economic power by using and discarding others. Both reveal shocking webs of complicity and oppression, and both challenge contemporary audiences to recognize the past in order to imagine something better. Boiled down to a lesson, both plays teach us not to allow such things to happen again. But, of course, such lessons are reductive. The impact of both plays comes from their capacity to haunt us: *The Komagata Maru Incident* makes us witnesses to a traumatic spectacle that we cannot stop and *End Dream* is a terrible ghost story in which Janet Smith and Wong Foon Sing refuse to go away. These terse snapshots of Canadian history remind us of what the larger panoramas of *Walsh* and *Fair Liberty's Call* insist is, to paraphrase Joyce's Stephen Dedalus, the nightmare of history from which we must awake (*Ulysses* 42).

III

Both *Walsh* and *Fair Liberty's Call* are large plays, epic in their scope and purpose; both examine originary moments in the imagining of an emergent national identity and nation state. Both tackle issues of "blood and belonging," issues, as Michael Ignatieff reminds us, that permeate our so-called post-nationalist age, returning us, continually, to the challenge of nationalism (9). And both situate their identity politics on the border that literally (cartographically, politically) separates, while juxtaposing and relating, Canada and the United States. Twenty years elapsed between the writing of these plays, so it is all the more interesting that Pollock returned, in

1994 with *Fair Liberty's Call*, to the history of an 18th century war, rebellion, and conflicting set of loyalties that had informed the Indians' claim on pre-Confederation Canada and that surfaced dramatically during the 1870s context of *Walsh*. Like the United Empire Loyalists, who left the United States after the American Revolution to remain loyal British subjects in what would become the Canadian province of New Brunswick, the Sioux claimed the right to seek asylum in the Canadian Northwest after the battle of the Little Big Horn in 1876. They too were loyalists during the American Revolution and again in the War of 1812.[6] 1776 and 1876 are, thus, pivotal dates in Pollock's vision of Canadian history, watershed moments of greater significance for the present than the building of a railway (E.J. Pratt's choice of epic subject) or the Great War, and to read these two plays together is to understand how these moments crystallize the failure and potential of a Canadian imagined community.

But I have still more reasons for wanting to focus on these two plays. Although each can be called a history play (as *Walsh* repeatedly has), neither is simply that. Even *Walsh*, despite its shortcomings, reaches beyond documentary and history play to embrace a complex dramaturgy that unsettles easy categorization.[7] In *Walsh*, I would argue, we see Pollock's earliest probings, not only of historical fact but also of history as a hegemonic discourse and as a discipline that presumes to tells us who we are—and might be—as individuals and as a nation. Through the writing and revising of *Walsh*, Pollock learned how history can be changed by theatre so that, by the early 1990s with work like *The Komagata Maru Incident* under her belt and the lessons of *Whiskey Six Cadenza*, *Blood Relations* and *Doc* behind her, she was ready to challenge Canadian history again.[8] To look back at *Walsh* from the perspective of *Fair Liberty's Call* is to see just how bold an experiment it was for its day, how far Pollock has come in her philosophy of performance, and how the dramatic challenges faced in *Walsh* are taken up and overcome in the later play. *Walsh*, I believe, is a highly performative play, one that explores a subtle mix of presentational and expressionist techniques as a means for combining history and theatre. It prefigures *Fair Liberty's Call* as theatre. If I were to remount it today, at the beginning of the 21st century, I would stage it as Major Walsh's expressionist nightmare, with Walsh, the individual figure, representing a Canadian history scripted by the winners. But first the play itself—

The story informing this play is relatively brief and brutally simple. After the American army's defeat at the Little Big Horn in 1876, where George Armstrong Custer was killed during his attack on the Hunkpapa Sioux, the Indians, led by Chief Sitting Bull, moved north across the border to escape further American violence. They arrived at Fort Walsh in what is today southern Saskatchewan, where they sought permission to stay. They were essentially refugees, albeit fleeing across a border imposed on them, and they believed they had a legitimate claim on the British Queen and on Ottawa for loyal services rendered in the past. Major Walsh, Superintendent of the North West Mounted Police agreed and put their case to the Prime Minister. Sir John A. MacDonald, however, insisted that the Sioux return to the States and that, if they could not be reasoned into leaving, they could be starved into it. The Sioux were forced south to their deaths so that Canada could placate a vengeful United States, and

Major Walsh left the force to become a businessman in Winnipeg. He returned to the force with the onset of the Klondike Gold Rush in the Yukon and he served in Dawson City as Commissioner from 1897 to 1898. His life and career encompassed two of the most significant events in the history of the Canadian Northwest—the rejection of the Sioux (which made its own contribution to the famous Riel Rebellion of 1885) and the Klondike Gold Rush. Both events signalled serious American challenges to Canadian sovereignty, Canadian attempts to consolidate their authority, and a clear recognition that dealing with Americans meant sacrifice and appeasement.

Walsh opens, not with the Little Big Horn or with Sitting Bull's arrival at Fort Walsh, but in a Dawson City saloon during the winter of 1897–98. The Prologue, added after the premiere, is crucial to the play we know now and I want to examine it closely. It serves many purposes in the play by providing necessary information for audiences/readers who do not know their history, by introducing all the actors who will perform—one set of roles in Dawson City, another twenty years earlier at Fort Walsh—and by establishing James Walsh as a damaged survivor of the 1870s. In her precise, detailed stage instructions, Pollock tells us that the Prologue must flow without a break into Act One (9); she calls for a saloon scene straight out of Robert Service, with a good-hearted whore, a music-playing kid, and a prospector fresh from the creeks with his poke full of gold nuggets; and she stipulates a careful use of music, lighting and freezes. However, the truly frightening presence in Pollock's Dawson City saloon is not Dangerous Dan McGrew but James M. Walsh, the "grafter" (12), whose mind we enter as the play begins. The stage instruction is worth quoting in full:

> *The scene is from WALSH's point of view, and the freezes are momentary arrests in the action and are broken by the character's speech or action following. The impression given is similar to that experienced when one is drunk or under great mental stress. CLARENCE stands outside of the prologue scene, never taking his eyes off WALSH. He has on his red tunic and he exists only in WALSH's mind. He is not part of the prologue scene and his scream is heard only by WALSH.* (9)

In short, the scene about to unfold is an expressionist one emanating from the soul and performed in the tormented memory of Walsh. The people around him will merge, with "*no break in staging*" (9), into the people around him at Fort Walsh to suggest that the *entire* play is performed on the stage of this man's mind and that history, like Walsh, is and continues to be haunted and conditioned by the past.

Pollock reinforces this temporal blurring and expressionist carry-forward into Acts One and Two through many small touches and a few high profile scenes. The music for "Garryowen," General Custer's marching song, played by Billy on his harmonica during the Prologue in deliberate defiance of Walsh (13), is the first music we hear and it will recur, like a leitmotif, throughout the play to taunt Walsh and to remind us of what he/we might like to forget. Clarence, the new recruit to the Mounties, who was with Walsh when the Sioux arrived, represents the Major's conscience and better self. He is, as Walsh understands, the kind of man who should never make a military police force his life (*Walsh* 119) because, if he does, he will have to play a role that will destroy him, as Walsh has done. In this symbolic role, as Walsh's soul or conscience, Clarence will stand apart in the Prologue because he was forsaken, like Sitting Bull, in the past. Yet he persists on the periphery of Walsh's mind and memory and only Walsh will hear his scream of protest and despair. Certain phrases are also repeated (about the lack of food or requests for help, for example), echoing, like the music, back through time and blurring, or unifying, the three parts of the play.

But by far the most galvanizing scene in the play is the one in which Walsh lashes out in rage and frustration to knock another man to the ground and plant his booted foot on the prostrate man's back. In the Prologue that man is the Prospector, who has asked the Commissioner for a donation to help a starving boy; in Act Two that man is Chief Sitting Bull, who has come, in extremity, to ask for food for his starving people. The same actor performs both roles. Walsh refuses help on both occasions, and Clarence screams "Noooooooo!" (16, 113) as he witnesses Walsh's violence. It is this violent act, more than any other, that haunts Walsh and, thus, Canadian history, but there is another scene, one that has no direct mirror image in the Prologue, that informs my reading—and proposed expressionist staging—of the play. Towards the end of Act Two, and just before Walsh learns of Sitting Bull's murder, Pollock inserts a brief discussion of a mock performance: to entertain eastern dignitaries coming west to celebrate the completion of the railway, Walsh is planning an Indian-Wild-West-style hijack of the train with a dramatic rescue by "the force" (125–27). One of his men brings him a board with toy soldiers and train so Walsh can illustrate his script-writing, but the climax of this scene is surely Walsh's order:

> **WALSH.** When you open a railroad, you do it in style, I say! Bloody train will be full of Easterners and we'll scare the pants off every one of them! I want a good show! (127)

In this bitterly ironic play-within-the-play, itself a scene within the nightmare Walsh relives in Dawson City, Pollock reminds us, not only of the pathetic depths to which a man like Walsh, an organization like the NWMP, and the ideals proclaimed for the opening of the *Canadian* West, can sink, but also of the degree to which history *is* theatre—"a good show." If history is a "show" staged by this play, and surely that is one of Pollock's most incisive points, then the play itself is a performance of history *as performance*. This scene in which Walsh scripts a tawdry spectacle for eastern VIPs reaches back to the scene overtly staged in the 1897–98 Dawson City saloon of the Prologue. Thus, the entire play, I believe, is an elaborate and devastating performance, not *of* history, but of history *as* performance. Major Walsh, who made "the force" his life and career, like William Hopkinson, has chosen a self-destructive and symbolically odious role. By exposing his role as a role, Pollock insists that we reflect critically upon the roles we assume because, with hindsight, we may want to script others. In the *present* of Dawson City James Walsh remembers, *recognizes* (to use Pollock's word), a past that is both his and ours. Although Walsh, the man, does not appear to have changed—he does after all strike the prospector as he struck Sitting Bull—the very process of performance holds the potential for change, a potential that is held out with more hope in *Fair Liberty's Call*.

IV

If you "want to know ... where to put your eye ... so you can hear the ... heartbeat ... of a country ... comin' into ... country comin' into bein'" (Pollock, *Fair Liberty's Call* 19–20) you need only listen to and watch Pollock's 1995 masterpiece *Fair Liberty's Call.*[9] This play takes us back to the 1780s and to one of the most significant originary moments in Canadian history, a moment of choices, of decisions, of acceptances, a moment taut with memory and forgetting, a moment Pollock stages as remembering, bearing witness, and confessing. However, as Guy Sprung, who directed the play's premiere at Stratford in 1993, notes in his introduction to the published text, the play may

> look like a traditional history play set amidst the Loyalist immigration to Canada after the American Revolution [but Pollock] is less interested in a sequence of dates and events than in using history as poetry to explore the complex warp and woof of choice and responsibility in our country past and present. (7)

And I would agree. This play is less about the past than it is about the present. Canada, after all, is a country built on immigration and characterized by a very uneasy relationship with the United States. Like *Walsh*, though more profoundly and, in theatrical terms more successfully, it is a performance in which one chooses the roles to be played as much as the country in which one will live.

The play is set in the newly created province of New Brunswick; the date is 22 October 1785; the occasion is a commemorative reunion in which the men gathered will fuel their present resentments and plot their future ambitions by remembering the glories of battle in the Loyalist cause and the agonies of betrayal and defeat at Yorktown four years earlier.[10] Or, at least, that is what the patriarch George Roberts and two of his colonial, Loyalist associates anticipate. Had their expectations been dramatized as the action of this play, we might have had a traditional history play about the American Revolution of 1776 that split communities and families along political and philosophical lines and drove between 40,000 to 50,000 people north to Canada. On one side of this *de facto* civil war were those who chose to remain loyal to the British king; on the other, were those who rebelled against all aspects of colonial status, called themselves "Patriots," and defined themselves in the available 18th century rhetoric of the day as fighting for *liberty.*[11] In the eyes of American Rebels, there was no middle ground, no room for tolerance or debate; liberty meant independence from a tyrant. Men like Roberts, Major Abijah Williams and Daniel Wilson (the latter two having fought in Tarleton's Legion), had to recant or leave once Britain signed the 1783 peace treaty with the Rebels, thereby confirming the transformation of the Thirteen Colonies into the United States of America. If George Roberts and his cronies had written this play, their reunion and Remembrance Ritual in 1785 would have celebrated this history and cemented Roberts' position within the potential elite of New Brunswick.

But Roberts is not in control of history, his family, or the play. And the stories Pollock privileges contain much more than he wants to see, hear, or accept. Unlike *Walsh*, no single male figure dominates this play and, as Kathy Chung notes, the roles of women are crucial to the multiple roles and possibilities performed by the play because it is the women who "seem most able to imagine alternative structures and choices" (153). The female characters are Joan Roberts, the traumatized wife and mother; Annie, the elder daughter who manipulates masculine perceptions through song and talk; and Emily, the younger daughter who will only appear as Eddie, an identity she assumed to serve her father's interests after her Loyalist brother, Edward, committed suicide. Of these three women, Eddie is the hardest, most practical, and most overtly rebellious. It is she who wrote the so-called seditious letter (33) opposing the Committee of Fifty-five and claiming the rights of all in their new home; it is she who will ask the tough questions (such as, "Is any opposition rebellion?" 48); and it is she who will reject her father: "I'm not willin' to live for you" (73). She will do and say these things, and more, to allow something new to be born, something her mother, sister and Wullie, her black Loyalist comrade (a former slave), can all see when they heed her advice to "look up close" at this "new world" (78).

The central stories of *Fair Liberty's Call* are, in fact, the stories of Eddie, Wullie, Annie and Joan, who cannot recover from the losses and betrayals she has endured. Underlying their stories is not the war itself, although Eddie will describe some terrible battle scenes, but the human context of complicated loyalties, betrayed trusts, and vicious (racist and classist) manipulation of the weak by those who want power. In the new world of New Brunswick, manoeuvres are underway to ensure that the winners will not be *all* Loyalists but only those who are part of, or in favour with, the Committee of Fifty-five. George Roberts is prepared to do almost anything to secure his preferment and access to a large estate, but Eddie rejects her father's ambition as perpetuating an evil hierarchy and entrenching an unjust system that would evict a Loyalist soldier's widow, turn thousands of immigrants into tenants, and continue slavery for Blacks. As it happened, the Committee of Fifty-five did not get their way in New Brunswick, but Pollock situates her drama within the context of that possibility, and it is the struggle for access to land and freedom for all that drives the play. It is, as it were, this *present* reality in the New Brunswick of 1785 that matters, not the past American war or the defeat of the Loyalists at Yorktown or any of the other battles between Loyalists and Rebels, battles that George Roberts and Major Williams want to celebrate.

By the time the play ends, we will have learned about the horrors witnessed by the women of this family, their oppression by a patriarchy deaf to all but its own version of reality, and their vision for the future in a new home. Thanks to Annie and Joan, Major John Anderson, a Rebel soldier who has infiltrated their planned Loyalist celebration seeking revenge for his brother's murder, will be convinced to forgive the past and leave without exacting his price (the death of one of the assembled Loyalists). Through Wullie we will learn about the racist double standard applied *by the British* to slaves:

> **WULLIE.** If you be a slave and owned by a Rebel, and if you run away and fight for the Loyalists, you'd be freed by the Loyalists. But if you did the same thing, and were owned by a Loyalist, you wouldn't be freed, no sir. Fightin' for the Loyalists won't buy you freedom 'less you be Rebel-owned. (21)

Moreover, a former slave must be able to prove he was "Rebel-owned." Unable to prove this, black Wullie will not only be denied land, he will, if Major Williams and his kind get their way, be returned to slavery by the very interests he fought to protect.

It is through Eddie, however, that the elitist powers will be exposed most emphatically for what they are, even when they are embodied in her own father. Eddie knows that the greatest enemy is not a Rebel soldier (like Anderson) but, in fact, the rhetoric, as Major Williams puts it, of "Loyalty to our country, trust in Parliament and the King" (49). At its most ironic core this play is not anatomizing the ideology of the American Revolution, the butcheries of war, or even the human scramble to survive. It is exposing the lie of liberty *in Canada*, where an elitist few seek to rob the many of everything. Loyalty to country, for Williams, Roberts, and the would-be elite, means supporting their greed; anything else will be "sedition and treason" (48). Trust in Parliament and King, insisted on by Williams and Roberts, will be misplaced and ultimately betrayed, as Eddie sees all too clearly. In a key exchange with her father, she calls a spade a spade:

> **EDDIE.** Is any opposition rebellion?
> **GEORGE.** It's not the time for questionin'! It's a time for restorin' order and rank and stability. It's time to get on with our lives.
> **EDDIE.** So our promised land, our great new province, this country will become the fiefdom of a few, is that it?
> **GEORGE.** Our position—
> **EDDIE.** Former position—
> **GEORGE.** —gives us rights, can't you see that?
> **EDDIE.** It's not what I'm lookin' at. (48)

To consider how Pollock creates her complex vision of Canada, I must turn to the form of the play because it is there, in its dramaturgy, sets, staging and theatrical shape, that its success and power lie. *Fair Liberty's Call* is built in a circle (which reminds me of the Sioux cosmology and its lost promise of harmony in *Walsh*). It opens with the voices of the Roberts women, Joan, Annie and Eddie, and it returns to their voices at the end. Many images (verbal and visual, heard and seen) recur to connect both parts of the play and to affirm the female script for a "country comin' into bein'" (20). But there are also some crucial differences between the beginning and the end; the circle described by the play re-imagines beginnings instead of closing on a regressive cycle of masculine remembering, privilege and revenge. The most important of the differences is the position and voice of Wullie. He is seen but not heard in the opening sequence (19–20). He is seen, heard, and active at the close, and he is the only male to interact with the Roberts women as they clear the stage of the men's ceremonial trappings (flags, weapons, trophies, uniforms) to perform another, a healing ritual. This ritual has several parts. First, Joan must learn to accept that her daughter Emily has been "changed" into Eddie and that her new home is here in New Brunswick by looking closely at and by touching both her daughter's face and the earth of this place. Second, *both* copies of Wullie's indenture papers must be destroyed, not just by Eddie (who killed Frank Taylor, the man who had tricked Wullie into signing himself back into slavery, and destroyed Wullie's copy of the paper, 57), but by Wullie himself.[12] In a highly symbolic act that mirrors Eddie's earlier burning of the document (57), Wullie tears up Taylor's copy of the indenture (the paper that Eddie folded up and has kept in her pocket from the opening scene of the play, 20, and now gives to him), thereby participating in his own freeing. Third, Joan, Annie and Wullie must make a choice *for Canada*—as Wullie puts it, "we could always stay about here. Try to make a place" (79). Finally, these three acts/decisions/choices must be consolidated, confirmed, celebrated by an act of ritual recognition, and it is, fittingly, the mother, Joan, who performs this ritual. With words that recall her opening description of "the red woman with the baby on her back" (20, 79), Joan accepts this woman's offering—"a bowl full of earth" (79)—which she must swallow in a gesture of sacred communion: "Eat, she says. Swallow. [...] And I do" (80).

The action contained (a word I choose deliberately) within this dramatic circle is dominated by the men. It is they who change the set from the opening "*dark-hued swirl of colour* [that] *represents the 'virgin' land*" (19) into a war memorial for their Reunion. It is they who argue over the past and the Committee of Fifty-five's patronage. And it is they who will be reduced to obscene squabbling when the American Rebel, John Anderson, reveals himself and demands his human sacrifice, either in the person of the man who slaughtered his brother at Waxhaws or in the person of a scapegoat. Having wanted to commemorate the past as a means of forging strategic alliances of privilege in New Brunswick, these *Gentlemen* are forced to confess or choose a sacrificial victim ... and they fail. Instead, Anderson is talked into forgiveness by the women, who protect his departure by disarming the men and scattering their horses—acts of sabotage, insurrection, and rebellion if ever there were any! The men's war trophies are then cleared away to restore "*the stage to some semblance of its virgin state at the beginning of the play*" (78), so that the women, with Wullie, can perform the final rites of the play.

In another analysis of *Fair Liberty's Call* I might focus on the form itself to argue that Pollock has pitted a masculine plotline against a feminist one and allowed the latter to triumph.[13] But I am less interested in labels and terminology, whether history play, docu-drama, presentational or feminist dramaturgy (and there are elements of all these in this play), than I am in accounting for Pollock's imagining of Canada and in tracing the performative advances this play makes on *Walsh*. There are, as I see it, a few crucial differences between the two plays, and together these differences contribute to the greater hope and potential held out by *Fair Liberty's Call*. Where *Walsh* performed one man's symbolic entrapment in a vicious circle of history, with one violent act begetting another, *Fair Liberty's Call* enables multiple performances of/within a representative and symbolically important community. It stages, to rephrase Benedict Anderson, a microcosmic community in the process of imagining itself anew. Absolutely key to this imagining are its White women and its racial others, the Black man and the Red woman (although her *First* Nations position is not directly addressed), who imagine and enable a dream of community that could include them all. No absent, oppressive elite is allowed to rule; no White male desire for hierarchy, wealth, privilege and power is allowed to prevail; and no vengeance or retribution has been permitted to stain this "*virgin*" land. To achieve this imagining of community, Eddie has changed (in fact, *freed*) herself and through this transformation encouraged all the others who will listen and see—her mother, sister, and her Black comrade—to do the same. But something more has changed, something carried in the very language of the play and signalled by its seemingly innocent title. *Liberty*, the 18th century battle-cry of the American Rebels, has been redefined by Eddie, Joan, Annie and Wullie, as the call of the future in which men and women may be truly free because they have put the ideology of "liberty," as played out in the polarized, brutal world of the Revolution, behind them to seek out rights and justice and *fair* liberty for all in "a new world" (78).

V

At the start of this discussion I described what I see as two poles in Sharon Pollock's work: history and theatre. What her work over the past thirty years or so tells us is that these two interests, and the tension between them, are of lasting importance in her oeuvre. [14] At the same time, she has refined, honed, and shaped her use of history to serve increasingly theatrical and performative ends. If I am correct in my reading of *Walsh* (and a full expressionist production would be a splendid test), then even at this early juncture Pollock was using the stage to comment on the scripting and performing of histories by locating the history of Major Walsh and the Sioux refugees within the mind, memory, and soul of the central, but symbolically representative character. *Walsh* embodies a tragic view of history in much the same way that certain German expressionist plays do (say, Kaiser's *From Morn to Midnight*); the central, suffering Soul, caught up in a cycle of events he cannot control, must perform a role he hates but is doomed to play to its bitter end, and he will die betrayed, abandoned, lost (see Grace, *Regression and Apocalypse*, 54–56). *Fair Liberty's Call* differs from *Walsh* in the ways I have already mentioned, but, more importantly, it is less expressionist than symbolic, even mythic, and it leans towards the comedic in its communal, ritualized affirmation of life. Where history controls performance in *Walsh*, theatre rewrites, and reperforms history in *Fair Liberty's Call.* Between these two plays Pollock has learned how to tap the ritual roots of drama so that theatre can liberate us from history.

Or that, at least, is the promise held out by this play. It is also why I think it is such an important play now. Without preaching or sentimentality (criticisms leveled at early productions of *Walsh*), *Fair Liberty's Call* reminds Canadians, indeed *all* modern nations at the turn of the 21st century, how fragile true liberty is, what a sacred trust it is, and how much can be lost by a stubborn refusal to *imagine* a better world. Wisely, Pollock is not pretending that all is well in late-20th century Canada. She relies on our knowing that slavery did exist here, that the First Nations were betrayed and oppressed, that non-white immigrants faced, and still face, discrimination, and that extreme appeals to rights, patriotism and loyalty are dangerous.[15] Neither is she criticizing the United States (although the binary thinking so characteristic of American policy in the 1770s and ever since is rejected by the play), or condemning Britain for signing away, in 1783 (a signing away that typified Britain's treatment of Canada for 200 years), what was not theirs to give in order to achieve stability in Europe. She is not laying blame but dramatizing the promise of inclusivity, understanding, growth, tolerance, and a multiplicity of stories (and answers). When Joan asks Anderson, in *Fair Liberty's Call* (67), if he believes that a lion can lie down with a lamb, Pollock is evoking the symbolism of a peaceable kingdom that Northrop Frye describes as a Canadian ideal (248–49). In practice we have failed that ideal, but it is the artist's duty to remind us of that failure and that promise. If Pollock is Canada's answer to Ibsen, as Robert Nunn once speculated she might be (42), it is because of the scope of her vision, the timelessness of her subjects, and the power with which she makes history live as theatre and, thus, in an art that continues to matter.

(2003)

Notes

1 The first of the epigraphs to my article has frequently been cited by scholars, but I have juxtaposed the two to signal my sense of the complexities informing Pollock's *use* of historical document.

2 I have explored Pollock's use of performativity and its relation to Butler's concept in "Creating the Girl from God's Country" and "Sharon Pollock's Portraits of the Artist," but see also Butler, Case and Worthen. The key point to stress here is that performativity in a Pollock play stages the dynamic, often dialogic, nature of identity and the socially prescribed roles, or scripts, that individuals are expected to embody.

3 The idea of Canada as a "peaceable Kingdom" is discussed by Northrop Frye in *The Bush Garden* (248–49). Frye is alluding to the allegorical painting by Thomas Hicks called "The Peaceable Kingdom" (c 1830) which depicts a lion lying down with a lamb in a new world garden.

4 The context for the Janet Smith case was one of Exclusion Acts, Head Tax, and laws forbidding white women from being hired by Chinese businesses. For a discussion of these racist policies see Li, and for a fictional rendering of the times see Wayson Choy's *The Jade Peony*. Another unpublished play about Janet Smith is Kate

Schlemmer's *Disposing of the Dead*, produced by Pink Ink and Axis Theatre at Vancouver's Waterfront Theatre in November 1996.

[5] Pollock directed the premiere of the play on 8 March 2000 with Calgary's Theatre Junction. Terry Gunvordahl designed the striking sets and lighting, Bob Doble designed the sound, with Daniele Vlaskalic as Janet, Jovanni Sy as Wong Foon Sing, Jarvis Hall as Robert Clarke-Evans, the threatening, domineering husband and employer, and Laura Parkin as Doris, his alcoholic and jealous wife. The Chinese interpreter, who often spoke in Cantonese, was played by Anthony Chan.

[6] Various First Nations fought with the British and Loyalists during the American Revolution and again in 1812, when the United States attempted to invade the British colonies to the north.

[7] The most nuanced reading of this play, to my mind, is Salter's. Reviews of *Walsh* productions vary. Godfrey praised the 1983 Theatre Calgary production; Whittaker liked both the original Theatre Calgary production in 1973 and the 1974 Stratford premier (with a revised script); Freedman, however, was scathing and Kareda called Sitting Bull, in the original production, a "catastrophe" (qtd. by Page, 15).

[8] For a good discussion of *Walsh* and *Fair Liberty's Call*, see Nothof, "Crossing Borders." Several scholars consider the changes Pollock made to *Walsh*; see, for example, Gilbert, Page and Salter. In my view *Whiskey Six Cadenza* does not fulfill its promise as history or as theatre because the historical issues (Prohibition, mining hardships) lack the importance and epic scale of the issues addressed in *Walsh* or *Fair Liberty's Call* and the complex theatre metaphors of the play exceed their necessary grounding in fact or character. For a more positive reading of the play, see Walker, 167–76.

[9] These haunting words, said by Joan, Annie and Eddie, are heard as "*a taped montage*" over the opening speeches of the play and while we watch Eddie silently take a piece of paper from her pocket, wipe blood from it, and then fold it to put back in her pocket (19–20). Although we do not yet appreciate what we are hearing and seeing, these words, this scene, and this piece of paper will return in the closing moments of the play, when we will finally understand the symbolic, ritual importance of what we have just witnessed.

[10] New Brunswick was created in 1784 as a separate province from Nova Scotia because of the large influx of Loyalists into the Maritimes, but as early as 1783, under the leadership of Edward Winslow, it looked as if a Committee of Fifty-five wealthy families, which had come together in New York City prior to their exodus, would be allowed to control the majority of land and set themselves up as the elite ruling class. However, their ambitions were curtailed by a British policy granting a more equitable distribution of Crown lands (see Moore, 190–200). The battle at Yorktown, Virginia in 1781 was a serious defeat for the British and their Loyalist supporters, but it was not the end of the Revolution or the only reason why Loyalists fled the Thirteen Colonies. Far more decisive for the Loyalists' future was the 1783 Treaty of Separation signed by Britain and setting out terms for the independence

of the United States of America. This Treaty, more than any one battle, sealed the fate of families like the Roberts who were betrayed by Britain as well as by the American Patriots. Numbers vary for the Loyalists who came to Canada, but historians place the influx at between 40,000 and 50,000. Of these some returned to the States, but a large majority of those who settled in New Brunswick stayed. Loyalists faced violent persecution and the confiscation of all property in the States; return, therefore, was not easy. Pollock has drawn deeply on this rich, complex, and little-known history for dates, certain facts, songs of the day, and even for names. For historical details see Brown and Senior, and Moore.

11 As always in these things, the American revolution was a war of rhetoric. The term "liberty" carried enormous ideological baggage and was invoked by both sides of the struggle. It became, in American revolutionary practice, part of the rhetoric of dissent. Those who fought for liberty could only be "Patriots," another loaded term; everyone else was a traitor. No viable middle ground was allowed and freedoms of many kinds—to speak out, to debate, to disagree in any way—were curtailed. Pollock's use of the word "liberty" in her title is ironic and nuanced.

12 This business of the indenture papers, one copy kept by Wullie, the other by Taylor, constitutes some of the most significant stage business in the play. When Eddie burns Wullie's copy (57), I am reminded of Catherine in *Doc* who frees herself and her father from the guilt of the past by burning a letter. For me this burning remains troubling, insufficient and incomplete. In *Fair Liberty's Call*, however, the document must first be read, then destroyed twice, and the past it represents is unequivocally evil. In short, its destruction *works.*

13 There are many approaches to this splendid play and mine here is only one, partial reading. In a specifically feminist, structural analysis I would want to focus more closely on Act Two, where the stage, characters and language are split and counter-pointed to illustrate the profound differences between a masculine and feminine logic. Moreover, the series of confrontations that charts the escalating aggression among the men is gradually absorbed and deflected by the reasoning of the women who turn a hostage-taking into freedom and forgiveness. When they *act* it is to confiscate the men's weapons, release their horses, and allow Anderson his freedom. Significantly, it is only the cross-dressed (transgendered?) Eddie who can and will pass from one side to the other. For a theoretical discussion of feminist structures and "feminine endings," see Case, and McLary.

14 In her most recent work, *Moving Pictures* and *Angel's Trumpet*, Pollock takes historical figures, in both cases women artists, and explores their lives *as* women and artists. In these plays, Pollock's interests in the figure of the artist, feminism, and history come together in powerful theatrical experiences. I have discussed *Moving Pictures* in "Creating the Girl from God's Country."

15 One of the most extraordinary plays recently published in Canada is George Elliott Clark's *Beatrice Chancy*, which is set in 18th century Nova Scotia and reveals the full horror of slavery on Canadian soil.

Works Cited

Anderson, Benedict. *Imagined Communities: Reflections on the Origin and Spread of Nationalism.* London: Verso, 1991.

Bessai, Diane. "Canadian Docu-Drama." *Canadian Theatre Review* 16 (1977): 7–10.

Brady, Owen E. "*Fair Liberty's Call.*" *Theatre Journal* 46.2 (1994): 272–74.

Butler, Judith. "Performative Acts and Gender Constitution: An Essay in Phenomenology and Feminist Theory." *Performing Feminisms: Feminist Critical Theory and Theatre.* Ed. Sue-Ellen Case. Baltimore: Johns Hopkins P, 1990. 270–82.

Brown, Wallace and Hereward Senior. *Victorious in Defeat: The Loyalists in Canada.* New York: Methuen, 1984.

Case, Sue-Ellen. *Feminism and Theatre.* New York: Methuen, 1988.

Choy, Wayson. *The Jade Peony.* Vancouver: Douglas & McIntyre, 1995.

Chung, Kathy K.Y. "'Lookin' to a better world for our children': The Concept of Inheritance in *Fair Liberty's Call.*" Nothof, *Sharon Pollock* 151–66.

Clark, George Elliott. *Beatrice Chancy.* Victoria, B.C.: Polestar, 1999.

Frye, Northrop. *The Bush Garden.* Toronto: Anansi, 1971.

Gilbert, Reid. "Sharon Pollock." *Profiles in Canadian Literature* 6. Ed Jeffrey M. Heath. Toronto: Dundurn, 1986. 113–20.

Godfrey, Stephen. "Debate soars above earthbound historical drama." *The Globe and Mail* 29 January 1988. D11.

Grace, Sherrill. *Regression and Apocalypse: Studies in North American Literary Expressionism.* Toronto: U of Toronto P, 1989.

———. "Creating the Girl from God's Country." *Canadian Literature* 172. 33 (2002). 98–117.

———. "Sharon Pollock's Portraits of the Artist." *Theatre Research in Canada/Recherches théâtrales au Canada* 22.2 (2001): 124–38.

Grace, Sherrill and Gabriele Helms. "Documenting Racism: Sharon Pollock's *The Komagata Maru Incident.*" *Painting the Maple: Essays on Race, Gender, and the Construction of Canada.* Ed. V. Strong-Boag, S. Grace, A. Eisenberg, and J. Anderson. Vancouver: U of British Columbia P, 1998. 85–99.

Ignatieff, Michael. *Blood & Belonging: Journeys into the New Nationalism.* Toronto: Viking, 1993.

Joyce, James. *Ulysses.* London: The Bodley Head, 1960.

Knowles, Richard Paul. "Replaying History: Canadian Historiographic Metadrama." *Dalhousie Review* 67.214 (1987): 229–43.

Li, Peter. *The Chinese in Canada.* Toronto: Oxford UP, 1988.

McClary, Susan. *Feminine Endings: Music, Gender, and Sexuality.* Minnesota: U of Minnesota P, 1991.

Moore, Christopher. *The Loyalists: Revolution, Exile, Settlement.* 1984. Toronto: McLelland and Stewart, 1994.

Nothof, Anne. "Crossing Borders: Sharon Pollock's Revisitation of Canadian Frontiers." *Modern Drama* 38.4 (1995): 475–87.

———. "Interview with Sharon Pollock." in Nothof, *Sharon Pollock* 167–79.

———, ed. *Sharon Pollock: Essays on her Work.* Toronto: Guernica, 2001.

Nunn, Robert. "Performing Fact: Canadian Documentary Theatre." *Canadian Literature* 103 (1984): 51–62.

———. "Sharon Pollock's Plays: A Review Article." 1984. Nothof, *Sharon Pollock* 27–43.

Page, Malcolm. "Sharon Pollock: Committed Playwright." Nothof, *Sharon Pollock* 12–25.

Pollock, Sharon. *Doc.* Toronto: Playwright Canada, 1984.

———. *End Dream. Sharon Pollock: Three Plays.* Toronto: Playwrights Canada, 2003. 97–163.

———. *Fair Liberty's Call.* Toronto: Coach House, 1995.

———. Introduction, *The Komagata Maru Incident.* 226.

———. *The Komagata Maru Incident. Six Canadian Plays.* Toronto: Playwrights Canada, 1992. 224–86.

———. *Walsh.* Vancouver: Talonbooks 1973.

Rubin, Don. "Celebrating the Nation: History and the Canadian Theatre." *Canadian Theatre Review* (Spring 1982): 12–22.

Salter, Denis. "(Im)possible Worlds: The Plays of Sharon Pollock." *The Sharon Pollock Papers*, ed. Apollonia Steele. Calgary: U of Calgary P, 1989. xi–xxxv.

Schlemmer, Kate. *Disposing of the Dead.* Unpublished play, 1996.

Walker, Craig Stewart. *The Buried Astrolabe: Canadian Dramatic Imagination and Western Tradition.* Montreal: McGill-Queen's UP, 2001.

Whittaker, Herbert. "*Walsh* beautiful, tedious too." *The Globe and Mail* 13 November 1973. 16.

———. "*Walsh* serves up sad history straight." *The Globe and Mail* 25 July 1974. 13.

Worthen, W.B. "Drama, Performativity, and Performance." *PMLA* 113.5 (1998): 1093–1107.

Appropriated Voice in Sharon Pollock's *Angel's Trumpet*

by Anne Nothof

> They were all happy to exist in a man's world—they preserved their individuality through men and not by opposition to them. They would all three have made alternatively good courtesans or good wives not by the accident of birth but through the greater accident of finding their man or not finding him.
>
> (F. Scott Fitzgerald, *Tender is the Night* 53)

In all of her plays, Sharon Pollock is interested in the significance of the recording process as much as in the recorded subject. In her programme note for the premiere production of *Angel's Trumpet* by Theatre Junction at the Dr. Betty Mitchell Theatre, Calgary in March 2001, she points to the question that is central to the play: "[W]here does the truth lie? In the living of our lives, or in the multiple ways and means we have of recording them?" [1] *Angel's Trumpet* continues Pollock's exploration of creative women who struggle against social inhibitors and prescribed roles to express their own desires and needs, playing out their lives in multivalent, self-created roles. In *Moving Pictures* (1999) Pollock places the life of Canadian filmmaker Nell Shipman on stage; in *End Dream* (2000) she plays out the last minutes in the life of a Scottish nanny as that character dreams her own murder. The subject of *Angel's Trumpet* is Zelda Sayre Fitzgerald—painter, writer, dancer, wife and mother. *Angel's Trumpet* is further complicated by the issue of the appropriation of another's creativity, and of another's life. It raises the question of whether the encoding of another's life as "fiction" is an act of exploitation. Scott Fitzgerald writes the life of his wife, Zelda, as fiction, and when she attempts to reclaim it in her own writing, he insists on ownership—both of the words and of the woman. In showing Zelda's resistance to appropriation and objectification by her husband, Pollock plays her as continually reinventing herself and always in process. Zelda performs her life as self-conscious autobiography. Resistance to appropriation is effected through shifting, multiple role-playing. [2]

In *Angel's Trumpet* Pollock portrays the aesthetic and emotional relationship of Zelda and Scott as confrontational and destructive—a struggle over the artistic ownership of lived experience. In her programme note she provides an interpretation of this conflict that reveals her preoccupation with appropriation and exploitation—the "use" that artists make of the lives of others: "[...] the nature of the ownership of a life and its transformation into a literary (or dramatic) text, and whether one individual's urge to self-expression can be justifiably sacrificed if it's deemed necessary for the self-expression of a genius." In effect, she also challenges her own use of Zelda's life to interrogate personal and public aesthetic and moral conundrums.

Zelda's life has been freely inscribed in the novels and stories of her husband, whereas her own works remain literary and autobiographical curiosities. Despite the attempts of her grandchildren to recuperate her writing and painting in collections published in the 1990s, her life is still more an object of scrutiny than her art, as is evidenced by the publication of yet another biography in 2002 entitled *Sometimes Madness is Wisdom: Zelda and Scott Fitzgerald: a Marriage* by Kendall Taylor, and an essay entitled "How Crazy Was Zelda?" by clinical psychiatrist Peter D. Kramer, published in the *New York Times Magazine* in 1996, which occasioned a flurry of letters in defence of Zelda. In the 1970s feminist critics recast her as a symbolic victim of patriarchal oppression and as a paradigm for suppressed creativity—another woman trapped behind "Yellow Wallpaper" and driven mad by her male "caregivers." Her death by fire in Highland Hospital was transmuted into an image of transcendence, Jane Eyre's alter ego reborn from the flames.

In the introduction to *The Collected Writings* Zelda's daughter, Frances Fitzgerald Lanahan Smith (Scottie), denies the accuracy of this martyr script—although it "reads well, and will probably remain part of the 'Scott and Zelda' mythology forever" (v). From Scottie's point of view, her mother "was surprisingly emancipated" (vi) for a woman born in 1900 in the American South. She more or less did what she pleased in her personal and social life, acting out the part of a flapper in the 1920s—a role which she characterized in one of her essays entitled "What Became of the Flappers?": "I believe in the flapper as an artist in her particular field, the art of being—being young, being lovely, being an object" (*Collected Writings* 398). Scottie interprets her parents' relationship as symbiotic, one of mutual love, dependence and exploitation. In her opinion, her father "greatly appreciated and encouraged his wife's unusual talents and ebullient imagination" (v). He arranged a showing of her paintings in New York in 1934; supported the production of what he considered her "woefully bad" farce, *Scandalabra* (qtd. in Milford 278); edited her short stories; and paid for her ballet lessons in France for three years when she was in her late twenties. According to Scottie, although "[h]e did raise a terrible row when she published her novel, *Save Me the Waltz* [...] this sort of competition is traditionally the bane of literary romances" (vi). Zelda's letters to her husband, most written when she was voluntarily hospitalized, are full of her expressions of love for him, of her admiration for his writing talent, and of apology (although her "contrite tone" may be read as ironic):

> Your dear letter made me feel very self-condemnatory. I have often told you that I am that little fish who swims about under a shark and, I believe, lives indelicately on its offal. Anyway, that is the way I am. Life moves over me in a vast black shadow and I swallow whatever it drops with relish, having learned in a very hard school that one cannot be both a parasite and enjoy self-nourishment without moving in worlds too fantastic for even my disordered imagination to people with meaning. (*Collected Writings* 465)

Despite this apparent self-deprecation, however, Zelda wanted to serve something greater than herself, and to lose herself in the process. In her autobiographical novel, *Save Me the Waltz*, her heroine, Alabama, experiences a forgetfulness of self that creates a truer self through her rigorous ballet practices: "By springtime, she was gladly, savagely proud of the strengths of her Negroid hips, convex as boats in a wood carving. The complete control of her body freed her from all fetid consciousness of it [...]. Her life outside was like trying to remember in the morning a dream from the night before" (*Collected Writings* 127).[3]

Both Zelda and Scott wrote novels based on their marriage: *Save Me the Waltz* by Zelda in 1930, and *Tender is the Night* by Scott in 1932. Zelda sent her MS, considered by her biographer Nancy Milford to be "so deeply autobiographical, the transmutation of art into reality is incomplete" (224), to Scribner's before Scott had seen it. Her novel had been written over a period of two months while she was hospitalized for schizophrenia. Fearing that her novel would pre-empt his own, based on similar material, and on which he had been working for the past four years, Scott wired Scribner's that Zelda's novel would "seriously compromise what literary future she may have and cause inconceivable harm in its present form" (qtd. from Milford 217). When this attempt to block publication failed, he insisted that Zelda cut or change a significant portion.

Angel's Trumpet focuses on one confrontational episode between Zelda and Scott, based on the account provided in Nancy Milford's 1970 biography *Zelda.* In 1933 Scott Fitzgerald requested that Zelda's psychiatrist, Dr. Rennie, meet with them at their home in Baltimore, ironically named "La Paix," to prove that she was incapable of making her own decisions, and to assert his authority over her course of "treatment." In particular, however, he wanted to establish, personally and legally, whether he could stop her writing—because it affected her health, and because it undermined his own writing career. Milford describes Dr. Rennie as "intensely interested in literature" and an aspiring playwright (260). He was fascinated by both husband and wife, and tried to check the deterioration of their relationship, which he saw as having three parts: the struggle between them as creative artists, each jealous of the other; the conflict caused within Zelda by trying to have a career as a writer, while at the same time fulfilling her obligations of home and marriage; the conflict caused by each not performing the "roles" required of each other (see Milford 261).

Pollock dramatizes this "interview" in terms of a trial, with the doctor (renamed Renton) as arbitrator or referee more than a judge. Initially, he provides Scott with the opportunity to state his case, questioning him on significant details. The "character" of Zelda is created through this male interaction while she sits silently, her back to the audience, or prowls around the periphery of the room. Once Zelda begins to speak, Dr. Renton says little, functioning as an unwilling and conflicted witness to the verbal and emotional violence, ineffectually attempting to interject some reason into the process, and easily silenced by Scott. The other witness is a silent stenographer who exactly records the words of Scott and Zelda. Pollock specifically identifies the significance of the stenographer in the stage directions: "*The sound* [of the keys] *as*

LAHEURSA transcribes and records the meeting provides an aural counterpoint to, and comment on, the spoken words, as well as on their transformation from spoken to written with attendant interpretive variance" (168). The fictional name of the stenographer suggests her heuristic function—"allowing or assisting to discover" (*The Oxford Canadian* 662). Her black coat has a red lining, suggesting her creative, transformative significance—like Zelda's red ballet slipper that lies on the floor beneath a charred and skeletal minimalist sculpture, and her dress "in shades of red to pink" (169), anticipating the fire that consumes her in the hospital fifteen years after this meeting. Laheursa speaks the first word in the play—"Zelda"—announcing the woman whose life will be the subject of public scrutiny; then she is silent. Only the tapping of the keys indicates the recording of the interrogation and response. It is Scott who insists that every word be recorded: "It has standing with Zelda and me. The words. Material. Concrete. Captured. Not ephemeral. Eternal. Enduring. I endure. I endure" (172). At the end of the play, however, Laheursa hands the complete transcript to Zelda, who scatters the pages, suggesting that the words belong finally to her, to do with as she wishes. Although Scott has instigated the recording of her words, he cannot own them. They are transcribed by someone (significantly a woman under his direction), but in the transcribing they are transferred to a more public domain, to be "read" by whoever has access to them. In delivering them to Zelda, Laheursa signals that since they are the words that record her life, she should disseminate them as she wishes. Pollock's stage directions describing Zelda's response suggest both her acknowledgement and disinterest: "*ZELDA looks at the first page, it drifts to the floor, similarly so the second. All of the manuscript pages slowly rain from ZELDA's hands down onto the red slippers as music grows*" (224). She denies Scott ownership of her words.

Pollock uses the words of Zelda and Scott from Milford's excerpts of the 114-page transcript to paint their backgrounds. Scott Fitzgerald had given the young resident physician, Dr. Rennie, a detailed case history, describing Zelda's wild youth, her promiscuity, her unusual relationship with her parents. Many of Zelda's and Scott's words in Pollock's play are taken verbatim from this transcript; for example Scott's rhetorical question, "Shall we go back to Zelda hanging off her mother's teat till the year she was three? Spoilt rotten by ... her mother Minnie! Her father Judge Sayre, and the whole wretched family who now blame me for her condition" (186–87). Zelda's responses are described by Milford, and dramatized by Pollock as unruly but meaningful:

> If her thoughts were unruly, they nevertheless carried enormous meaning to Scott and it was from an emotional rather than a rational language of meaning that she wrote. Its limits, and they were severe, were that she depended on too private a mode of communication. (Milford 212)

In effect, then, Milford as biographer functions as the stenographer/transcriber of their confrontation, and Pollock transposes the recorded words into art. She effects the artistic aspirations of her subject, Zelda, who explained in a letter to Scott that she wanted "to open some new facet of the stark emotion or to preserve some old one in the grace of a phrase" (*Collected Writings* xxvi).

Initially, Zelda is silent in *Angel's Trumpet*. Scott begins the trial with a command—"Now. To begin" (169), and instructs Dr. Renton how to position the three chairs for each participant—like a stage manager or director of the play to follow. He bullies Dr. Renton into compliance, threatening to sabotage his professional ambitions and to stonewall his chances of publishing. He clearly outlines his priorities—the survival of his work, his child, himself, his wife. He delineates his own role as protector and provider, and Zelda's as helpmate, mother and muse. By engaging in "competitive work" she has undermined his authority. However, although his words are threatening and egotistical—"if the ultimate price to be paid for my survival, is her sanity ... then that is the price that must be paid" (183)—Pollock tempers his autocratic posturing with his memory of an earlier, almost idolatrous relationship with Zelda:

> I admit it! I loved her courage, the supreme self-confidence and untutored defiant intelligence. I loved the absence of any feeling of inferiority, the lack of self-doubt or regret, I loved the sincerity and the selfishness. Utterly selfish. I loved the flawless skin, the savage eyes, and the burnished hair, I loved the covetous glances, I loved knowing what others sought, I had. (188)

It is also evident, however, that Scott has created Zelda to suit his own needs and desires.

When she finally does speak, Zelda rejects his objectification of her: "He thought he could wear me like a rose" (188), although she also admits that she "played the role well when it suited" (188). Early in their marriage both played other roles in a drama that vacillated between farce and tragedy: "Each of us thought we were the major character in our own sensational tale [...]. I was his fictional girl, and I loved him" (194). Zelda has enjoyed and exploited the roles provided for her by Scott, but she now struggles towards creative and personal independence, to speak and write her own words, instead of reading a script he has provided. The verbal duel which comprises the rest of the play bears a strong resemblance to Edward Albee's *Who's Afraid of Virginia Woolf?* The Fitzgeralds' past disappointments and failures—infidelities, alcoholism, abortions—become ammunition in the struggle for survival. The balance between mutual destructiveness and co-dependence is precarious. Zelda reminds Scott that he has used her words—from letters and diaries—in his stories and novels, that she has provided the model for Daisy in *The Great Gatsby*. She asserts that her own words should count, that she should count. She will write out of her whole body and mind:

> I will write! With this!
> *Her hand to heart. Her actions will grow increasingly violent as she mounts an attack on herself.*
> And this! *(clutches her stomach)*
> And this! *(both arms embrace herself)*
> And these! *(strikes her legs and falls to her knees)*
> And this! And this! And this! *(holds both her hands out and up, hitting at herself)* What these have seen and heard! *(her eyes and ears)*
> [. .]
> And what has come from here! *(her mouth)*
> While splintered shards of meaning
> *Striking her head with both hands, flailing at herself as SCOTT struggles to hold her, speaking softly under her words, crooning to her as if she were a baby, while she continues over his words.*
> turn and twist in here but sometimes still and beautiful! Muddled! Disjointed! Out of tune and out of time you tell me but it's all I have to Shape and Mold! What else can I make something from, but this Poor Thing? It's all I have, why can't I? It's mine! Why not? (220)

Scott comforts her and whispers his love for her, but undermines her need to write her life with his opinion of her as a third-rate writer, whereas he is a writer "of some talent and genius" (221). As is typically the case in Pollock's plays, both sides of the case are convincingly expressed. Despite Zelda's emotional appeal for self-expression, Scott's judgment of their writing has been echoed in subsequent critical assessments. Zelda's life and art have been of interest only because of her association with him. Pollock's personal view of Zelda's art, however, is sympathetic; "her writing is very rich with metaphor and interesting insight and intuitive leaps" marked by "wonderfully creative and free descriptions of the thought processes" (qtd. in Clark ES6). Her words *are* worth hearing.

Zelda remains undefeated in *Angel's Trumpet.* Like the actress, Kate, who assumes the direction of the murderous scenario in Pollock's *Saucy Jack*, she foresees her antagonist's final exit, in this case Scott's anti-climactic death in his Hollywood apartment: "Putting his writing aside, eating a chocolate bar, while reading the football news from Princeton. His fluttering heart? Like a sparrow in a bully's fist. Stopped" (223). And she envisions her own death as an apotheosis: "Highland Hospital. Top floor. Doors locked. Windows barred. Six women consumed by fire. Zelda Sayre. Fitzgerald. Identified by a slipper that lies beneath some bones. Realized at last! Transformed! Transcendent in the flames!" (223). She has lived and died like the wild young women she emulated in Owen Johnson's 1914 novel *The Salamander*: "adventurous, eager and unafraid" (qtd. from Mallick's review of *Sometimes Madness is Wisdom*). Pollock was particularly intrigued by Zelda's reference to herself as a salamander—a mythical creature "that can live in fire and be transformed by it. It cannot actually die" (qtd. from Clark ES6). Zelda's life is transformed through her own words, and those of Scott Fitzgerald, and these in turn have been transformed into a dramatic investigation of the process of creativity.

Like Scott Fitzgerald, Sharon Pollock uses Zelda's words in *Angel's Trumpet* to make her own point about appropriation of voice. She speculates on the "property" which is transposed into art, using the words of one of Zelda's many letters to Scott, in which she cites Aristotle to clarify her opinion on the relationship between life and art, in effect sanctioning Scott's "transposition" of *her* life: "he said that all emotion and experience were common property—that the transposition of these into form was individual and art [...] to open some new facet of the stark emotions or to preserve some old one in the grace of a phrase seem nearer the artistic end" (qtd. in Gordon). For Pollock, "the conundrum of the artist" (Clark ES6) in *Angel's Trumpet* is complicated by the constraints and assumptions of society in respect to women's roles, which result in an inhibiting self-censorship and a compliance that often results in exploitation. In Pollock's play, Zelda plays out the highly conflicted role of self-assertion and self-denial: she is both artist and model, integral voice, and appropriated voice. As Pollock explains in Bob Clark's review of *Angel's Trumpet* for the *Calgary Herald*:

> Recently it's been a female character who is unable to conform to what is expected of her (or whose) sense of herself doesn't conform to what she's told she should be .... Here is someone who began as a very strong individual ... and who gradually through pressure begins to self-censor and to become what others say they [sic] are—as a means of defence or even as a means of perverse victory when they have very little avenue for real victory. (ES6)

Pollock appraises the personal price paid by a willful, creative woman for her art. And, as in her other dramatizations of strong-minded, imaginative women—*Blood Relations, Moving Pictures, End Dream*—the price is high: madness, isolation, or early death. Zelda's death by fire at the age of 48 is presaged from the beginning of *Angel's Trumpet*—from the flame that flares from Scott's cigarette lighter, and the red slipper which she holds in her hand.

The play's title also alludes to Zelda's creative and destructive proclivities: Angel's Trumpet is a poisonous lily that grows in the American South where Zelda was born in 1900, one of six children of a judge in Montgomery, Alabama. Zelda was fascinated with bold and exotic southern flowers, and was particularly fond of calla lilies as subjects for her paintings. They exhibit a disturbing, menacing beauty, recalling the psychic distortions of the works of Vincent van Gogh, whose work she found both repellent and seductive: "Those crawling flowers and venomous vindictive blossoms are the hallucinations of a mad-man—without organization or rhythm but with the power to sting and strangle" (qtd. in Milford 215).

In *Angel's Trumpet*, Zelda's schizophrenia functions as both a metaphor for creativity and as the consequence of a repressed creativity. Her illness signals the appropriation of her life and words by the individual on whom she was emotionally dependent and whose dominance she resisted. *Angel's Trumpet* may also suggest the Last Judgment and Zelda's religious obsessions and visions, which she expressed through her portraits of contorted nude angels. In the end, however, the last judgment of her life and art is left with the audience.

(2004)

Notes

[1] My thanks to Sharon Pollock for providing a copy of the unpublished MS of *Angel's Trumpet* for the first draft of this paper, presented at the conference of the Association for Canadian Theatre Research at the University of Toronto, May 2001. Sharon Pollock also directed the world premiere of *Angel's Trumpet.*

[2] In her essay, "Sharon Pollock's Portraits of the Artist," Sherrill Grace locates these fragmented elements of self-representation, self-invention and self-discovery in Pollock's plays through the practice of "autobiographics" (125).

[3] This philosophy has some resonance with that of Margaret, the farm wife in Pollock's play *Generations* and (one is tempted to suspect) with Pollock's own belief.

Works Cited

Clark, Bob. "Beautiful damned: New Play explores the ill-fated marriage of Scott and Zelda Fitzgerald." *Calgary Herald* 3 March 2001: ES6.

Fitzgerald, F. Scott. *Tender is the Night.* New York: Charles Scribner's, 1933, 1971.

Fitzgerald, Zelda. *The Collected Writings.* Ed. Matthew J. Bruccoli. Tuscaloosa: U of Alabama P, 1991.

Gordon, Mary. "Introduction." Zelda Fitzgerald, *Collected Writings* xv–xxvii.

Grace, Sherrill. "Sharon Pollock's Portraits of the Artist." *Theatre Research in Canada/Recherches Théâtrales au Canada* 22.2 (2001): 124–38.

Kramer, Peter D. "How Crazy Was Zelda?" *New York Times Magazine.* 1 December 1996. http://query.nytimes.com/gst/fullpage.html. Accessed 28 January 2008.

"Legend of Zelda." March 1, 2006. http://www.poprocks.com/zelda/zeldabody.html. Accessed 28 January 2008.

Mallick, Heather. "Zelda: Beautiful, Brilliant and Booze-Battered." Rev. of *Sometimes Madness is Wisdom: Zelda and Scott Fitzgerald: a Marriage* by Kendall Taylor. *The Globe and Mail* 1 Sept. 2001: D9.

Milford, Nancy. *Zelda: A Biography.* New York: Harper and Row, 1970.

Oxford Canadian Dictionary, The. Toronto: Ed. Katherine Barber. Toronto: Oxford UP, 1998.

Pollock, Sharon. *Angel's Trumpet. Sharon Pollock Three Plays.* Toronto: Playwrights Canada, 2003. 166–224.

———. Programme note for "Angel's Trumpet." Calgary: Theatre Junction, February 2001.

Indigenous Women Living Beyond the Grave: From Pollock to Pechawis

by Michelle La Flamme

for Vanessa Lee Buckner[1]

Throughout her career Sharon Pollock has consistently managed to write plays that explore complex power dynamics surrounding gendered and racialized relationships in Canada's historical and contemporary landscape. The essays in this volume attest to the fact that much of the criticism on Pollock's work focuses on her interest in politics, power, privilege, and feminist struggles. In *The Making of Warriors*, Pollock uses the stories of "warrior" characters to document the existence of two historical figures who risked social ostracism and death by standing up for their political ideals. Originally written as a radio play (1991), and later revised for the second stage production in Edmonton in 2003, *The Making of Warriors* dramatizes the intersections between three women's lives: an innocent witness/bystander, a Canadian Aboriginal political martyr, and a white American abolitionist.[2] By weaving together their stories, Pollock's play offers a transnational and crossracial feminist vision of collective political action.

The stage version of *The Making of Warriors* has just been published (2008) and is usually overlooked in the scholarship that addresses Pollock's feminist vision. I am interested in Pollock's representation of indigeneity and start my analysis by placing this representation in the context of the structure of the play and then thinking through Pollock's method for including an indigenous character within the inclusive feminism that the play advances. My secondary interest is in placing Pollock's representation of indigeneity within the context of other Canadian performances that, like Pollock's play, double as elegies for murdered Aboriginal women. These plays and performances mark moments of collective remembering in Canadian theatre history and are important means of commemoration that have the potential to transform the trauma of the past.

The characters in *The Making of Warriors* are identified in their respective roles as Eloise, a kind of everywoman figure who is a witness/innocent bystander, Sarah Moore Grimké, a nineteenth-century American suffragette who is enraged at the abuse of slaves and takes up the abolitionist cause, and Anna Mae Pictou Aquash, an Aboriginal activist from Nova Scotia who became involved in the American Indian Movement. Grimké and Aquash are based on real women and Eloise is a fictional character. By offering this diverse set of perspectives, Pollock asks her readers and audience to position themselves somewhere within this spectrum: Do we silently witness the tragedies that befall others, do we take up the cause of the "Other," or are we within the category of "Other," according to the largely white hegemony in North America?

In order to address the structural features of Pollock's play and her representation of indigenous activist Anna Mae Aquash, a brief note on the genesis of this play is needed. *The Making of Warriors* was first commissioned by CBC radio for "Morningside" as part of a festival of plays linked to the Second International Women Playwrights' festival of 1992. According to Ann Jansen, the medium allowed Pollock to play "with the narrative and timely possibilities of drama on radio for a purpose, to reshape the histories at hand" (90). Jansen argues that radio drama allows for "various styles of narration and [that] its fluid time-shifting, can break the usual forward momentum of a told story" (87). It is important to keep in mind that the form of Pollock's drama, the choral delivery of the lines and its content were developed initially for radio. Pollock used the medium of radio and this form of delivery to create an internal coherence from these disparate stories by assembling the disembodied voices of three women. Their choral speeches threaded their disparate lives into a single unified voice of resistance that was wonderfully suited to the medium of radio.

Pollock utilizes four principal methods to structure *The Making of Warriors* in both the stage and radio script. She uses overlapping dialogue and choral delivery of lines to offer an interconnected multiple character-driven narrative that presents the feminist struggle for emancipation as an ethos that transcends history and unites women across racial and national boundaries; she uses a third-person perspective to offer a crossracial examination of three women; she develops the role of the witness character who sees what she later discovers was the scene of the murder of Aquash, in order to create tension between the binaries of silence/voice and action/passivity as a means for meditating on the audience's complicity in silencing this story; and, she brings Aquash's story to bear on the other narratives in a way that allows the impact of her life to extend beyond the moment of her death. This final structural feature connects Pollock's play to two other Canadian plays that use different narrative means to represent the death of Aboriginal women as the start of intergenerational emancipation: Yvette Nolan's *Annie Mae's Movement* and Marie Clements's *The Unnatural and Accidental Women.* I will compare Pollock's representation of indigeneity to other representations of indigenous women in the latter half of this essay.

Because both Grimké and Aquash were real historical women, Pollock's versions of their lives are interesting to analyze. I am particularly interested in how the biography of Aquash is retold through Pollock's vision of her as a warrior. By pairing Grimké's and Aquash's struggles for emancipation in their respective "warrior" narratives, Pollock invites the audience to consider the ways in which their "warrior" narratives contain similar elements despite the century that separated these two historical figures. Such a narrative strategy is inevitably emancipatory because Pollock has refused to allow these two women's stories to fade into obscurity. As Jansen accurately notes, their activities and their lives are "on the margins of history: Grimké's activities are recorded, but little known, while Aquash's murder was hushed up and her story has faded from public discourse" (90). By bringing these stories to bear upon each other, Pollock's play unmasks the historical silencing of their struggles in Canada and the United States, in the nineteenth and twentieth centuries, and across racial lines, to present a crossracial, transhistoric and transnational feminist performance.

Pollock adds a third woman, Eloise, who is neither a warrior nor a character based on the life of an actual woman, to provide the audience with a person they can identify with. The witness role of this character highlights the audience's role as listener/spectator because it is placed within the context of the "warrior" stories. The murder of Aquash is made palpable through Eloise's recollections of what she saw at the scene where the murder took place. Using Eloise's recollections as the means by which we imagine the murder scene is a somewhat more ominous method of presenting Aquash's murder and it is a fitting choice for a radio play which, by necessity of the medium, demands some form of aural representation. Hearing Eloise tell us what she saw when she drove past the murder scene encourages audience members to identify with this innocent bystander and wonder what they would have done in similar circumstances.

Although the title refers to warriors, according to Cynthia Zimmerman, the play is "about idealists, activists, not soldiers" (92). The three strands of the radio narrative include "historical dramatization, a documentary account, and a personal reminiscence" (92). Sarah Moore Grimké's life is dramatized, Anna Mae Pictou Aquash's life is delivered in the form of a news report, and Eloise's lines are delivered as personal reminiscence. In the very structure of the play, Pollock has shown a certain amount of what Zimmerman refers to as "self-consciousness about the vantage point, [and] the limited perspective, of the storyteller" (92). Pollock writes about these women in such a way that we believe "the ideals they fought for did not die with them" (93). In bringing these stories forward, Pollock is heralding the hope for new warriors to emerge. How Pollock achieves these ideals, and the way in which she utilizes indigeneity to further these large ideals, will be evident after a close analysis of the structural features that Pollock employs in order to bring these women's stories to the stage.

The first stage production of this play was difficult for the actors because Pollock had initially written it for radio and the script had no stage directions. However, this omission also offered freedom to the actors who worked on the first production of *The Making of Warriors* by Calgary's Native theatre company, Crazy Horse Theatre. During rehearsal they had a certain amount of latitude to interpret the dialogue and they were encouraged by the director, Coral Larsen, to find innovative ways to stage this play.[3] There are two other aspects of the stage production that are noteworthy here. *The Making of Warriors* was the first play that was written by a non-Native woman to be produced by this company at the Pumphouse Theatre in October 5–14, 2000. A crucial aspect of the allure of this play for Aboriginal audiences can be attributed to Pollock's representation of the Aquash character. The lines Aquash delivers bring the history of women who were involved in the American Indian Movement into focus. Secondly, the fact that Crazy Horse Theatre chose to mount this play and, interestingly, cast Aboriginal women in each of the roles, suggests that Pollock's work has something of value for Aboriginal communities. The stage production of this play and this unique casting choice transformed the disembodied voices of the radio play into a play that brought the thematic issue of Aboriginal embodiment, symbolically and, quite literally, to the stage.

Interestingly, Pollock sketches crucial moments in the lives of the white characters, but the sketch given of Aquash's life is left to the basic facts of her existence. Liz Nichols reviewed the stage play and has referred to Pollock's narrative structure as "a hybrid of documentary, dramatization and editorial." The play is also a fictionalized biography that opens with the act of remembering and witnessing, after which we are drawn into the stories and lives of three women. Aquash's lines concentrate on the retelling of the complicated political events that led up to, and resulted in, the November 1972 occupation of the Bureau of Indian Affairs in Washington. The following seventy-one day occupation of the village of Wounded Knee on the Pine Ridge Reservation that began February 27, 1973 is referred to as historical fact by the Aquash character. This occupation involved supporters of the Oglala Sioux Civil Rights organization and members of the American Indian Movement, including Aquash. In the play, we are informed by Aquash that the FBI arrested her and requested information about other AIM members in exchange for dropping the charges against her. In Pollock's retelling of Aquash's involvement with the FBI, the character refuses to divulge the requested information about the other AIM members and remains true to her principles. Pollock has chosen to represent this character as a warrior rather than as a traitor.

Although there has been, and continues to be, a dispute about Aquash's involvement with the FBI and the murderers have never been positively identified, Pollock's *version* of the events surrounding Aquash's death are presented as facts and not as subjective opinions. Pollock's presentation of the biographical details of Aquash's life sets the context for her fictionalized version of the events that led to the murder. This biographical information creates a higher truth-value for the claims about her refusal to implicate members of AIM in exchange for her own freedom. Because Pollock has this character deliver the factual aspects of Aquash's life (her date of birth, her political activities, her movement across the border at key moments in her life) *and* these details regarding Aquash's unbroken commitment to her ideals, the disputed "facts" regarding her complicity with the FBI, are represented as "truth." Pollock creates a barely discernable slippage between facts and fiction in order to present her own version of the truth about Aquash's death, and by doing so she implicates the FBI in murder and, consequently, establishes Aquash as a martyr/warrior rather than as an AIM traitor.

Pollock's politicized counternarrative undermines the official and legal view that Aquash was killed by John Graham, a member of AIM.[4] Once she has established the "truth" of her version of the events by embedding them within the biographical details of Aquash's life, Pollock offers a number of different theories as to *why* Aquash was killed:

> **ANNIE.** Some people say
> Anna Mae Pictou Aquash would have been a key witness
> Countering government charges against the leaders of the
> American Indian Movement
>
> **OTHER.** Some people say the killing is an execution style slaying
> **OTHER.** Some people say the authorities' handling of the case is curious.
>
> **ELOISE.** Some people say the conduct of the FBI raises serious questions.
> [...]
> **ANNIE.** Anna Mae Pictou Aquash is not forgotten
>
> **OTHER.** We haven't forgotten. (252–53 ellipsis added)

Although Pollock's use of a third person voice constructs a kind of objectivity by offering these different theories, the clear implication in the play is that Aquash was murdered by the FBI and that the details of her murder were covered up. However, the play brings her story back into focus and demonstrates that she has not been forgotten because Pollock uncovers the "truth" about this warrior for the audience.

In addition to Pollock's inclusion of her own version of the "truth" about Aquash with the *facts* of Aquash's life, she also uses the third-person perspective for the lines that Aquash delivers. This latter narrative choice suggests that Pollock has refused to be a spokesperson for this Aboriginal woman, yet she is still able to bring Aquash's voice/story into the play. In this respect, Pollock has consciously avoided appropriating the voice of the Aboriginal character and manages to recall the life of this "warrior" by using the third person and, in effect, linguistically "speaking nearby" so as to not appropriate her voice. Filmmaker Trinh Min-ha coined the term "speaking nearby" to describe a strategy that she has used in her film *Reassemblage* where she, as a Vietnamese woman, documents the story of African women by consciously "speaking nearby" rather than *for* the women.[5] Min-ha describes "speaking nearby" as an "attitude in life" (327). She states that this form of speaking about the "Other" is "a speaking that does not objectify, does not point to an object as if it is distant from the speaking subject or absent from the speaking place. A speaking that reflects on itself and can come very close to a subject without, however, seizing it or claiming it" (327). By choosing this strategy for representing Aquash's life, Pollock has refused to accept the silencing of this Aboriginal woman's story while simultaneously preventing herself from speaking for and/or appropriating her voice. Despite the difficulties of staging a play that was originally written for radio and the difficulties for the actor playing Annie in the third-person, Pollock's project allows for a crossracial perspective on "warriors" that is at once recuperative and emancipatory.

The choice to represent Aquash's life in the third person had an interesting effect on the Aboriginal woman who played this character in the Crazy Horse production. While Eloise introduces herself as a middle-aged white woman and Sarah introduces herself as "Sarah Moore Grimké" from Charleston, South Carolina, Aquash states: "Anna Mae Pictou Aquash is a native woman, a Mi'kmaq." At no point in the play does she, like the other women, reflect on the effects of the events that occur around her. She is simply a mouthpiece for the official version of the facts of her existence. In rehearsal, Michelle Thrush, who was cast as Aquash, found that speaking about her in the third person, as if the character was devoid of interiority, was quite challenging. Embodying this character and yet delivering lines about her from the third-person perspective was profoundly unsettling for her as an Aboriginal woman (Thrush). Nonetheless, the Crazy Horse production of this play was attended by Aboriginal and non-Aboriginal audiences who were able to find ways to identify with the stories represented on stage.

Other productions of Pollock's play have brought this multi-perspectival narrative to other audiences. For the second production, Pollock further revised her radio script to create a newer version of the play. *The Making of Warriors* was directed by Heather Inglis for the Edmonton production in February of 2003 and theatre critic Colin Maclean suggested that the success of this production was due to Pollock's expert storytelling and the use of props and set design. Maclean noted Inglis's "ingenious" use of "a stark basement (the PITS gallery) with cement floors, low ceilings and exposed light bulbs," the effective use of television sets, and stark lighting that was used in this production to evoke "a feeling of dark intimacy" (50). This set design was also noted in a review by Liz Nichols who remarked on the intimacy that was established between the audience and the actors in this production. The audience was "sitting among the cast in chairs of every description: rocking, basket, director's, [and] arm [chairs]." The play was re-mounted for the Edmonton Fringe Festival in August of 2003.

Pollock's interest in investigating the role of the witness is evident in this stage play because the drama opens with the act of witnessing an imagined murder. The play begins with Annie, Eloise, Sarah and a character simply named "Other" giving a vivid description of the imagined visceral experience that Aquash had when she was about to be shot:

> **ANNIE.** She is kneeling
> **ELOISE.** The gravel is biting into her knees
> **OTHER.** She is feeling
> **SARAH.** a slight pressure behind her right ear.
> **ANNIE.** She is looking
> **OTHER.** at the stars
> **ELOISE.** She is looking at the stars.
> **SARAH.** Looking

ELOISE. she is listening to the wind.
OTHER. She does not
ANNIE. hear she does not hear
OTHER. hear
ANNIE. She does not hear the shot.
Silence as they listen. They do not hear a shot. A beat and the light shifts as the group turns from the scene they've just viewed.... (231 ellipsis added)

Because we do not see the murder enacted on stage, we, like Eloise, have to imagine it. Pollock's attention to the physical and aural sensations that Aquash may have experienced just before being murdered, in some ways, brings the death more forcefully into the minds of the listeners in the radio play format. In the stage production, this scene brings the audience into close proximity with the Aquash murder through their own vicarious role as witness to the actors imagining the murder.

Pollock's thematic interest in the role of witness is further developed in Sarah Grimké's story when she recalls being traumatized by witnessing the beating of one of the slaves on her father's plantation. However, unlike Grimké who takes up the abolitionist cause as a result of the events she witnesses on her father's plantation, Eloise is caught in the trauma of witnessing and returns to it in order to relieve the tension that she is plagued with by *not* having done anything. Although the audience may find it difficult to identify with the rather remarkable lives of Grimké and Aquash, Pollock provides a third character that the audience can identify with.

Eloise is an ordinary woman who is recognizable as an innocent bystander/Everywoman character. In one scene, she recalls driving slowly past a group of white men and witnessing something red at the side of the road as the men glared at her:

ELOISE. I was driving. I didn't stop. Why should I stop? I felt as if it wouldn't be wise to stop. There were ten or twelve of them. White men. Just standing on the shoulder of the road, and as I passed, they stared at the car and I stared back. It was late in the afternoon.

OTHER. February 24th, 1976.
OTHER. 4:30 in the afternoon.

ELOISE. Yes, about 4:30 in the afternoon, and a golden grey glow hung in the air. It was that time of year. And after I passed I stared in the rearview mirror. I saw them staring back, watching the car disappear into the golden-grey luminescence. They no longer saw me yet I saw them, I saw them shift in the rear view mirror, shift their ambiguous neutral gaze from the receding car to something on the shoulder of the road. It was red. Partly red. A red... (238–39 ellipsis in original)

Multiple looking-relations are established at this moment in this play: Eloise notices that the police noticed her noticing them while we watch the performance. Eloise's recollection of this witnessing highlights the powerful role of the witness and makes manifest the audience's subsequent complicity in witnessing the witness recollect these events on stage. She returns to this trauma and, with the audience as witness, confesses the guilt she feels about not stopping to discover what had happened, who was murdered, and why.

Eloise's witness trauma is referred to throughout the play, and the painful recollection that plagues her is summarized in the following lines that she repeats throughout the play: "I didn't stop. I kept driving." Stuck in this moment of guilt-laden reflection, Eloise repeats this refrain until she is able to return to this moment at the climax of the play when the other two women's voices join in documenting the last days of Sarah Moore Grimké and the murder of Anna Mae Pictou Aquash. This is the first moment where the murder of Aquash is revealed to Eloise and the audience. At this point, Eloise realizes the gravity of what she had witnessed and the audience understands why her witness trauma has been so profoundly unsettling for her. Finally, Eloise (and, by extension, the audience) comes to the realization that the red bundle she witnessed at the side of the road was Annie's ski jacket or the blood that spilled on the ground from the gunshot to the head that ended Aquash's life. Eloise's trauma was not simply based on the fact that she drove past a group of men gathered at the side of the road; it is based on the fact that she, as a woman, did not inquire into what turned out to be the murder of another woman. This tension between action and passivity is manifest in the characterization of the women. While we celebrate the outspoken Grimké character's abolitionist ethics and applaud Aquash's political stance on Aboriginal sovereignty, we question Eloise's passivity. The contrast between action and passivity creates an internal tension in the play and this action/passivity binary is enhanced by the tension Pollock establishes between falling silent and using one's voice to stand up for one's ideals.

Ann Jansen's analysis of Pollock's use of silence in the original radio play highlights the nature of the medium. She states, "[b]eing silenced is central to *The Making of Warriors*—and silence is a powerful tool on radio, where characters not heard from or mentioned for a time disappear" (91). In the stage production, however, silence becomes a thematic issue and a means for Pollock to comment upon the possible consequences that follow from giving voice to one's ideal. The social and political efforts to silence women who agitate for social change provides a counterpoint to the celebratory gesture of speaking up and acting upon one's ideals. At the same time, silence is integral to this play: the murder of Aquash is a means of silencing her; her refusal to offer the FBI information is an act of conscious political silencing for a larger objective; the silent role of the witness Eloise implicates the audience; and, the larger social silencing of these women's lives highlights the North American historical silencing of the "truth" about these women "warriors."

By remembering and retelling Aquash's story, Pollock insists that the history of her execution and, more importantly, the untold story of her fictionalized defiant refusal to implicate her fellow activists, is brought to audiences. Fittingly, the play ends with the three women's voices addressing the legacy that these women have left and reminding the audience of the threads that bind these women's lives together:

> **OTHER.** Sarah Moore Grimké died in 1873 at the age of eighty-one
> **SARAH.** No stopping
> **ELOISE.** Never
> **ANNIE.** Anna Mae Pictou Aquash
> **ELOISE.** Lives! (253)

In this scene, Pollock uses the choral delivery of these lines to demonstrate the power of feminist collaboration.The feminist unification that is achieved by the choral delivery of these lines is represented again in the final symbolic gesture. After these triumphant lines, the stage directions read "*they burn the rope that had bound Anna's hands as lights dim and their voices fade and overlap*" (253). This final gesture, like the choral voices, unites these women's stories and lives.

Jansen notes that Pollock's "overlapping dialogue, intercut scenes, and echoing words and phrases" are techniques that the playwright used "to highlight similarities between the two women's struggles, while building an insistent, purposeful rhythm to the play" (90). Although her comments are referring to the radio play, the same is true of the stage production because both use choral delivery to bring together these women's voices and stories. She suggests that "[w]hile each has a specific role in relation to a story, on occasion the three speak as a chorus or comment on events in the other story. Their subjects' lives are brought closer by this means…" (90). As another example of this choral delivery, the final lines of the play are delivered by the three characters, and Pollock's stage directions state that they are "*speaking some words as individuals, other words together*" (253).[6] The choral delivery of the closing lines of this play also makes the audience aware of their own role as witness by way of the pronoun "you":

> We won't forget
> remember
> yes do
> remember
> yes that
> remember
> one two three
> out of many
> Anna Mae Sarah
> and
> you
> out
> of man
> you out of many bring
> stories
> bring courage

brings stories
bring courage and stories (253–54)

Although *The Making of Warriors* opens with the imagined murder of Aquash, in this final speech, Pollock urges us to consider the ways in which Aquash's story does not, and did not, end with her death. As a martyred warrior, Aquash still has the power to affect change through inspiring others to continue with struggles for emancipation for Aboriginal people. Pollock's decision to close both the radio play and the stage play in this way offers hope that feminists and women "warriors" do indeed change society and, by extension, that the play will affect change in the audience as well.

The story of Anna Mae Pictou Aquash was also brought to Canadian stages in Yvette Nolan's play *Annie Mae's Movement,* which provides an interesting comparison with Pollock's representation of Aquash. Nolan's play was first presented as a staged reading at Native Earth Performing Arts' Weesageechak Begins to Dance festival of new plays in Toronto, February 17–22, 1998, and premiered in Whitehorse, Yukon, September 17, 1998. Nolan's play has had a number of productions and most recently was staged as part of the 2006 Honouring Theatre event that offered a trilogy of plays by Aboriginal artists from Canada, Australia and Samoa. It was produced again in October of 2007 at the Firehall Theatre in Vancouver. In Nolan's version, Aquash is also represented as one of the "disappeared" warriors in the struggle for Aboriginal empowerment. Nolan, like Pollock, uses the character of Anna to suggest that the "disappeared" women warriors will not be left on the margins of history. Both playwrights suggest that the retelling of Aquash's courageous story will inspire others.

Where Pollock addresses transnational and transhistoric feminist struggles in her play, Nolan investigates feminist struggles *within* the American Indian Movement itself. Nolan delves further than Pollock into the patriarchy of the American Indian Movement by documenting the complex position Aquash was in as a woman in the largely male-dominated organization. Nolan's Aquash offers her own perspective on her political views and feminist ideals in the opening monologue:

> **ANNA.** You gotta stand up, you gotta fight for what's important, no matter who wants you to shut up. We have to fight, even if it seems like we're fighting ourselves. Or else we will disappear, just disappear. (4)

One of the many differences between Pollock's and Nolan's versions of Aquash's life is that the Aquash character in Nolan's play is given an interiority and first-person perspective on the need to resist erasure within the organization itself. In addition, Pollock names her character Annie, the more informal name that was used by Aquash's friends and family. Nolan uses the more formal and legal name Anna to refer to the same character.

Another difference between these two plays is the presentation of Aquash's murder. Pollock does not stage the murder; instead, she presents it through the "imagined" murder that opens the play and she brings the murder into the narrative through the role of the witness at the scene of the murder after Aquash has been shot. While I recognize that Pollock originally wrote *The Making of Warriors* as a radio script, she could have represented the murder on stage in the later adaptation of the play for the stage production. She chose, instead, to keep the original presentation of the death as both imagined and available through the recollections of Eloise so that a murder was not shown on stage. In *Annie Mae's Movement*, Nolan stages the murder after this prophetic speech:

> **ANNA.** My name is Anna Mae Pictou Aquash, Micmac nation from Shubenacadie, Nova Scotia. My mother is Mary Ellen Pictou, my father is Francis Thomas Levi, my sisters are Rebecca Julien and Mary Lafford, my brother is Francis. My daughters are Denise and Deborah. You cannot kill us all. You can kill me, but my sisters live, my daughters live. You cannot kill us all. My sisters live. Becky and Mary, Helen and Priscilla, Janet and Raven, Sylvia, Ellen, Pelajia, Agnes, Monica, Edie, Jessica, Gloria and Lisa and Muriel, Monique, Joy and Tina, Margo, Maria, Beatrice, Minnie, April, Colleen… You can kill me, but you cannot kill us all. You can kill me.
> *There is a gunshot. She falls, curls into a foetal position. Blackout.*
> (41–42)

There are four aspects of Nolan's choice that deserve attention here. By pairing this hopeful speech with the dramatic murdering of this character on stage, she implicates the audience as witness to this murder in ways that Pollock avoids. By naming family, friends and Aboriginal playwrights and claiming that "You can kill me, but you cannot kill us all" (42), the character suggests the powerful and enduring effect that her life has had, and will continue to have, on Aboriginal women. In Nolan's play, Anna has a first-person perspective on her existence before her staged death. After an intense interrogation, when her death becomes inevitable, Aquash reflects on the power of women to make change and ruminates on the effect that her death will have on other activists. This first-person perspective enables the actor and the audience to consider the possibility of Aquash's conscious awareness of her role as a martyr for a larger cause. Lastly, the final speech extends the life of Annie Mae beyond the point of her physical death in order to suggest that her martyrdom was not in vain. Although Nolan and Pollock use different narrative strategies to document their refusal to accept the silencing of women *and* each playwright differently positions the audience as witness to the Aquash murder, they both use her death as a marker and political touchstone of feminist resistance in a way that provides both a defiant and a tragic example of what it means to be a woman warrior.

The second contemporary Canadian play that can usefully be compared to Pollock's *The Making of Warriors* is Marie Clements's *The Unnatural and Accidental Women*. The play was written in 1997 and a staged reading was given at the Vancouver East Cultural Centre in the same year. It premiered in 2000 at the Firehall Arts Centre in Vancouver and was first published in 2001. Clements's play, like *Annie Mae's Movement* and *The Making of Warriors,* offers a vision of Aboriginal women whose influence extends beyond the point of death. Clements, like Pollock and Nolan, has managed to write beyond the death of these women by employing specific narrative techniques. Although Clements's play is not about Aquash, the murder of Aboriginal women is the focus of the drama and it is this point that I want to use to draw a comparison between these three plays. In *The Unnatural and Accidental Women*, the tragedy of the women's deaths is transformed by Clements's use of a fictional revenge plot in which the murdered Aboriginal women, who appear as ghosts, execute the man who has murdered them.

Although the basis of this play is factual, Clements takes creative license to extend the power of these murdered Aboriginal women to affect change beyond the grave by giving them an embodied and active presence as ghost murderers. The "truth" about these murdered women is that the killer, Gilbert Robert Jordan, was only sentenced for one of the eleven murders, served six years, and was released.[7] However, by choosing to construct a play in which the murderer is killed on stage, Clements effectively rewrites the events in a way that empowers the Aboriginal women who were murdered.

Like Pollock, Clements has consciously avoided representing the murder of the women on stage; she chooses to focus on the last few hours in their lives before they were killed. The indication that the women have been murdered is represented by way of slides that document the "official" versions of the coroner's reports which state that each woman died of "unnatural and accidental" causes. Only one murder is shown on stage and that is the murder of the killer. In this respect, Clements' vision is similar to both Nolan's and Pollock's in that the playwright, in each case, refuses to close the play with the horrific murder(s) of the Aboriginal women while simultaneously finding a way to foreground the murder(s) in the performance.

The Making of Warriors, Annie Mae's Movement and *The Unnatural and Accidental Women* use the power of drama to document the lives of real Aboriginal women. Aquash's story has been rescued from the margins of history as an emancipatory gesture by Pollock and Nolan because the plays bring the lives of murdered Aboriginal women to the stage. In this respect, both plays function as memorials for the "disappeared" Aboriginal women in Canadian society. Other Canadian artists have more explicitly used performance as a means to create memorials for the Aboriginal women who have been victims of violence in Canada. The two performances I will discuss next use the lighting of candles and a ritualized naming of the missing women as both performance art and elegy.

Aboriginal performance artist Rebecca Belmore has created a performance art installation entitled "Vigil" that commemorates missing and murdered Aboriginal women in Vancouver.[8] Belmore set her performance in an alley in the downtown Eastside where Aboriginal women's bodies have been found. She wore a white tank top that revealed the names of some of the murdered women written on her body in black. She vigorously scrubbed the cement in preparation for the ceremonial naming of the deceased while an audience member lit a candle for each woman. Once the candles were lit, Belmore put on a red dress and nailed parts of it to telephone poles that lined the alley. She then ripped the dress so that pieces of red fabric remained on the poles. To close the performance, she read the names of the women from her own body, one at a time. With the recitation of each name she used her mouth to rip the thorns and leaves from red roses for each of the women. The candles, the red bits of fabric on the poles, the violently discarded roses and the names of the women formed the core of this performance. Belmore also used her own body as a script that memorialized the murdered women and brought the notion of embodiment to the centre of the performance. The performance piece was videotaped and became a video installation that was presented as part of the Talking Stick Festival in Vancouver, 2002.

Memorializing and naming missing Aboriginal women is still represented in performance today. Aboriginal performance and new media artist Archer Pechawis also memorialized Aboriginal women who have gone "missing" in his performance "Elegy" which was first presented at the Talking Stick Festival in Vancouver, 2006. On his website, Pechawis states that this performance is: "a memorial to the missing women of Vancouver's Downtown Eastside. Using video projections and an original score by drummer/singer Anthony Favel and cellist Cris Derksen, 'Elegy' is a meditation on the lives of these women and on the tragically indifferent response of the Vancouver Police Department."[9]

Again, the performance involved the lighting of candles and a ritualized naming of the missing women. As Derksen spoke the name of each woman, the name was also projected onto a screen behind the performance and Pechawis lit a candle for each of the women. Pechawis and Belmore used the medium of performance to document real Aboriginal women's lives in such a way that the performance explicitly functioned as memorial rituals for the Aboriginal community and Canadian society. Pechawis and Belmore created their performances specifically for Aboriginal audiences within cities where there is still an enormous amount of grief about murdered Aboriginal women and so, it is fitting that they more explicitly use performance as community ritual and commemoration for Vancouver's Aboriginal community. Playwrights Pollock, Clements and Nolan use the medium of theatre less explicitly to document and memorialize the lives of these women. However, each of these playwrights has, in her own way, used performance to confront audiences with the issue of missing Aboriginal women in order to ensure that we remember their lives, their deaths and their names.

In conclusion, Pollock's *The Making of Warriors* offers a transhistoric and transnational feminist drama by way of four important structural features. Pollock uses a hybrid form of dialogue to suggest the interrelatedness of these women's lives and she uses a choral delivery of lines to fuse these different women's lives into a single narrative. By using a third-person perspective for the lines that Aquash delivers, Pollock finds a way to speak about her without appropriating the voice of the "Other." Pollock investigates the power of the gaze through her dramatization of the role of the witness, Eloise, in ways that invite the audience to consider our own gaze and complicity in silencing this story. Lastly, by offering a dramatization of Aquash's life that presents a series of facts within the context of Pollock's *interpre-*

tation of her as a martyr who was executed by the FBI, Pollock sets in motion a revisionist narrative that, ultimately, allows the story of Aquash's warrior activism to extend beyond the grave.

Pollock brings the murder of Aquash into the play by opening the play with actors imagining the sensations of the murdered woman and later brings the murder of Aquash into the narrative by way of the traumatic recollections of what the witness saw at the scene of the murder. Because the play was originally written for radio, the decision to present the murder this way makes sense. In contrast, Nolan's Aquash character is murdered on stage and members of the American Indian Movement are implicated in the murder. The influence of the deceased is evident in the closing lines of both plays and in Nolan's play, Aquash is given a first-person perspective on the intergenerational empowerment that her story will have on women. Clements, like Pollock and Nolan, has created a play that extends the influence of murdered Aboriginal women beyond the grave but Clements, like Pollock, chooses to *not* represent the murder of an Aboriginal woman on stage. Where Pollock and Nolan use prophetic speeches about their warriors living on at the close of their plays, Clements uses a fictionalized revenge plot in order to extend the power of the murdered Aboriginal women.

Each playwright uses different narrative, rhetorical and dramatic means in order to suggest that these Aboriginal women have not been murdered in vain. Each playwright presents a feminist vision that suggests other women will be inspired (like the playwrights themselves) to remember and retell these stories of resistance. Each playwright addresses the murder of Aboriginal women in performances that function as national commemorations. Together, these performances document, historicize and elegize the deaths of Aboriginal women in Canada. As live performances, they create moments of collective remembering in Canadian theatre history and, as a result, they are important examples of commemoration that have the potential to transform the trauma of the past. The recent remount of Yvette Nolan's play *Annie Mae's Movement* (May, 2008), directed by Alanis King in Saskatoon and produced by Saskatchewan Native Theatre Company (SNTC), indicates the enduring interest that Canadian theatre audiences, especially Aboriginal audiences, have in the figure of Anna Mae Pictou Aquash. The final lines spoken by Anna in Nolan's play offer a means by which to contemplate the power of the feminist vision in each of these plays, and within the work of these two important Aboriginal performance artists: "You can kill me, but you cannot kill us all" (42).

(2008)

Notes

[1] I dedicate this essay to the memory of my cousin Vanessa Lee Buckner (born 1960 died 1987).

[2] All page references to the published play are based on the stage adaptation as it appears in Pollock, *Sharon Pollock's Collected Works.*

[3] The information about the rehearsal of this production was offered by Thrush.

[4] In December of 2003 John Graham was arrested for the murder of Aquash. In 2005, Federal Justice Minister Vic Toews ordered the extradition of former Yukon resident John Graham, who is wanted in the United States for the murder of Nova Scotia Mi'kmaq activist Anna Mae Pictou Aquash. To date, he is still facing extradition to the United States for the murder of Aquash and several Aboriginal activists have lobbied to appeal the extradition order. Graham claims that he is a scapegoat for this murder and there is a John Graham Defense Committee set up to assist in challenging the court extradition order. For more information on his position see John Graham Defense Committee: http://www.grahamdefense.org/index.htm.

[5] For an elaboration on this aesthetic convention of "speaking nearby" see Min-ha and Chen.

[6] I have chosen to focus on the choral delivery of the three primary characters in this essay. Although these lines, and other key lines in the play, include the voices and presence of the OTHERS on stage, I have decided to focus on the three women characters and examine the impact of their choral delivery. Other areas of enquiry might include an analysis of the role that the OTHERS have within this play and the ways in which these OTHERS function as a chorus as defined by Aristotle.

[7] For more information on the details of this gruesome crime, see "Gilbert Paul Jordan." The issue of the notorious "barbershop killer" has also been represented in film and television. First, the killer and the details of these murders were fictionalized in the first episodes of the television series, "Da Vinci's Inquest." More recently, Carl Bessai's 2006 film adaptation of Clements's play, "Unnatural and Accidental," brings these women's lives to a whole new audience. The television series and the film indicate a contemporary revival of the interest in addressing the murder of Canadian Aboriginal women. In addition, the recent trial of Robert Pickton has also brought the issue of murdered Aboriginal women into contemporary popular culture by way of the media.

[8] For further details on this performance or to watch a video of the performance, see Belmore.

[9] To view stills of this performance or to watch a video of this performance see Pechawis.

Works Cited

Belmore, Rebecca. Grunt Gallery. October 15, 2007. http://www.rebeccabelmore.com/home.html. Accessed August 2007.

Clements, Marie. *The Unnatural and Accidental Women.* Vancouver: Talonbooks 2005.

Gilbert Paul Jordan. Wikipedia. http://en.wikipedia.org/wiki/Gilbert_Paul_Jordan. Accessed August 2007.

Jansen, Ann. "Change the Story: Narrative Strategies in Two Radio Plays." *Contemporary Issues in Canadian Drama.* Ed. Per Brask. Winnipeg: Blizzard Publications, 1995. 86–102.

John Graham Defense Committee. "John Graham Defense Committee." 2004. http://www.grahamdefense.org/index.htm. Accessed August 2007.

Maclean, Colin. "Stark Backdrop Highlights Warriors." *The Edmonton Sun* 13 February 2003: 50.

Min-ha, Trinh T. and Nancy Chen. "Speaking Nearby." *Feminism and Film.* Ed. E. Ann Kaplan. New York: Oxford UP, 2000. 317–35.

Nicholls, Liz. "Awakening the Warrior Within: Three Women's Lives Intertwine in Salute to Restless Spirits." *Edmonton Journal* 12 February 2003, final ed.: C2.

Nolan, Yvette. *Annie Mae's Movement.* Toronto: PUC Play Service, 1999.

Pechawis, Archer. APXO.net. October 15, 2007. http://www.apxo.net/home.html. Accessed August 2007.

Pollock, Sharon. *Sharon Pollock: Collected Works, Volume Three.* Ed. Cynthia Zimmerman. Toronto: Playwrights Canada, 2008.

———. *The Making of Warriors. Airborne: Radio Plays by Women.* Ed. Ann Jansen. Winnipeg: Blizzard, 1991. 99–132.

———. *The Making of Warriors. Sharon Pollock: Collected Works, Volume Three.* Ed. Cynthia Zimmerman. Toronto: Playwrights Canada, 2008. 227–54.

Thrush, Michelle. Personal interview. October 20, 2007.

"Unnatural and Accidental." Dir. Carl Bessai. Raven West Films, 2006.

Zimmerman, Cynthia. "The Making of Warriors." *Playwriting Women: Female Voices in English Canada.* Vol. 3. Toronto: Simon & Pierre, 1994. 60–98.

Suggested Further Reading

Belliveau, George. "Daddy on Trial: Sharon Pollock's New Brunswick Plays." *Theatre Research in Canada/Recherches théâtrales au Canada* 22.2 (2001): 161–72.

———. "Investigating British Columbia's Past: *The Komagata Maru Incident* and *The Hope Slide* as Historiographic Metadrama." *BC Studies* 137 (2003): 93–106.

Bennett, Susan, ed. *Feminist Theatre and Performance.* Toronto: Playwrights Canada, 2005.

Clement, Susan, and Esther Beth Sullivan. "The Split Subject of *Blood Relations.*" *Upstaging Big Daddy: Directing Theatre as if Gender and Race Matter.* Ed. Ellen Donkin and Susan Clement. Ann Arbor: U Michigan P, 1993. 259–76.

DeFelice, Jim. "Remembrance of Things Past: Time, Space and Character in Sharon Pollock's *The Komagata Maru Incident, Blood Relations,* and *Doc.*" *Sharon Pollock. wwr Magazine* 2.1 (2005): 8–9.

Dolan, Jill. *Presence and Desire: Essays on Gender, Sexuality, Performance.* Ann Arbor: U of Michigan P, 1993.

Eakin, Paul John. *How our Lives Become Stories: Making Selves.* Ithaca: Cornell U, 1999.

Egan, Susanna. *Mirror Talk: Genres of Crisis in Contemporary Autobiography.* Chapel Hill: U of North Carolina P, 1999.

Gilbert, Reid. "Sharon Pollock." *Profiles in Canadian Literature, 6.* Ed. Jeffrey Heath. Toronto: Dundurn, 1986. 113–20.

Grace, Sherrill. "Creating the Girl from God's Country: Sharon Pollock's Nell Shipman." *Canadian Literature* 172 (2002): 98–117.

———. "Sharon Pollock's *Doc* and the Biographer's Dilemma." *Theatre and AutoBiography.* Ed. Sherrill Grace and Jerry Wasserman. Vancouver: Talonbooks, 2006. 275–88.

———. "White Men Talking." *Journal of Northern Studies* 1–2 (2007): 9–26.

——— and Gabriele Helms. "Documenting Racism: Sharon Pollock's *The Komagata Maru Incident.*" *Painting the Maple: Essays on Race, Gender, and the Construction of Canada.* Vancouver: UBC Press, 1998. 85–99.

——— and Jerry Wasserman, ed. *Theatre and AutoBiography: Writing and Performing Lives.* Vancouver: Talonbooks, 2006.

Loiselle, André. "Paradigms of 1980s Québécois and Canadian Drama: Normand Chaurette's *Provincetown, Juillet 1919, J'avais 19 ans* and Sharon Pollock's *Blood Relations*." *Québec Studies* 14 (1992): 93–104.

Minami, Yoshinari. "Canadian Plays on the Japanese Stage." *Performing National Identities: International Perspectives on Contemporary Canadian Theatre*. Ed. S. Grace and A.R. Glaap. Vancouver: Talonbooks, 2003. 181–97.

Nothof, Anne. "Canadian Radio Drama: Prick Up Your Ears." *Theatre History in Canada/L'Histoire du théâtre au Canada* 11.1 (1990): 59–70.

———. "Ironic Images: Sharon Pollock's Stratford Productions." *Canadian Theatre Review* 114 (2003): 21–25.

———. "Postcolonial Tragedy in the Crowsnest Pass: Two Rearview Reflections by Sharon Pollock and John Murrell." *Great Plains Quarterly* 26.4 (2006): 235–44.

Pollock, Sharon. *Sharon Pollock: Three Plays*. Toronto: Playwrights Canada, 2003.

Saddlemyer, Ann. "Two Canadian Women Playwrights." *Cross-Cultural Studies: American, Canadian and European Literatures: 1945–1985*. Ed. Mirko Jurak. Ljubljana: English Department, Filozofska Fakulteta, 1988. 251–56.

———. "Crime in Literature: Canadian Drama." *Rough Justice: Essays on Crime in Literature*. Ed. M. L. Friedland. Toronto: U of Toronto P, 1991. 214–30.

Sharon Pollock. Special issue of *wwr Magazine* 2.1 (Summer 2005). www.womenwritingreading.org. Accessed 28 January 2008.

Stone-Blackburn, Susan. "Feminism and Metadrama: Role Playing in *Blood Relations*." *Canadian Drama* 15 (1989): 169–78.

Striff, Erin. "Lady Killers: Feminism and Murder in Sharon Pollock's *Blood Relations* and Wendy Kesselman's *My Sister in This House*." *New England Theatre Journal* 8 (1997): 95–109.

Zimmerman, Cynthia. "Sharon Pollock: The Making of Warriors." *Playwriting Women: Female Voices in English Canada*. Toronto: Simon and Pierre, 1994. 60–98.

———, ed. *Sharon Pollock: Collected Works, Volumes One, Two and Three*. Toronto: Playwrights Canada, 2005, 2006 and 2008.

Notes on Contributors

Sherrill Grace is Professor of English and Distinguished University Scholar at the University of British Columbia. Her most recent books include *Canada and the Idea of North*, reprinted in paperback in 2007, and *Theatre and AutoBiography* (2006), co-edited with Jerry Wasserman. Her biography of Sharon Pollock, *Making Theatre: A Life of Sharon Pollock*, will appear with Talonbooks in 2008.

Rosalind Kerr is associate professor of Dramatic Theory in the Department of Drama at the University of Alberta. She publishes on early modern Italian actresses and contemporary Canadian theatre. She has edited three volumes for Playwrights Canada Press: *Queer Theatre In Canada* (2007); *Lesbian Plays: Coming of Age in Canada* (2006) and *Staging Alternative Albertas: Experimental Theatre in Edmonton* (2002).

Michelle La Flamme is a performer and educator who is of African-Canadian, Métis and Creek ancestry. She is very involved with the Aboriginal arts community and has worked for (IMAG) Indigenous Media Arts Group and with Margo Kane at Full Circle First Nations Performance for a number of years. She has been the Coordinator of the IPAA (Indigenous Performers Arts Alliance) and was recently Project Coordinator for the Indigenous Language Revitalization program at UBC. She has been a guest lecturer in Germany and has also taught in The Netherlands and Spain. Recently, she has been teaching in the English department, Theatre department and First Nation Studies at UBC. In 2006 she graduated from UBC and was awarded the Paul Stanwood Prize for the best doctoral thesis in the Department of English. She is revising her thesis, "Living, Writing and Staging Racial Hybridity" for publication with Wilfred Laurier University Press (2008).

Madonne Miner teaches and writes about twentieth-century literature, most often from a feminist perspective. She has published on women's bestsellers, drama and short stories; her book, *Insatiable Appetites: Twentieth-Century American Women's Bestsellers*, analyzes women's bestsellers from feminist and psychoanalytic perspectives. Currently, she serves as Dean of the College of Arts and Humanities at Weber State University.

Rita Much has taught at UBC, the University of Toronto, Ryerson and McGill and is now a tenured professor of Theatre History at Dawson College in Montreal. She is editor of *Women on The Canadian Stage: The Legacy of Hrosvit*; co-author of *Hot Ice (Shakespeare in Moscow, A Director's Diary)*; and co-author of *Fair Play: 12 Women Speak (Conversations with Canadian Playwrights)*.

Anne Nothof is a professor of English at Athabasca University in Alberta, Canada, where she has developed and taught undergraduate and post-graduate distance education courses in literature and drama. She has published critical essays in journals such as *Theatre Research in Canada/Recherches théâtrales au Canada*, *Modern Drama*, *Mosaic* and the *International Journal of Canadian Studies*, and in two texts on postmodern theatre: *Siting the Other* and *Crucible of Cultures*. She has contributed essays on Canadian theatre for Camden's *History of Literature in Canada* and the *Cambridge History of Canadian Literature*. She has edited a collection of essays on Canadian playwright, Sharon Pollock for Guernica Press, a collection of essays on Alberta theatre for Playwrights Canada Press, and an issue of *Canadian Theatre Review* on Alberta theatre. For NeWest, she has edited a collection of Pollock's plays, and for Playwrights, a collection of Alberta plays, entitled *The Alberta Advantage*. She is a board member and editor for NeWest Press, board member for AU Press, and past president of the Canadian Association for Theatre Research. She is also editor for the Canadian Theatre Encyclopedia (www.canadiantheatre.com).

Sharon Pollock was born in Fredericton, New Brunswick, but has lived and worked in Calgary, Alberta since 1966. She has written more than 30 plays for the stage, radio and television, and during her career she has acted, directed, and served as artistic director with Theatre Calgary and Theatre New Brunswick. She has won two Governor General's Awards (for *Blood Relations* and *Doc*) and many other national and international awards and prizes, including four honorary degrees. Her plays have been translated and performed abroad, as well as across Canada and the United States. *Sharon Pollock: Collected Works*, (three volumes), is published by Playwrights Canada Press. Her most recent play, *Man Out of Joint*, premiered in Calgary in 2007.

Pat Quigley is the Director of Education and Archives at the Stratford Shakespeare Festival, a position she has held since 1986. She was formerly a high school English and drama teacher and also taught at the Faculty of Education at the University of Western Ontario.

Denis Salter joined the Department of English Drama and Theatre program at McGill in 1987 where he was the program's director from 1989–93. He is a widely published specialist on modern drama, dramaturgy and criticism, Victorian and Edwardian stage history, Shakespeare in performance, and Canadian/Québécois theatre. He serves on the editorial and advisory boards of *Theatre Research in Canada/Recherches Théâtrales au Canada*, *Comparative Drama*, *Theatre History Studies*, *Nineteenth Century Theatre and Film*, *Theatre*, *Studies in Theatre and Performance*, *The Theatre in the Americas* series, the Theatre Museum Canada, and the online *Canadian Adaptations of Shakespeare Project*. He is the Quebec representative on the Canadian Association for Theatre Research (CATR) board. With Ted Little as Editor he is the Associate Editor of *alt.theatre: cultural diversity and the stage*, a quarterly magazine published by Teesri Duniya Theatre; with Glen Nichols, he is the co-editor of the Canadian drama entries posted on the online *Literary Encyclopedia*. He is a two-time winner of the Richard Plant essay prize (2002, 2003) awarded by the Canadian Association for Theatre Research and an Honorary Member of the Henry

Irving Society in the UK. His current research is on problematic keywords in evidence-based (Canadian) theatre historiography and on the development of critical methodologies to decode the meanings of nineteenth-century Shakespearean promptbooks.

Craig S. Walker is Professor of Drama and English at Queen's University, where he has worked since 1992. He holds an MA in English and a PhD in Drama from the University of Toronto, and has worked as a professional actor and director at many theatres. He is the author of *The Buried Astrolabe: Canadian Dramatic Imagination and Western Tradition* (McGill-Queen's UP, 2001) and is co-editor, with Jennifer Wise, of the two-volume and concise editions of *The Broadview Anthology of Drama* (Broadview Press, 2003 & 2005).

Jerry Wasserman teaches English and Theatre at the University of British Columbia in Vancouver where he is Acting Head of the Department of Theatre and Film. His extensive publications on Canadian theatre include *Modern Canadian Plays* (4th ed.); *Twenty Years at Play: A New Play Centre Anthology*; *Theatre and AutoBiography: Writing and Performing Lives in Theory and Practice*, co-edited with Sherrill Grace; and *Spectacle of Empire: Marc Lescarbot's Theatre of Neptune in New France*. He reviews theatre for *The Province* newspaper in Vancouver and is also an actor with more than 200 professional credits for stage and screen.

Herb Wyile is an Associate Professor in the Dept. of English at Acadia University in Wolfville, Nova Scotia. He has published articles in numerous journals on regionalism, historical fiction, postmodernism, and Atlantic-Canadian literature. He is the author of *Speculative Fictions: Contemporary Canadian Novelists and the Writing of History* (2002) and *Speaking in the Past Tense: Canadian Novelists on Writing Historical Fiction* (2007). He has also co-edited three special issues of journals, *A Sense of Place* (*Textual Studies in Canada* 9), *Past Matters* (*Studies in Canadian Literature* 27.1), and a forthcoming collection on Atlantic-Canadian Literature.

Cynthia Zimmerman has been a commentator on Canadian playwriting and on the voice of women on the Canadian stage for her whole career at Glendon College, York University, where she is a professor in the English department. Her most recent books are *Sharon Pollock: Collected Works*, in three volumes, and *The Betty Lambert Reader*, all published by Playwrights Canada Press. Currently she is working on a Carol Bolt collection, a book to commemorate and celebrate Bolt's significant contributions.